HOMER AND THE
RESOURCES OF MEMORY

Homer and the Resources of Memory

Some Applications of Cognitive Theory
to the Iliad *and the* Odyssey

ELIZABETH MINCHIN

OXFORD
UNIVERSITY PRESS

OXFORD

UNIVERSITY PRESS

Great Clarendon Street, Oxford OX2 6DP

Oxford University Press is a department of the University of Oxford.
It furthers the University's aim of excellence in research, scholarship,
and education by publishing worldwide in

Oxford New York

Athens Auckland Bangkok Bogotá Bombay Buenos Aires Calcutta
Cape Town Chennai Dar es Salaam Delhi Florence Hong Kong Istanbul
Karachi Kuala Lumpur Madrid Melbourne Mexico City Mumbai
Nairobi Paris São Paulo Singapore Taipei Tokyo Toronto Warsaw

with associated companies in Berlin Ibadan

Oxford is a registered trade mark of Oxford University Press
in the UK and certain other countries

Published in the United States
by Oxford University Press Inc., New York

© Elizabeth Minchin 2001

The moral rights of the author have been asserted
Database right Oxford University Press (maker)

First published 2001

British Library Cataloguing in Publication Data
Data available

Library of Congress Cataloging in Publication Data
Minchin, Elizabeth.
Homer and the resources of memory: some applications of cognitive theory to the *Iliad*
and the *Odyssey*/Elizabeth Minchin.
p. cm.
Includes bibliographical references (p.) and indexes.
1. Homer—Technique. 2. Epic poetry, Greek—History and criticism.
3. Storytelling—Psychological aspects. 4. Oral tradition—Greece. 5. Oral-
formulaic analysis. 6. Cognitive psychology. 7. Memory. I. Title.
PA4175.M56 2001   883'.01—dc21   00-040064

ISBN 0-19-815257-4

1 3 5 7 9 10 8 6 4 2

Typeset in Imprint
by Joshua Associates Ltd., Oxford
Printed in Great Britain
on acid-free paper by
Biddles Ltd., Guildford & King's Lynn

To the memory of my grandmother, Hope Hely

Preface

How could a poet who worked in an oral tradition maintain the momentum of his song? How could a poet such as Homer weave a tale which filled an evening or, perhaps, a whole long night? The answer lies in memory, as we know. But this bald explanation does not do justice either to the complexity of memory or to the richness of the Homeric epics. Now that so much more information has become available to us, from several fields, about the workings of the mind it will be useful to us to identify with greater precision those contributions which memory makes to the composition and performance of oral traditional song.

In recent years I have been engaged in a systematic review of a number of compositional elements common to the *Iliad* and the *Odyssey*. I have taken each of the principal modes which we can identify in the epics—the poet's invocations, his typical scenes, his lists and catalogues, his small descriptive passages, his similes, and the anecdotes which are told within the structure of the larger epic—and I have analysed them as elements of a story which was performed for a listening rather than a reading audience. I have shown that the demands made on the poet, who does *not* rely on rote memory when he performs, and his ambition to sing a 'monumental' song have led him to adopt certain memory-based strategies which have left their traces in the text. What we discover is that the poet in an oral tradition makes intense and creative use of those resources of memory which are available to us all—episodic memory, auditory memory, visual memory, and spatial memory—to assist him both in the preparation of his song and at the moment of performance. In conducting this study I have drawn heavily on work in the now vast field of cognitive psychology and in two sub-disciplines of linguistics, discourse analysis and pragmatics. My discussion, in the light of such research, will allow us to understand more clearly the processes of epic composition in an oral context and to account for certain remarkable features of the text of the *Iliad* and the *Odyssey*—and some of the pleasure we find in them.

The central chapters of this book each began their lives in a different form. Chapter 1, now much expanded, was first published in *Classical Antiquity*; Chapter 2 appeared in an earlier guise in Ian Worthington's volume of papers from the first Orality and Literacy conference, *Voice into Text*; Chapter 3, now expanded in a number of ways, was published in Anne Mackay's volume, *Signs of Orality*, from the second such conference, Epos and Logos; Chapter 4 is to appear in the papers of the third meeting, in Janet Watson's *Speaking Volumes*; Chapter 5, on invocations, was published in an earlier form in the *Classical Journal*; and Chapter 6, on ring composition, first appeared in the journal *Helios*. I thank the editors and publishers of these volumes for allowing me to draw on this material. In order to bring these chapters together into a monograph, a considerable amount of writing, rewriting, and reshaping has been necessary. I thank the reader appointed by Oxford University Press for his or her valuable suggestions on how I might achieve this goal.

I wish to acknowledge the encouragement of a number of people over the years since I began thinking about Homer in this way: Colin Mayrhofer, who set me on this path; Beryl Rawson, Frances Muecke, and Oliver Taplin, who in their different ways have brought me to this point; and the participants in the three Orality and Literacy–Epos and Logos conferences, who have been the sounding board for many of my ideas. I thank a number of others for their assistance at various stages: Brian Gray, Pam Gray, Tony Liddicoat, Karen Ottley, Judy Slee, and Janet Watson. And, not least, I am more than grateful for the understanding and support of my family, who have lived with Homer for the last twenty years.

Canberra   E.M.

September, 1999

Contents

Abbreviations

Introduction

WORKING FROM MEMORY?

The *Iliad* and the *Odyssey* are remarkable works. The scope and grandeur of the poems and their persuasive depiction of a largely imagined heroic world have engaged and absorbed audiences through the centuries. But they are remarkable, also, as poems which were composed and performed without the aid of writing. Epic tales about the quarrel of Achilleus and Agamemnon and about the adventures of Odysseus were told and retold for audiences in the Aegean world in the period which followed the collapse of the Mycenaean world of the Late Bronze Age; they were passed from generation to generation by singers, or bards; and at some late point in the life of this oral tradition they were performed on a grand scale, as two monumental songs, by the singer whom we know as Homer.[1] Homer's tales were in the course of time recorded, so that it is possible for us, more than two thousand years later, to read a version of each of those great performances. To us today the singing of a narrative poem of such length, in a metrical language and without the support of written notes, represents an extraordinary achievement. And it raises the question: how could Homer, or any singer of traditional tales, have performed as he did, relying for the most part on memory?[2] It is the question which underpins this book, in which I consider the resources of memory which supported the poet as he composed and sang.

---

[1] For a brief but excellent discussion of the background to the epics, see G. S. Kirk, *The* Iliad*: A Commentary*, i (Cambridge: Cambridge University Press, 1985), 1–16. See also O. Dickinson, 'Homer, the Poet of the Dark Age', in I. McAuslan and P. Walcot (eds.), *Homer* (Oxford: Oxford University Press, 1998), 19–37, esp. at 35–7 (Addendum).

[2] For a summary of arguments against the likelihood of extensive use of writing by the poet of the *Iliad* and the *Odyssey*, and for brief comment on the possibility that Homer used writing on a small scale, in order to record themes, topics, or points, see Kirk, *The* Iliad*: A Commentary*, i, at 13.

My study draws on research in three areas: Homeric studies, cognitive psychology, and linguistics. In this introductory chapter I shall single out for attention a number of scholars whose work in their respective fields has opened up my line of enquiry. The first of these is Milman Parry. His investigations of the language of Homer, over sixty years ago, and the fruitful comparisons which he made with the then living Serbian oral tradition have changed the course of Homeric studies. The second scholar, contemporary with Parry, is Frederick Bartlett, an experimental psychologist. His work on memory—or, more accurately, the activity of remembering—has in recent years been reconsidered and developed in ways which are highly relevant to the Homerist or, indeed, to the student of any oral tradition. The third and fourth are Erving Goffman, a sociologist, and J. L. Austin, a philosopher. Goffman's accounts of the ways in which people interact in conversation and Austin's important discussion of the ways in which we use discourse to achieve our goals in transactions of all kinds have been taken up in the newer research fields of sociolinguistics, discourse analysis, and pragmatics; and developments in these fields have in turn opened the way to new appraisals of the oral aspects of traditional epic.

HOMERISTS ON HOMER: FORMULAS AND THEMES

It was Milman Parry who drew together earlier studies of metre and language, namely those of Heinrich Düntzer, Antoine Meillet, and Matija Murko to set out for us in systematic form compelling evidence that the language of the Homeric epics was in substantial part formulaic.[3] Under

---

[3] The development of Parry's thought may be traced most conveniently in his collected works: A. Parry (ed.), *The Making of Homeric Verse: The Collected Papers of Milman Parry* (Oxford: Clarendon Press, 1971); and see the editor's introduction, esp. at pp. xxii–xxiv. On the formulaic system which underpins the Homeric hexameter, see 'L'épithète traditionnelle dans Homère: Essai sur un problème de style homérique', Thèse pour le doctorat ès lettres présentée à la Faculté des Lettres de l'Université de Paris (Paris, 1928), appearing in translation as 'The

the influence of the anthropologist and psycholinguist, Marcel Jousse, Parry perceived the broader significance of his observations; he recognized that a diction marked by the metrical language patterns which he had isolated in Homeric verse was consistent with the nature of oral poetry.[4] He argued that this recurrent formulaic language which characterizes the epics had been developed over generations specifically for the transmission of traditional epic songs. Parry claimed, in short, that the Homeric style is typical of the style of oral poetry.[5]

Parry's oral–formulaic theory is now widely, although not universally, accepted. Most scholarly discussion concerning the nature of the Homeric epics has, in Parry's wake, been founded on the assumption that they are the work of an orally-trained poet.[6] It is an assumption which is fundamental to my own study.

Before his death, Parry had extended his interest beyond

Traditional Epithet in Homer', in A. Parry (ed.), *Homeric Verse*, 1–190. A valuable supplement to Adam Parry's introduction to his father's collected works is the discussion in J. Miles Foley, *The Theory of Oral Composition* (Bloomington and Indianapolis: Indiana University Press, 1988), ch. 1.

[4] See M. Jousse, *Le Style oral rythmique et mnémotechnique chez les Verbo-moteurs* (first published Paris, 1925), trans. E. Sienaert and R. Whitaker (New York: Garland, 1990). For Parry's debt to Jousse, see e.g. 'The Traditional Epithet in Homer', in A. Parry (ed.), *Homeric Verse*, esp. at 22–3.

[5] On this see M. Parry, 'Studies in the Epic Technique of Oral Verse-Making. I. Homer and Homeric Style', *HSCP* 41 (1930), 73–147, reprinted in A. Parry (ed.), *Homeric Verse*, 266–324.

[6] Throughout this volume I shall use the terms 'poet', 'narrator', and 'singer' interchangeably to refer to Homer. For discussion in narratological terms of the identity of poet and narrator in the epics, see I. de Jong, *Narrators and Focalizers: The Presentation of the Story in the* Iliad (Amsterdam: B. R. Gruner, 1987), ch. 1. For a survey of literature on the formula in Homer, see M. Edwards, 'Homer and Oral Tradition: The Formula, Part I', *Oral Tradition*, 1 (1986), 171–230; 'Homer and Oral Tradition: The Formula, Part II', *Oral Tradition*, 3 (1988), 11–60. Amongst Homerists who are sceptical of Parry's proposals, see D. Shive, *Naming Achilles* (New York and Oxford: Oxford University Press, 1987), who reassesses Parry's evidence of formulas as a first step towards re-establishing Homer as a literate poet. On the question of whether Homer himself composed orally, see R. Finnegan, *Oral Poetry: Its Nature, Significance and Social Context* (Cambridge: Cambridge University Press, 1977), who insists on an oral–literate continuum and notes (69–72) that formulaic style is not an infallible sign of oral composition; but see the recent work of M. Sale, 'In Defence of Milman Parry: Renewing the Oral Theory', *Oral Tradition*, 11 (1996), 374–417. In the light of Sale's quantitative studies and the arguments based on them, we are in a position to argue that the Homeric poems are indeed part of an oral tradition.

the smaller, syntactic-phonological unit of composition, the formula, to a larger unit which, he inferred, played the same role as the formula, but at the level of narrative structure. Following Walter Arend, he referred to these larger units as 'typical scenes'.[7] A typical scene, according to Parry, is a description of a recurrent action sequence which, each time it occurs within the *Iliad* or the *Odyssey*, is narrated 'with many of the same details and many of the same words'.[8] Parry and, subsequently, Albert Lord, his field assistant, proposed that the typical scene or, in Lord's terminology, the theme, was similar to the formula. Like the formula, each typical scene was learned by an apprentice singer so that he might reproduce an action sequence in song with relative ease.[9] Thus the oral poet could readily generate a standardized account of the harnessing of horses, the preparation of a meal, the making of a bed, or the procedures of dressing. Parry's thinking on the nature of the theme was taken up by Armstrong, Gunn, Edwards, and Fenik, all of whom have explored typical scenes in a variety of ways.[10] And Lord continued to develop his own thinking on this characteristic feature of oral epic. As a result we have studies which identify typical features in Homeric narrative structures, studies which emphasize the atypical in the midst of the typical, and a comparatively small number of longitudinal studies which describe and assess the thematic content of a sustained passage.

[7] See W. Arend, *Die typischen Scenen bei Homer* (Berlin: Weidmannische Buchhandlung, 1933).

[8] M. Parry, 'On Typical Scenes in Homer', *Classical Philology*, 31 (1936), 357–60, reprinted in A. Parry (ed.), *Homeric Verse*, 404–7, at 404. This is an extended review of Arend's work, *Die typischen Scenen bei Homer*.

[9] Parry, 'Typical Scenes', at 406; A. B. Lord, 'Composition by Theme in Homer and Southslavic Epos', *TAPA* 82 (1951), 71–80; *The Singer of Tales* (Cambridge, Mass.: Harvard University Press, 1960; Atheneum edn., 1965), ch. 4. Lord has always insisted that themes are learned but not memorized: on this see 'Homer as an Oral–Traditional Poet', in *Epic Singers and Oral Tradition* (Ithaca and London: Cornell University Press, 1991), 72–103, at 77.

[10] See e.g. J. Armstrong, 'The Arming Motif in the Iliad', *AJP* 79 (1958), 337–54; B. Fenik, *Typical Battle Scenes in the* Iliad: *Studies in the Narrative Techniques of Homeric Battle Description* (Wiesbaden: Franz Steiner, 1968); D. M. Gunn, 'Narrative Inconsistency and the Oral Dictated Text in the Homeric Epic', *AJP* 91 (1970), 192–203; M. Edwards, 'Type-Scenes and Homeric Hospitality', *TAPA* 105 (1975), 51–72. For a comprehensive survey of the literature on the type-scene, see M. Edwards, 'Homer and Oral Tradition: The Type-Scene', *Oral Tradition*, 7 (1992), 284–330.

We have, therefore, ample data, formulaic and thematic, which might serve as evidence of the compositional process which produced the Homeric epics. We recognize the formulaic language of Homer as the language of an oral poet who composes in performance; and we have come to see that the poet's typical scenes were an economical strategy for effecting the forward movement of his song. Parry's interpretation of the evidence, however, for a time created problems for those Homeric scholars for whom the aesthetic merits of the poems were paramount. He believed that the sole function of the ornamental epithet was to serve the demands of metre, and that, as a consequence, it had virtually no meaning of itself. And because the typical scene was linked by Parry and Lord with the formula, since they viewed the type-scene as an extended formula, it became subject to the same limitations. If we accept Parry's view that typical scenes are learned for the sole purpose of singing traditional epic, the formula and the typical scene alike are no more than prefabricated, multi-purpose, units of composition. It was an unhappy corollary of Parry's hypothesis, therefore, that for some years we almost lost sight of Homer, the poet who, as was once thought, had shaped his own individual versions of the quarrel of Achilleus and Agamemnon and the return of Odysseus to his homeland. Parry had emphasized the binding force of tradition, to which, he argued, the 'poets' of each generation of necessity conformed; Parry's poet was, at best, a craftsman who built a song from his repertory of learned phrases and themes: the extent of his repertory represented the limits of his capacity to sing. The notion of a confining tradition became a confinement in itself; it discouraged scholars from considering the Homeric epics as the products of a creative mind. And criticism in the wider sense—that is, the attempt to understand and to evaluate works which have aroused admiration and affection over the centuries—seemed to many scholars to be, in Griffin's words, 'naïve or impossible'.[11]

---

[11] See J. Griffin, 'Freshly Perceived Epics', *TLS* 4, 433 (March 18–24, 1988), 312. On this point see also J. Miles Foley, *Immanent Art: From Structure to Meaning in Traditional Oral Epic* (Bloomington: Indiana University Press, 1991),

In more recent times, however, there have been moves to re-focus oral-formulaic theory and to consider the poems not as texts of oral poems but as records of oral communication. Richard Martin and Egbert Bakker, for example, have recognized the value of trying to recapture the experience of traditional oral epic. That is, in their different ways, each attempts to place the words of the poet in the context of performance, giving consideration both to the poet who sings and to the audience which follows the tale.[12] This general issue was raised and discussed in Lord's study, *The Singer of Tales*. Lord there provided many insights into the singer's understanding of his role, through his accounts of interviews with his subjects in the field. But, as Martin observes, the question of communication in performance has on the whole been neglected by Homerists.[13] Indeed, it has only recently become apparent that research of great relevance to the ancient epics is being conducted in the fields of cognitive psychology and linguistics, and that a close understanding of cognitive and pragmatic issues—those issues which are central to communication in general and to oral communication in particular—is crucial if we are to appreciate the style, as well as the quality, of the Homeric epics. As Bakker observes, the poet's interaction with his audience should be no less important to us as a subject for study than his mastery of his formulaic language.[14]

at pp. xii, 2–5; I. De Jong, 'Homer as Literature: Some Current Areas of Research', in J. P. Crielaard, *Homeric Questions* (Amsterdam: J. C. Gieben, 1995), 127–46, esp. at 130–2. Griffin's claim is, nevertheless, overstated. De Jong gives the example of Edwards, whose research into the type-scene (e.g. 'Type-Scenes and Homeric Hospitality') has demonstrated Homer's artistry 'precisely in the use he makes of the traditional, oral style' (132).

[12] See e.g. R. Martin, *The Language of Heroes: Speech and Performance in the Iliad* (Ithaca and London: Cornell University Press, 1989); 'Similes and Performance', in E. Bakker and A. Kahane (eds.), *Written Voices, Spoken Signs: Performance, Tradition, and the Epic Text* (Cambridge, Mass.: Harvard University Press, 1997), 138–66; E. Bakker, *Poetry in Speech: Orality and Homeric Discourse* (Ithaca and London: Cornell University Press, 1997); 'The Study of Homeric Discourse', in I. Morris and B. Powell (eds.), *A New Companion to Homer* (Leiden: E. J. Brill, 1997), 284–304; 'Homeric ΟΥΤΟΣ and the Poetics of Deixis', *Classical Philology*, 94 (1999), 1–19.

[13] See Martin, *Language of Heroes*, 4; cf. the introductory comments of S. R. Slings, 'Written and Spoken Language: An Exercise in the Pragmatics of the Greek Sentence', *Classical Philology*, 87 (1992), 95–109, at 95.

[14] Bakker, 'Homeric ΟΥΤΟΣ', at 4.

Bakker has for the most part used current studies of everyday discourse to elucidate certain surface features of the epic. Although the language of the Homeric poems might be described as 'special speech', to distinguish it from the 'ordinary speech' of everyday, the two modes— 'special' and 'ordinary' speech—have much in common. For they both translate the workings of the mind into language for a listener.[15] Martin, on the other hand, has chosen to study the utterances of the heroes themselves. In considering Homer's heroes as poetic performers in their own right, he aims to 'discover the parameters' of their performance and to compare Greek notions of performance with our own.[16]

I propose in this volume to follow the path which has been laid out by these two scholars, taking as my starting point the hypothesis that these great epics were songs performed before a live audience; and that it is essential to take this into account in any analysis of the poems. I shall bring to the fore further evidence for the close parallels that exist between 'ordinary', everyday storytellings and the 'special' storytelling of Homer; and use these parallels to illuminate certain surface features of the poems. My approach to this task is in some ways similar to Bakker's, since, for reasons which I set out below, I base my discussion on findings in cognitive psychology and linguistics.[17] But whereas Bakker is interested in analysing in terms of spoken discourse certain features of Homeric style, such as the singer's use of particles, or the demonstrative οὗτος, or the appositional nature of his discourse, my interest lies in larger units of discourse: typical scenes, anecdotes, lists, invocations, descriptive passages, and similes. Like Martin, I examine these elements in their performative context; but, by contrast with Martin, the focus of my interest is the poet, whose circumstances are perhaps much as Albert Lord described them. Here is a man who needed to earn his keep through

[15] Bakker, 'Homeric Discourse', 300–1.
[16] Martin, *Language of Heroes*, 10.
[17] See e.g. E. Bakker, 'Homeric Discourse and Enjambement: A Cognitive Approach', *TAPA* 120 (1990), 1–21; 'Discourse and Performance: Involvement, Visualization and "Presence" in Homeric Poetry', *Classical Antiquity*, 12 (1993), 1–29; and, most important, *Poetry in Speech, passim*.

song. His task was to perform before an audience which had to be persuaded to listen and whose span of attention was in direct relationship to the quality of his song; his only resources were his voice, his 'special' epic dialect, his repertoire of stories, and his memory.[18]

The poet, or narrator, is the focus also of Scott Richardson's recent discussion of Homeric composition.[19] Richardson's analysis of the epics has been influenced by a number of theorists, principally, Gérard Genette and Seymour Chatman. For Richardson, the narrator is the link between story and discourse.[20] His study is a documentation from a theoretical perspective of the act of narration in the Homeric epics. He has gathered information on the poet's habits of narration, his conception of his task as creator of illusion, and his role as guide to the tale he tells.[21] And he examines the narrative for signs of Homer's presence in the discourse: he observes those occasions on which the poet has chosen to stand back from the story and keep his activity hidden and those on which he has chosen to show his hand.[22] A number of the conclusions which Richardson has drawn about the poet's habits and intentions are echoed in my discussion, especially in later chapters. But his approach is quite different from mine. Whereas Richardson has taken little account of oral-formulaic theory and has confined his study to the activity of the narrator as revealed by the text on the page, I shall be considering the narrator as a performer; and I shall begin my study not with the printed word, as Richardson does, but with the poet's mind.

WHAT IS MEMORY?

When we use the term 'memory' in everyday, non-specialist discourse, we appear to imply that memory is a single

---

[18] See Lord, *Singer*, ch. 2.

[19] S. Richardson, *The Homeric Narrator* (Nashville, Tenn.: Vanderbilt University Press, 1990).

[20] Richardson draws on structuralist theory to distinguish between the two terms: 'story' refers to what is depicted in the narrative; 'discourse' refers to the manner of the communication.

[21] Richardson, *Homeric Narrator*, 197–8.   [22] Ibid., 5.

unified phenomenon. Frances Yates, for example, in *The Art of Memory*, uses 'memory' in this general way;[23] and I have used the term in a similar fashion, in the sub-title of this introductory chapter. But, as cognitive psychologists observe, memory is not one system; it comprises a range of complementary systems, which have in common the capacity for storing information.[24] As we live our lives in the everyday world, much of the data we acquire and store are fed into memory by our senses. When we hear a sound or when we see an object, for example, we register auditory or visual information. This material will be held briefly in the auditory or the visual systems of short-term memory, which contribute to the functions of working memory.[25] But it is possible also that some of this information will pass into the long-term memory systems for the storage of sights and sounds; these are the systems which give us access to auditory memories, of voices and tunes, and visual memories, of faces and scenes.[26] A further function of visual memory, or possibly a separate memory system, is spatial memory; this is a form of memory which has been recognized, and exploited, from early times.[27] The spatial system is concerned with our memory for places and their relationships to one another.[28] The last of the memory systems relevant to this study is by no means the least

[23] See F. Yates, *The Art of Memory* (London: Routledge & Kegan Paul, 1966). Yates is, in fact, describing two of several systems of memory: spatial and visual memory.

[24] See A. Baddeley, *Human Memory: Theory and Practice* (Hove and London: Lawrence Erlbaum, 1990), 4–8.

[25] Working memory, with its limited capacity, is that complex system which is designed to cope with the present situation; its function is, quite simply, the exercise of remaining alert. On short-term memory, see Baddeley, *Human Memory*, ch. 3.

[26] See Baddeley, *Human Memory*, ch. 2, at 13.

[27] On the ancient world's interest in spatial memory, see Yates, *The Art of Memory*, esp. chs. 1 and 2; J. P. Small, *Wax Tablets of the Mind: Cognitive Studies of Memory and Literacy in Classical Antiquity* (London and New York: Routledge, 1997), chs. 7–9.

[28] See U. Neisser, 'Domains of Memory', in P. Solomon, G. Goethals, C. Kelley, B. Stephens (eds.), *Memory: Interdisciplinary Approaches* (New York and Berlin: Springer-Verlag, 1988), 67–83, at 76–7. D. Rubin, *Memory in Oral Traditions: The Cognitive Psychology of Epic, Ballads, and Counting-out Rhymes* (New York and Oxford: Oxford University Press, 1995), 57–9, draws a careful distinction, with references, between spatial memory and memory for image.

important. It is the system which processes and stores our general knowledge about the world: semantic, or episodic, memory.

All oral traditions depend on the resources of memory for the preservation and the transmission of their songs. My aim in this study of memory and oral song is to throw further light on the processes of storytelling in the epic tradition which we associate with Homer. My procedure will be to draw on the results of research into the nature and functions of the different memory systems which I have described above and to develop these findings in the specific context of the Homeric epics. My first point of reference will be the work of those cognitive psychologists who are interested in how we remember sequences of events, the components of a list of items, or of place-names; my second will be work on visual and auditory memory, which will throw light, respectively, on how we recall and generate descriptive passages and similes and how we 'learn' and recreate list-songs. I shall refer also to research in certain sub-disciplines of linguistics, which are concerned, amongst other things, with what it means to perform before an audience (even before an audience of one) and with the ways in which we shape the stories we tell so that they will be memorable. This exercise is primarily intended to advance our understanding of the composition of the epics and our appreciation of their art; at the same time, however, the application of cognitive theory to substantial segments of texts of acknowledged quality will be of interest to cognitive psychologists, as such an exercise provides a detailed case-study of the activities of the mind.[29] Let us begin with an account of episodic, or semantic, memory, that particular system which guides the comprehension and generation of narrative.

---

[29] See W. Chafe's statement of personal views in 'Some Things that Narratives Tell Us about the Mind', in B. Britton and A. Pellegrini (eds.), *Narrative Thought and Narrative Language* (Hillsdale, NJ: Lawrence Erlbaum, 1990), 79–98, esp. at 96–7; and note the recent contribution to interdisciplinary work in the cognitive sciences of C. Emmott, *Narrative Comprehension: A Discourse Perspective* (Oxford: Clarendon Press, 1997), whose aim is to 'show that the mind plays an important role in reading full-length texts' (xi).

STUDIES OF MEMORY FOR NARRATIVE IN PSYCHOLOGY AND COGNITIVE SCIENCE

The cognitive sciences have been particularly interested in how people understand and remember narrative, since research in this area may open the way to a broader understanding of cognitive processes. As a Homerist, I too am interested in the understanding and recall of narratives: hence my readiness to explore the ideas of cognitive psychology and to import them into an investigation of the *Iliad* and the *Odyssey*, two fine examples of the art of storytelling. I shall not, however, be the first to do so. In *Memory in Oral Traditions*, which I have cited above, David Rubin has summarized much relevant work in cognitive psychology for those who are interested in transmission in oral traditions of all kinds, including the oral epic tradition which produced the Homeric epics. I shall be making reference to his important book throughout my discussion of how memory has supported the singer of the *Iliad* and the *Odyssey*.

Since the 1970s evidence has been accumulating which suggests that knowledge of everyday activities and of conventional actions and reactions is fundamental to the process of comprehension. It has become obvious to the cognitive psychologist that people understand new experiences and new material in terms of existing structures in memory.[30] It has become clear, too, that if memory guides the processes of comprehension, it guides also the processes of composition. The starting point for any study of composition, therefore, should not be the language in which the story is ultimately expressed (which has until recently been accepted as the pathway to understanding the creative process); rather, we should begin with the mind which generates the whole. Storytelling, as I have suggested above, is a 'mind-based' activity.[31]

---

[30] See Baddeley, *Human Memory*, 335.
[31] The phrase is David Levy's. See D. Levy, 'Communicative Goals and Strategies: Between Discourse and Syntax', in T. Givón (ed.), *Discourse and Syntax* (New York: Academic Press, 1979), 183–210, at 184.

For all that it is exciting, this perspective is not new. In recent decades research in cognitive studies has returned to the work of Frederick Bartlett. In his book, *Remembering*, Bartlett proposed that when people remember new material they do so in terms of structures which are already in place in their memory; he called these memory structures 'schemas'.[32] To Bartlett a schema is a mental model of some part of our experience; it holds sequential information about events in the everyday world.[33] Bartlett demonstrated the role of the schema in his study of recall, wherein subjects were presented with an unfamiliar narrative (in this case a narrative from an unfamiliar culture, North American Indian) and were asked to recall the tale after various intervals of time, ranging from fifteen minutes to, an extreme case, six and a half years. What he noticed was that his subjects, in their retelling of the tale, would distort it by omitting features which did not fit with their understanding of the world or by distorting other features in order to accommodate them to their expectations of the world. He concluded that we all store in memory information about everyday experience. He used the term 'schemas' to describe these clusters of data, which are distillations of the experiences we encounter in everyday life. He argued that an individual automatically refers to these schemas in the process of remembering and is therefore likely to overlook details which he or she does not recognize as part of any of these schemas. The schema is, therefore, a tool for comprehension and composition.

Some forty years after the publication of *Remembering* there was renewed interest in Bartlett's work, in parallel with developments in the new field of artificial intelligence. Bartlett's ideas were re-examined and a number of papers appeared, which took up and reviewed his proposal that the act of remembering was a constructive act of reference to a number of knowledge structures: his so-called schemas. It is

---

[32] F. Bartlett, *Remembering: A Study in Experimental and Social Psychology* (Cambridge: Cambridge University Press, 1932; reprint edn., 1950). For discussion, see Baddeley, *Human Memory*, 335–7.

[33] See Bartlett, *Remembering*, at 199–200, 300–4, 312–14. For discussion of Bartlett's experiment and its conclusions, see Rubin, *Memory*, 130–6.

now a fundamental conviction of cognitive research that knowledge of the everyday world is stored in organized form, and that it is episodic in nature, since it is organized around personal experience (or one's acquaintance with the personal experience of others) rather than abstract semantic categories. Episodes which are similar in nature and content, such as visiting a restaurant, will be remembered in terms of standardized, generalized episodes, or structures of expectation. These have been called variously scripts, schemas, frames, or modules.[34] Rumelhart, a cognitive psychologist, uses the term 'schema'; Marvin Minsky, a computer scientist, has proposed a schema-like entity, which he has called a 'frame'; Roger Schank and Robert Abelson have introduced the concept of the 'script'.[35] Schemas, frames, modules, and scripts all have much in common: in summary, these entities are said to represent knowledge and experience, not definitions; they include a fixed core of routine actions or events along with a variable aspect; and they are active recognition devices.[36]

These scripts or schemas, as Bartlett suggested, allow us to find meaning and to reconstruct narrative. Because the script holds information about commonly experienced social events, it solves the problem of search in memory. It is possible for us quickly to recognize, to organize, and to interpret incoming information, and to make predictions about what is to happen next, simply through reference to the appropriate script. If speakers can assume that other people have access to the same scripts as their own, it will not be necessary to provide microscopic detail of the action sequence they are referring to, or of every causal connection within it. They can leave it to the audience to refer to the

---

[34] See D. Tannen, 'What's in a Frame? Surface Evidence for Underlying Expectations', in R. O. Freedle (ed.), *New Directions in Discourse Processing* (Norwood, NJ: Ablex, 1979), 137–81, esp. the introductory remarks at 137–44.

[35] See D. Rumelhart, 'Notes on a Schema for Stories', in D. Bobrow and A. Collins (eds.), *Representation and Understanding* (New York: Academic Press, 1975), 211–36; M. Minsky, 'A Framework for Representing Knowledge', in P. H. Winston (ed.), *The Psychology of Computer Vision* (New York: McGraw-Hill, 1975), 211–17; R. Schank and R. Abelson, *Scripts, Plans, Goals and Understanding: An Inquiry into Human Knowledge Structures* (Hillsdale, NJ: Lawrence Erlbaum, 1977).

[36] For this summary, see Baddeley, *Human Memory*, 336–7.

script which has been invoked and, therefore, to fill in the intervening steps, the causal connections, which make discourse coherent. Scripts allow us to fill in detail which is not overtly expressed. If we say something like 'I haven't time to cook this evening. Let's call that new restaurant and see if they have a table', only by calling up the restaurant script from memory can we make sense of what has been said. The implication that one must reserve a table at a restaurant so that one may eat there at a particular time is buried in that script. Because it is part of the script, it is not necessary for us to complete the expression of this idea or to say more than was expressed in the words I have used above. In order to be understood we need do no more than allude to a single element of the script.

In concluding their discussion of scripts and memory, Bower, Black, and Turner claim that scripts are a 'powerful and potentially valuable theoretical approach' to an investigation of cognitive processes.[37] The concept of the script, or the schema, is, indeed, of critical importance for Homerists in their efforts to understand the mechanics of oral composition. Since the episodic nature of the scripts which we are said to store in semantic memory appears to be mirrored in the recurrent narrative sequences of epic the notion of the cognitive script may explain certain characteristics of the Homeric type-scene. I shall argue that the typical scene (such as dressing, or preparing a meal), which Lord has declared to be a chunk of discourse committed to memory by an apprentice singer with performance in mind, may in fact be a scripted entity which encapsulates a standardized record of routine activities and which the singer to be, like

---

[37] See G. Bower, J. Black, and T. Turner, 'Scripts in Memory for Text', *Cognitive Psychology*, 11 (1979), 177–220, at 218. For a comprehensive, although in some respects intuitive, account of the workings of a script-based memory, see Schank and Abelson, *Scripts*. Schank and Abelson's account of memory is incomplete, since they do not recognize the role of other memory systems, such as visual memory and auditory memory. Their recent account of script-based memory, 'Knowledge and Memory: The Real Story', in R. Wyer (ed.), *Knowledge and Memory: The Real Story* (Hillsdale, NJ: Lawrence Erlbaum, 1995), 1–85, meets with the same criticisms as the former work: see e.g. D. Rubin, 'Stories about Stories', ibid., 153–64; W. Brewer, 'To Assert that Essentially All Human Knowledge and Memory is Represented in Terms of Stories is Certainly Wrong', ibid., 109–19.

anyone else, will have learned early in his life. We may identify the typical scene with the schema of Bartlett, or the script of Schank and Abelson, or of Bower, Black, and Turner. Athough a young man destined to be a singer may not yet know the 'special' language which he will later use in performance to give traditional expression to any script, he can, from an early age, render in everyday language the sequence of events which characterize it.

If we compare the two hypotheses, that of experientially-acquired scripts, which began with Bartlett, and Lord's insistence on learned themes, we note that the former offers us a more probable account of a singer's learning activities. According to this hypothesis, a singer will acquire scripted material in the normal course of life; the metrical language which will give it expression is, by contrast, actively learned by the young singer during his apprenticeship, at the same time as he commits to memory the story-paths of the songs he proposes to sing.

SCRIPT, NARRATIVE, AND STORY

If we express in sequence the details of any script, the outcome is a narrative of sorts, in which one routine event follows another. A scripted sequence does not, however, make a story; at the most, it may be render an element within a story. A story is a particular kind of discourse which we can distinguish from discourse of other kinds— from the instruction manual, for example, or the lecture. If it is to be successful, it must be intrinsically interesting. Whereas a script is a repository of predictable actions, a story deals with what is worth reporting: the unexpected.

The essential feature of any story is the narrative which is at its heart. The path of the narrative comprises a sequence of events linked by elements of explanation; this is often conceptualized as a causal chain.[38] Any narrative may be

---

[38] For confirmation of causal chain theory through psychological testing of human comprehension and recall, see J. Black and G. Bower, 'Story-Understanding as Problem-Solving', *Poetics*, 9 (1980), 223–50, at 234–5; on the criteria for the inclusion of an event in the causal chain of a narrative, see T. Trabasso and

reduced to a causal chain: we can, for example, identify from the *Iliad* the chain of events which led to Achilles' withdrawal from the fighting around Troy, or the chain of events which led to his return. The events along the chain may be fleshed out in the telling, especially by reference to relevant scripts. It is possible that the exercise of composition may see a re-ordering of the events of the causal chain in the interests of surprise or suspense;[39] or it may see emphasis on, or development of, one element of the chain at the expense of others. But we, the audience, expect that it should always be possible to retrieve the causal chain: for it is essential to the narrative sequence.

We should note that not all the connecting links which are necessary to the continuity of the causal chain (I refer here to connections of reason, cause, or enablement) need be expressed in a story. Some may be implicit. But there should be enough cues in the text to allow us to identify the important links: for example, there should be sufficient information to allow us to recognize the mental or emotional state of an actor, which leads him or her to take a certain action, and to connect that action with a resultant state. In most cases some specific knowledge of the social world is necessary to provide the relevant link, or links, in the processing chain, and to supply explanations of what has happened and predictions of what might happen. This is the kind of knowledge which I described above, which is stored in memory as scripts or schemas. Reference to knowledge stored in episodic form is fundamental to our habit of narration and to our ability to comprehend what we hear.

L. Sperry, 'Causal Relatedness and Importance of Story Events', *Journal of Memory and Language*, 24 (1985), 595–611; T. Trabasso and P. van den Broek, 'Causal Thinking and the Representation of Narrative Events', *Journal of Memory and Language*, 24 (1985), 612–30.

[39] For discussion from a psychological point of view of how stories may be made more effective by storytelling strategies which give rise to surprise, suspense, or curiosity in the audience, see W. Brewer and E. Lichtenstein, 'Stories are to Entertain: A Structural-Affect Theory of Stories', *Journal of Pragmatics*, 6 (1982), 473–86. For further discussion of this kind of structure, with particular reference to the Homeric epics, see Epilogue, below.

STORYTELLING AS SOCIAL ACTIVITY

All oral storytelling is performance. Whether it is produced for an audience of one or an audience of a hundred, whether the context is informal or formal, a storytelling is an event in itself. Our recent scholarly interest in stories as a mode of social interaction may be traced back to the work of Erving Goffman. Goffman's work, *The Presentation of Self in Everyday Life*, has since its publication generated considerable interest in personal interaction and discourse strategies, at the level of everyday exchange and in performance proper.[40] Goffman argued that there are considerable overlaps between each of these contexts: we are always 'performing', to a greater or lesser degree. And in his essay, 'On Face-Work', he offers important insights into the ways in which conversation works.[41] Here Goffman observes that all spoken interaction is regulated by a 'system of practices, conventions, and procedural rules'.[42] These rules and conventions guide us in the unspoken etiquette of conversation and organize the flow of communication amongst participants. Goffman's perceptions have been fruitfully amplified and extended in linguistic research by scholars such as William Labov, to whose work I refer below, Richard Wardhaugh, Richard Bauman, and Deborah Tannen. J. L. Austin, on the other hand, is interested in language as an integral part of social interaction. In *How to do Things with Words* he analyses the difference between the superficial meaning of an utterance and its force.[43] The distinction which he makes between locutionary, illocutionary, and perlocutionary acts has stimulated considerable interest in the ways in which speech acts may be analysed and understood. It was Austin's observation that a speech act may have a perlocutionary force (that is, that it may be intended

---

[40] E. Goffman, *The Presentation of Self in Everyday Life* (Edinburgh: Edinburgh University Press, 1958), esp. ch. 1. And note also his *Interaction Ritual: Essays on Face-to-Face Behaviour* (Harmondsworth: Penguin, 1972), ch. 1; and *Frame Analysis: An Essay on the Organization of Experience* (Harmondsworth: Penguin, 1975).

[41] Goffman, 'On Face-Work', in *Interaction Ritual*, 5–45.

[42] Ibid., 33–4.

[43] J. L. Austin, *How to Do Things with Words* (Oxford: Clarendon Press, 1962).

to achieve a certain effect through its utterance) that has perhaps been most important of all.[44] Austin's work has been one of the foundation texts of pragmatics, that branch of linguistics which is concerned with how people use language to manage situations and to carry out plans. The principle on which the study of pragmatics is based is that pragmatic theory provides insight into any speech unit in terms of its relation to the goals and plans of both producer and receiver—of speaker or writer, and his or her audience.[45]

Storytellers, in telling a story, inevitably have a purpose in mind; they may be doing so in order to entertain, to boast, to win sympathy, to persuade, or as a token of intimacy. To fulfil their goals storytellers will plan and shape their stories so that they will catch and hold the attention of their audiences and convey unambiguously the point of their tale. For they are aware that their display will be judged for skill and, without doubt, for effectiveness.[46] Given that no one wants to experience the embarrassment of having told a story which is deemed to be uninteresting or pointless, storytellers proceed carefully in order to increase their chances of success.[47]

First, any storyteller will choose a sequence of events which promises to appeal; he or she will select a sequence which contains an element of the unexpected. As I noted above, we do not make stories of everyday happenings which follow the predictable course. Such stories contain no surprises; they are not interesting to us. We expect a story to include events which interfere with the normal, or, in

---

[44] J. L. Austin, *How to Do Things with Words*, 101–32.

[45] For standard references, see D. Sperber and D. Wilson, 'Pragmatics', *Cognition*, 10 (1981), 281–6; T. van Dijk, *Text and Context: Explorations in the Semantics and Pragmatics of Discourse* (London and New York: Longman, 1977).

[46] See R. Bauman, *Story, Performance, and Event: Contextual Studies of Oral Narrative* (Cambridge: Cambridge University Press, 1986), 3.

[47] For a brief discussion of the social consequences of a failed story, see W. Labov, *Language in the Inner City: Studies in the Black English Vernacular* (Philadelphia: University of Pennsylvania Press, 1972), 366; E. Goffman, 'On Face-Work: An Analysis of Ritual Elements in Social Interaction', in J. Laver and S. Hutcheson (eds.), *Communication in Face to Face Interaction* (Harmondsworth: Penguin, 1972), ch. 17; L. Polanyi, 'Linguistic and Social Constraints on Story-telling', *Journal of Pragmatics*, 6 (1982), 509–24, at 519–20. The storyteller feels rejected because his or her story has been rejected; the listeners are embarrassed.

cognitive terms, the scripted, course of events. We expect to hear about an individual who cannot attain his or her goals simply by following a script, or individuals whose goals are in conflict, or everyday sequences which have been disrupted by an unexpected and therefore remarkable event.[48]

Second, a storyteller must present the story in a way that enables his or her listeners to follow the course of the tale. There is abundant evidence that storytellers of all kinds work to a recognizable procedural format when they tell their stories. My description below of the format which underlies the presentation of a story is an encapsulation of an analysis of 600 oral anecdotes—that is, stories occurring naturally in everyday conversation—by William Labov and Joshua Waletzky.[49] From their studies of storytelling and story structure they identified a series of moves which are made by all storytellers, at least in a Western culture.

Experienced storytellers, according to Labov and Waletzky, will almost unfailingly mark the limits of their tales: they will mark a beginning and an end. At the outset they will alert their potential audience to the story-to-come, by making known the drift of the tale they will tell. Labov and Waletzky have used the term *abstract* for this element. Apart from catching the attention of listeners, the abstract will summarize and possibly evaluate the story which the storyteller proposes to tell. The next step is to prepare listeners for the narrative which will be at its heart by ensuring that they are acquainted with relevant background knowledge and motivational information. This segment is called *orientation*. The storyteller then moves to the narrative proper, in which Labov and Waletzky have identified two elements: *complicating action* and the *resolution* of the tale. With a so-called *coda* speakers seal off their tale and return the audience to the conversation which had been suspended for the duration of the story. So that listeners will

---

[48] See S. Hidi and W. Baird, 'Interestingness—A Neglected Variable in Discourse Processing', *Cognitive Science*, 10 (1986), 179–94.

[49] For further discussion of this substantial study of story structure conducted in the late 1960s and a full account of the properties of storytelling, see W. Labov and J. Waletzky, 'Narrative Analysis: Oral Versions of Personal Experience', in J. Helm (ed.), *Essays on the Verbal and Visual Arts* (Seattle: University of Washington Press, 1967), 12–44, at 32–41. See also Labov, *Language in the Inner City*, ch. 9.

understand the action as is intended, storytellers will include cues which enable their audience to draw conclusions about the nature and content of the narrative. These cues serve the purpose of *evaluation*.[50] Evaluative information does not appear in any one fixed position. It is usually presented at relevant points throughout the tale. This series of moves, which prompts the teller to present his tale in such a way that his audience may follow it and enjoy it, functions co-operatively with the processes of memory which monitor and organize the sequential flow of the narrative itself; these processes together serve the specific function of storytelling: that is, they bring about the successful interaction of story-teller and audience, both with each other and with the text.

IS THERE A SCRIPT FOR STORYTELLING?

It is clear that this knowledge—of how to present a story—is learned. And it is learned at the workface, so to speak. All of us have seen new storytellers (I am thinking here of children in their apprenticeship as storytellers) being questioned, prompted, and assisted by their sympathetic listeners, who are encouraging them to present a coherent account of experience. More precisely, these novices are being tutored in the craft of storytelling. Children most often omit from their tales or only partly render that element which Labov and Waletzky call orientation. It becomes the task of their listeners to urge them to provide the information against which the narrative may be understood. These exchanges between a child and his or her adult audience reflect our cognitive need for such data. Our insistence on what is necessary fulfils an educative role. We are instructing the child in framing a story so that it will be acceptable to its audience.

In the sense that our definition of a script to this point has specified a particular physical setting and prescribes actions

---

[50] For further discussion, including my own elaboration, of these properties of storytelling, see Ch. 6, below.

rather than discourse, the knowledge of how to structure a story is not like the scripts which we have met so far. What we are considering here is a generalized skill, a skill for telling stories. This kind of knowledge has been termed 'implicit knowledge', or, as Rubin expresses it, 'knowing how'.[51] 'Implicit knowledge', as the name itself suggests, is intuitive knowledge; it is the kind of expertise which has been acquired unconsciously over time; it represents the sum of past experience without specific reference to any single past event; and it may not lend itself to verbalization.[52] That is, we cannot readily find the words to describe the steps of the procedure in question, even though we are able to perform it. Implicit knowledge may be contrasted with 'explicit knowledge', the type of declarative, script-based knowledge which I have discussed above, and which encapsulates knowledge that may be readily communicated in words. Rubin defines such knowledge as 'knowing that'.[53] Both kinds of knowledge, implicit and explicit, are represented in memory as schemas or scripts. But the scripts which hold implicit knowledge differ from the action sequences of situational scripts, since they are more abstract. Such scripts do not comprise a series of specified actions; they do not lead directly to words; rather, they prescribe steps to be followed. The script for storytelling, therefore, might unfold thus: introduce the tale; orientate your listeners; set out the complicating action; tell how things turned out; give an overview. In my discussions in later chapters I shall use the term 'format' to distinguish this more abstract phenomenon from the declarative script.[54] Chapter 3, for

[51] See Rubin, *Memory*, 190–1. This kind of knowledge is described as 'memory expertise': see D. Rubin, W. Wallace, and B. Houston, 'The Beginnings of Expertise for Ballads', *Cognitive Science*, 17 (1993), 435–62, at 435, 436–7, 454–5.
[52] Rubin, Wallace, and Houston, 'The Beginnings of Expertise for Ballads', at 436–8, 452–7.
[53] Rubin, *Memory*, 191.
[54] For further discussion, see Ch. 3, below. During the last twenty-five years there has been much discussion of story structure, often in terms of 'story grammar'. The gradual trend away from strictly formal grammars to a model which recognizes psychological processes is reflected in my discussion above. For a survey of earlier attempts to describe the nature of story, see R. de Beaugrande, 'The Story of Grammars and the Grammar of Stories', *Journal of Pragmatics*, 6 (1982), 383–422.

example, offers a comparison of the description format which is part of both Homer's memory store and our own.

It is implicit knowledge which underpins our ability to present our stories in a familiar and acceptable fashion, as I have described above. It structures other discourse units also, such as individual speech acts. These patterns, which I shall discuss further in Chapter 1, are of the 'knowing how' kind. When we rebuke a child, for example, we generally express our rebuke in a predictable fashion. We use a scripted format to trigger a particular series of moves; these moves cue the appropriate words. Homer's expressions of speech acts appear to follow the same, script-based procedure; they are, for the most part, refined versions of everyday discourse.[55] I shall refer to them in following chapters as 'speech-act scripts' or 'formats'.

THE STORY FORMAT IN THE HOMERIC EPICS

In Chapter 6 I describe the format for stories in more detail. I propose there two modifications to Labov and Waletzky's analysis of the elements *abstract* and *coda*. What is most interesting to me in my enquiry into the role which memory plays in storytelling is that the features which Labov and Waletzky point out to us, and the scope which they offer for a series of correspondences within stories—that is, for repetition or near repetition of words or, indeed, ideas (for example, in the elements *abstract* and *coda*)—find a parallel in Homer. In Homeric studies and other areas of classical research, similar correspondences have been termed 'ring composition'.[56] Ring composition has been identified as a premeditated pattern on the surface of the text, a pattern

[55] I base my argument in part on my observation that the expression of many of the speech-acts in Homer is echoed in our own intuitive models for speech-acts today: compare Homer's pattern for a rebuke (*reproach, the problem, generalization, proposal*) with our own. For further discussion and references, see Ch. 1, below.

[56] For the first use of the term, see W. van Otterlo, *De Ringcompositie als Opbouwprincipe in de epische Gedichten van Homerus* (Amsterdam: Noord-Hollandsche Uitg. Mij., 1948). For further references and discussion, see Ch. 6, below.

created by the poet as he sings. It has been argued that he uses this pattern for either aesthetic or, possibly, mnemonic purposes. When the same element appears at the beginning and at the end of a story or a segment of text, this correspondence is referred to as a ring. I shall argue that the kinds of correspondences which we observe in Homer are not self-conscious and artful, as has been proposed; rather, they reflect the story format used by any teller of tales, whether he or she is telling stories informally, in the course of conversation, or formally, before an invited audience. This explanation of Homer's so-called rings, in terms of the pragmatics of storytelling, allows us to see that Homer followed a strategy very close to our own. In this respect, he is behaving as we all do, when we are telling stories.

We might ask whether Homer was at all aware of the story-framework within which he worked. I shall argue that he was, but to a degree only; for, as I noted above, implicit knowledge of this kind does not lend itself to ready verbalization. It is intuitive, rather than intentional. In my study, in Chapter 5, of the ways in which Homer distributes across his epics his invocations to the Muse or Muses, I conclude that there is a discernible pattern of usage. The poet in the *Iliad* appeals to the Muses in that prolonged period when he is putting his story together (this is the so-called element *complicating action*); throughout this stretch of narrative he occasionally interrupts his story to seek inspiration from the divinities and to assert to his audience his quality as a singer. But from the moment of climax, that moment which sets the tale onto its path towards *resolution*, Homer does not break into the story again. He is unwilling now to distract his audience's attention from the action of the narrative; he is confident that the tale itself will hold their interest. We observe the same phenomenon in the *Odyssey*. It appears, therefore, that Homer did distinguish, perhaps to the degree that we all make a distinction—that is, intuitively—between the developing story and its movement towards resolution.

AUDITORY MEMORY

A long digression arising out of comments on semantic, or episodic, memory and its role in storytelling has distracted us from a survey of the principal processing and storage systems of memory. I turn now to a second system: auditory memory.

Auditory memory encompasses our memory for sounds, for voices, for music, and for language. We have observed that language is processed through semantic memory (in terms of schemas, or scripts, as I have discussed above); but spoken language is processed also as an auditory phenomenon.[57] The relevance of auditory memory to the memorability of oral song has been discussed by Rubin, who shows how patterns of sound assist in prompting a singer's memory.[58] This prompting function will be of interest to us, when we consider Homer's performances of lists and catalogues within the epics, for list-singing challenges memory in an extraordinary way. The nature of the list does not allow the singer to create a causal chain of reason, cause, or enablement, which will cue successive items. To 'learn' a list for performance, therefore, a poet will rely to a significant degree on principles of association, classification, and organization, which in their own various ways make the list meaningful for the singer, and easier to learn. The importance of such strategies as these has been understood since ancient times.[59] But, as I have suggested, there is another source of support besides that of semantic memory. Surface features of the list, such as assonance, alliteration, rhyme, and rhythm, also favour learning and prompt memory. In that these phonological patterns limit possible choices for word or phrase, they reduce search time in auditory memory and promote the recall of strings of items. Remarkably, those 'tricks' of composition which aid the singer are highly esteemed by the audience. In Chapter 2 I shall make the

---

[57] Baddeley, *Human Memory*, 33–5.

[58] For discussion of auditory memory in relation to oral traditions, see Rubin, *Memory*, ch. 4; and see below, Ch. 2.

[59] See Yates, *The Art of Memory*, chs. 1 and 2. For further discussion, see Ch. 2, below.

point that the very features of list-singing which are of value
to the singer as prompts to memory (alliteration, rhyme, and
rhythm, for example) are the same features which give special
pleasure—auditory pleasure—to his audience.

VISUAL MEMORY: IMAGES AND WORDS

Nearly all of us are able to bring to mind images of people
we know, events we have experienced, and items we have
seen in the past. We keep a store of such visual information
in memory and from this store we are able to generate
images in our mind's eye. Mental imagery, an analogue
system which represents and manipulates visual and spatial
information, shares many properties with actual perception,
hence the use of the popular term 'seeing with the mind's
eye', to describe the process of visualization.[60] Epic song,
with its strongly delineated action and its readily imaginable
scenes, capitalizes on the unique properties of imagery and
our ability to reconstruct from memory scenes, actions,
items, and faces. It is easy for most of us, if we wish, to
'run through' or 'see' whole episodes of the Homeric epics;
as Rubin observes, imagery, whether visual or spatial (which
I have described above), is one of the most powerful
mnemonic aids.[61]

There are three respects in which an understanding of
visual memory is important to us in our discussion of
traditional epic. The first is in connection with the poet's
memory for his song. We must conceive of epic song as
Rubin has described it, as a movie which runs in the cinema
of the mind: the mind of the poet and of the audience.[62] The

[60] For discussion, see M. Farah, 'Is Visual Imagery Really Visual? Overlooked
Evidence from Neuropsychology', *Psychological Review*, 95 (1988), 307–17, who
discusses the phenomenology of 'seeing with the mind's eye'. She concludes that
imagery is visual in the sense of 'using some of the same neural representational
machinery as vision'.

[61] See Rubin, *Memory*, at 60–3. For brief discussion of spatial imagery, and
references, see above.

[62] See Rubin, *Memory*, 41–6, for relevant studies; for much the same metaphor
and further discussion, see S. Fleischman, *Tense and Narrativity: From Medieval*

story that the poet tells, therefore, is his account of that movie-like sequence. Sometimes the singer's perspective on the action will be panoramic. In the case of the *Iliad*, the poet might visualize mass fighting and strive to convey to his audience the confused scene that he sees. Sometimes— indeed, in Homeric epic, more often—he will focus quite closely on intimate scenes: a duel, a discussion in mid-battlefield, a quiet moment of regret and sorrow, an instant of revelation. At other times he will narrow his focus further, to recreate for us an item in the possession of one of his characters: a sword, a shield, a finely-worked robe, or a splendid silver bowl. This close perspective on the material world may seem charming but pointless, until we observe the poet at work. In my discussion in Chapter 3, I show how the poet constructs his passages of description and how he uses them to achieve his ends as a storyteller at certain high moments in the drama. Visual memory, semantic memory, implicit knowledge, and the poet's understanding of his craft all contribute to the success of such segments within the narrative.

An understanding of the operations of visual memory is important to us in a third way. Since memory is not only the storehouse of imagery but also the seat of language, we might ask ourselves how imagery and language interact *vis-à-vis* memory. For some years Allan Paivio has been investigating the roles of imagery and language in regard to memory and thought, and has observed that imagery has special advantages over language and linguistic processes.[63] He states, on the basis of evidence from numerous experiments, that it is easier to bring to mind and to remember 'pictureable' material than it is to recall less 'pictureable' material; and that mental images are more effective as a mnemonic device than verbal techniques such as rote

Performance to Modern Fiction (Austin: University of Texas Press, 1990), 266–74; and see also Richardson, *Homeric Narrator*, 197, who in his conclusion states that Homer presents his audience with something like the view of the story they would have if they were to watch it directly. That is, Homer gives the impression of a continuous, filmed sequence.

[63] See e.g. A. Paivio, *Imagery and Verbal Processes* (New York: Holt, Rinehart & Winston, 1971); 'The Mind's Eye in Arts and Science', *Poetics*, 12 (1983), 1–18, at 6.

rehearsal.[64] That is, material which is high in imagery value is easier to remember than abstract material.[65] Paivio points out, too, that concrete words and the images they evoke are valuable as retrieval cues for other associated information.[66] They can be used as symbols for broader concepts which can be organized around them. Thus an image can serve as a reference point, or 'conceptual peg', for other information.[67] Furthermore, Paivio notes that mental images are dynamic.[68] We can transform them or manipulate them; we can scan a scene which we hold in the mind's eye; we can focus on events to one side; and we can move back and forward through sequences with little effort. And yet an image, according to Paivio, takes up less space in memory than does a sequence of verbal description which contains the same information. When we access an image in memory we retrieve, in an instant, a bundle of complex information 'organized synchronously';[69] by contrast, when we access an abstract word, we retrieve one unit of information.

But, for all that, it is a verbal cue which most often initiates an image. Indeed, Paivio concludes that imagery itself rarely functions independently of language. To explain our ability to move so readily between images and words, whether we are describing scenes which are before our eyes or generating drawings from descriptions, and to explain the advantages of such an ability, Paivio has given expression to a 'dual coding' hypothesis of memory, which has provided the most successful account so far of the role of imagery in learning and memory tasks.[70] According to his theory, when

---

[64] For the term 'pictureable', see Paivio, 'The Mind's Eye', at 7–8. See also Farah, 'Is Visual Imagery Really Visual?'.

[65] Paivio, 'The Mind's Eye', at 8.

[66] This realization is not new: for analysis of the experience of Simonides, whose observations on the power of imagery and its relation to memory led him to devise his techniques for recall (Cicero, *de Or.* 2. 86), see Yates, *The Art of Memory*, ch. 1. And see also Ch. 2, below.

[67] Paivio, 'The Mind's Eye', at 13–14.

[68] Ibid., 15–16.

[69] For the phrase, see ibid., 8.

[70] See A. Paivio, *Mental Representations: A Dual Coding Approach* (New York: Oxford University Press, 1986). For an overview of the theory and its contribution to our understanding of the comprehension of metaphor, see A. Paivio and M. Walsh, 'Psychological Processes in Metaphor Comprehension and Memory', in A. Ortony (ed.), *Metaphor and Thought*, 2nd edn. (Cambridge: Cambridge

we name a familiar object, two kinds of memory traces will be evoked simultaneously, a visual response (we see an image) and a verbal response (we register a word). The advantage of such dual coding is the probability that recall for the material in question is increased because the concept has been stored in two ways: 'there are two paths to an idea rather than one'.[71] The two memory codes are individually advantageous in different contexts (in different tasks or in different aspects of the same task), since visual imagery stores information in a synchronous fashion, as we noted above; and the linguistic code stores it sequentially. Imagery, therefore, not only provides a vast repertoire of concrete memories which embody much of our knowledge of the world but it can be used, whether consciously or unconsciously, to facilitate recall.

The Homeric simile, like the descriptive passage, creates a moment of rest in the narrative. And, like the descriptive passage, it draws together image and word. The simile is, of course, expressed in words. But the comparison itself is always an image; Homer's similes, like our own, are 'pictureable'. In Chapter 4, where I discuss similes as a general phenomenon in discourse and consider the nature, the composition, and the function of simile in the context of the Homeric epics, my point of reference will be the importance of imagery in the mental functions of both the singer and his audience.

Albert Lord begins his work, *The Singer of Tales*, with the remark that what has been needed most in Homeric scholarship, following Milman Parry's work, has been a more exact knowledge of the way in which oral epic poets learn and compose their songs.[72] To be sure, this is one of the questions which has preoccupied Homeric scholars in recent decades. It is a question which might now be profitably reconsidered. Parry and Lord's collection of south-Slavic material has, of

---

University Press, 1993), at 307–28. For evaluation of the theory, see M. Marschak, 'Imagery and Organization in the Recall of Prose', *Journal of Memory and Language*, 24 (1985), 734–45, at 734; Baddeley, *Human Memory*, 106–9.

[71] Paivio, 'The Mind's Eye', 16–17, at 17.
[72] Lord, *Singer*, 3.

course, made possible substantial advances in this project. But equally important is the work of cognitive psychologists and linguists, who have provided us with a conceptual framework within which we can review the Parry–Lord hypotheses. We must remember that the functions of memory are not thoroughly understood; nor am I capable of doing more than reporting on the work of scholars in cognitive studies. But it is clear that, owing to developments in this large field, we are in a position at last to develop a far more realistic view of the way in which the poet of the *Iliad* and the *Odyssey* composed his remarkable songs and to account for some of their extraordinary features. And I suggest that we might have the blessing of Milman Parry himself, who once urged classical scholars that, if they wished to persuade others of the importance for humanity of Greek and Latin literature, they should 'quit their philological isolation' and 'join in the movement of current human thought'.[73]

David Rubin has made an invaluable contribution to the study of Homeric epic through his painstaking collection of relevant studies of memory, in the field of cognitive psychology. He draws together the information he has gathered in a concluding discussion, which takes the form of a theoretical review of the process of recall in oral traditions.[74] Here he tries to identify the factors in memory which contribute to a performer's recall of song and to his ability to maintain the continuity of performance. Because, as Rubin observes, people are not good at 'verbatim memory of language', we might ask how they manage as professional storytellers.[75] How do they succeed, as Demodokos did, in singing λίην . . . κατὰ κόσμον (all too right following the tale, *Od.* 8. 489)?[76] It appears, in fact, that professional storytellers work not so much *from* memory, but *with* memory. That is, when

---

[73] M. Parry, 'The Historical Method in Literary Criticism', *Harvard Alumni Bulletin*, 38 (1936), 778–82; reprinted in A. Parry (ed.), *Homeric Verse*, 408–13, at 413.

[74] See Rubin, *Memory*, at 304–7.

[75] Ibid., 306

[76] I shall refer throughout to the Oxford text of the Homeric epics, D. B. Monro and T. W. Allen (eds.) *Homeri Opera*, i–iv (Oxford: Clarendon Press, 1902); translations for the most part are those of R. Lattimore, *The* Iliad *of Homer* (Chicago: University of Chicago Press, 1951); *The* Odyssey *of Homer* (New York: Harper & Row, 1965).

singers are confronted with the task of drawing from
memory a sequence of events which will be the foundation
of a good story—and the words to express it—they employ a
number of memory-based functions: memory for typical
scenes (that is, semantic, or episodic, memory), visual
memory, spatial memory, and auditory memory. These
many sources, complementing each other, point them
towards the words they are seeking, so that they can tell a
story which is so well constructed and so well expressed that
it could be mistaken for the work of a bard who has had
special tutoring from the Muse, or from Apollo. This is the
compliment which Eumaios pays to Odysseus: ἦ σέ γε Μοῦσ'
ἐδίδαξε, Διὸς πάϊς, ἦ σέ γ' Ἀπόλλων (Surely the Muse, Zeus'
daughter or else Apollo has taught you, *Od.* 8. 488).

Rubin, in his study of ballads, keeps his focus on the
performer. It is the skilled singer who holds his attention.[77]
But we must remember that the memory-based skills on
which the singer draws in performance are resources which
we all share: we all have these skills and we all use them,
although not with the conspicuous success of the great
singer of oral epic in the ancient world. This knowledge,
that we share these skills with Homer, and that he worked in
the same tradition of storytelling that we know and practise,
makes the study of his singing both exciting and engaging.
On a practical level this knowledge allows us to test out the
hypotheses of cognitive psychology against our own experience, before we use them to make claims for Homer's
compositional practices.[78]

---

[77] Rubin, *Memory*, ch. 11.

[78] I report here on an informal experiment that I carried out in successive years
with classes of first-year Ancient History students who were studying the *Iliad* in
translation. By way of impressing on them the nature of oral composition, I asked
them, after they had read and discussed a number of Homeric scripts, similes, and
descriptive passages, to generate a small 'Homeric' episode of their own. The point of
the exercise was to lift the epic off the printed page—that is, to force students to think
of epic in oral terms—and to persuade them that, monumental as it is, the *Iliad* could
have been composed orally. The students quickly saw that what an oral poet needed
(apart from the language of epic and a collection of stories—both of which he had to
develop for himself) was his existing knowledge of routine action sequences and a
considerable body of implicit knowledge, such as I describe above, about the ways of
oral epic. It was remarkable then to observe how little time elapsed before these
students were able to imitate (in English) epic song. For a similar, but formal, study,
see Rubin, Wallace, and Houston, 'The Beginnings of Expertise for Ballads'.

In my account of how the different functions of memory individually contribute to Homer's recreation of the Achilleus-story and the Odysseus-story as monumental tales, I shall be observing also the diverse ways in which these functions of the mind have left their traces in song. Audiences over generations have learned to recognize these features and to value them: the poet's use of a 'special', formulaic language, his ritualized development of typical scenes, his familiar story format, his delight in imagery, his love of anecdote, and his enthusiasm for lists. In discovering more about the epic singer's capacity for, and approach to, his task, we shall come closer to understanding why such elements, familiar as they are to the audience, are the source of so much pleasure.

Homer's Typical Scenes: Homeric Theme and Cognitive Script

Within the Homeric epics it is possible to identify a number of 'typical scenes': action sequences such as contests, meals, journeys, visits, and funeral rites; procedures such as dressing, or harnessing horses; and, although they were not considered by Milman Parry and Albert Lord, various speech acts, such as rebukes, challenges, exhortations, prayers, and boasts. Parry and Lord referred to such stereotyped episodes as themes. In each of these repeated scenes we notice recurrent ideas or events, some or all of which are expressed each time Homer refers to that scene. Indeed, in the case of routines which describe social situations and mechanical operations, the language in which they are expressed is generally, and not surprisingly, the same as well.[1] In the case of speech acts it is less often the case that lexical similarity is thoroughgoing; for this reason their predictable organization was initially overlooked. Nevertheless, it is possible to observe repeated patterns of discourse in a wide range of individual speech acts; Richard Martin, for example, refers to the poet's conventional modes of expression as rhetorical 'genres'.[2]

[1] According to Parry, a typical scene is a recurrent sequence which is narrated 'with many of the same details and many of the same words': see A. Parry (ed.), 'On Typical Scenes in Homer', in *The Making of Homeric Verse: The Collected Papers of Milman Parry* (Oxford: Clarendon Press, 1971), 404–7, at 404. Apart from studies of individual themes, a number of which I have listed in my Introduction, the most remarkable sustained discussion of thematic structure is that of B. Fenik, *Typical Battle Scenes in the* Iliad: *Studies in the Narrative Techniques of Homeric Battle Description* (Wiesbaden: Franz Steiner, 1968). See also, more recently, S. Reece, *The Stranger's Welcome: Oral Theory and the Aesthetics of the Homeric Hospitality Scene* (Ann Arbor: University of Michigan Press, 1993).

[2] See R. Martin, *The Language of Heroes: Speech and Performance in the* Iliad (Ithaca and London: Cornell University Press, 1989) 44–5, at 44. Let us take as an example a number of rebukes from the *Iliad*: at *Il.* 5. 472–92; 7. 96–102; 13. 726–

For Albert Lord, themes are the building blocks of narrative: when strung together, they become the story.[3] Following Parry, he claimed that themes are clusters of ideas learned as a unit by the apprentice singer, who reproduces them faithfully when he sings;[4] they exist solely for the sake of the song.[5] Each theme, once learned, remains the possession of the singer; it is not accessible to all.[6] It is this assumption, that the Homeric typical scene is a poetic device confined to traditional epic song, which has prompted my review of the Parry–Lord account. For I believe, with Michael Nagler, that the typical scene or theme which we discern in Homer is more than a form of words coined as a response to the exigencies of oral performance.[7] It is important to our understanding of the mechanics of oral composition, therefore, that we look again at the relation of the typical scene to epic song, now in the light of recent work in cognitive research.

COGNITIVE RESEARCH AND THE 'TYPICAL SCENE'

One of the aims of cognitive studies is to come to terms with the processes which underlie communication: hence the

47; 24. 33–54. Despite the lack of thoroughgoing verbal parallels, note the pattern which underlies each rebuke: *reproach, the problem, generalization, proposal*. (For a similar outline of the rebuke pattern, see Fenik, *Typical Battle Scenes*, 120.) The most exhaustive study of speech acts is that of D. Lohmann, *Die Komposition der Reden in der* Ilias (Berlin: de Gruyter, 1970). His analysis of speeches, however, relies heavily on ring-composition as a structural principle (5–6): see e.g. his discussion of a rebuke at 21. For comment on ring-composition, see Ch. 6, below. For analysis, from a Parry–Lord viewpoint, of the patterns which underlie certain speech acts, see E. Minchin, 'The Interpretation of a Theme in Oral Epic: *Iliad* 24. 559–70', *G&R* 33 (1986), 11–19; M. Willcock, 'The Search for the Poet Homer', *G&R* 37 (1990), 1–13, at 7–11.

[3] A. B. Lord, *The Singer of Tales* (Cambridge, Mass.: Harvard University Press, 1960; Atheneum edn., 1965), 95–6. Although Lord's proposal has been sustained in scholarship in the years since the publication of *The Singer of Tales* (see e.g. Reece, *The Stranger's Welcome*, 2 and 190), a sound argument against the proposal that the theme is the building block of song has been raised by M. Finkelberg, 'A Creative Oral Poet and the Muse', *AJP* 111 (1990), 293–303, at 299. As she points out (n. 20), Lord has blurred the distinction between the 'facts' of a given story and its thematic development.

[4] Lord, *Singer*, 68–9, 78, 98.   [5] Ibid., 94.   [6] Ibid., 68, 71, 78, and 98.

[7] See M. Nagler, *Spontaneity and Tradition: A Study in the Oral Art of Homer* (Berkeley: University of California Press, 1974).

interest of the cognitive sciences—in which I include cognitive psychology and linguistics, as well as what we now know as cognitive science—in narrative. Stories of all kinds have been used by scholars in these fields to test hypotheses about the structure and the function of memory. The cognitive psychologist and the cognitive scientist investigate the way in which individuals compose and comprehend narrative sequences and the role which memory—that is, stored knowledge—plays in these operations. The cognitive psychologist's aim in this exercise is to understand the mechanisms of human understanding; the cognitive scientist aims to construct a system which models these mechanisms. If for no other reason than the fact that narrative is the focus of research in other fields, the ideas which emerge from these studies are worth examination; and they are illuminating.[8] I present below, in summary, an account of the organization of memory, in terms proposed by a cognitive scientist, Roger Schank, and his colleague, a psychologist, Robert Abelson.[9] Although Schank has continued to develop his hypothesis and to recast his programmes, I shall be referring to his earlier work with Abelson, since it is this material which addresses directly the relevant issues.[10] What is important to my discussion is not the particular theory of long-term memory which Schank and Abelson propose, but their clear presentation of ideas which are current and generally accepted in psychology about the storage of knowledge in episodic form.[11] Schank

[8] See G. Bower, J. Black, and T. Turner, 'Scripts in Memory for Text', *Cognitive Psychology*, 11 (1979), 177–220, at 218. See also the discussion, with references, in the Introduction, above; the work of Frederick Bartlett, described there, has been fundamental to much of the research which has since been done in the cognitive sciences.

[9] The exposition of their theory and an explanation of its application is to be found in R. Schank and R. Abelson, *Scripts, Plans, Goals and Understanding: An Inquiry into Human Knowledge Structures* (Hillsdale, NJ: Lawrence Erlbaum, 1977).

[10] For Schank's later study of the workings of memory, see R. Schank, *Dynamic Memory: A Theory of Reminding and Learning in Computers and People* (Cambridge: Cambridge University Press, 1982); see also R. Schank and R. Abelson, 'Knowledge and Memory: The Real Story', in R. Wyer (ed.), *Knowledge and Memory: The Real Story* (Hillsdale, NJ: Lawrence Erlbaum, 1995), 1–85.

[11] See D. Rubin, *Memory in Oral Traditions: The Cognitive Psychology of Epic, Ballads, and Counting-out Rhymes* (New York and Oxford: Oxford University Press, 1995), 26–8, for studies in cognitive psychology which accord with Schank

and Abelson base their discussions on the hypothesis which arose out of Frederick Bartlett's work, described in my Introduction, that each person acquires a vast store of knowledge about routine sequences of events in the everyday world and that he or she draws on this knowledge to make sense of actions or events in the real world or in the world described in stories.

Narrative texts have become interesting to cognitive science, therefore, because of their content and the way that this content is presented. As a cognitive scientist might see it, a narrative is a chain of events which are related in terms of cause and effect.[12] The chain exists in the mind of a speaker, who attempts to communicate this linked sequence to his or her listeners, so that they in turn can reconstruct in their minds the same sequence and the same interrelationships. But the chain of cause and effect which the speaker had in mind at the outset, and which his or her listeners construct for themselves as they hear the tale, is in some respects different from the narrative as the speaker expresses it. This is because much of the information which is transferred during the telling is implicit: no storyteller will spell out all the details of every action performed in the course of events; nor does he feel it necessary to indicate the motivation behind each action to which he refers. He expects that his listeners can—and will—make certain connections without instruction.[13] The cognitive sciences ask, therefore, what sort of knowledge it is which, for the most part, can be left unspoken, even though it is essential to the coherence of the narrative, and

and Abelson's hypotheses about the storage of episodic data and the ways in which we use such data. For discussion of the reservations which some cognitive psychologists hold about other aspects of Schank and Abelson's account of memory, see my Introduction.

[12] For discussion of the causal chain fundamental to narrative, see my Introduction, above. By 'event' in this context I refer not to a real-world happening but to a cognitive construct which 'mediates between experience and language': see S. Fleischman, *Tense and Narrativity: From Medieval Performance to Modern Fiction* (Austin: University of Texas Press, 1990), 97–100 (a survey of the literature on 'event' and its definition), at 99. Note that the sequential nature of 'events' is fundamental to the notion of story.

[13] For introductory discussion and examples, see Schank and Abelson, *Scripts*, 9–11; Rubin, *Memory*, 24–5, 28.

how it is organized in memory so that it can be readily retrieved.

The kind of information which is referred to here has been described as 'world knowledge' or 'cultural knowledge'. Such knowledge includes information about our physical environment, about survival skills, and about the social world—about how people react to various stimuli, about what happens in all kinds of social contexts, and about how one should act in those contexts.[14] Schank and Abelson are immediately concerned with how we store and access knowledge of this kind. They work from the assumption that if memory is to function efficiently, it must be organized according to certain principles. They have proposed, therefore, an organizational system of knowledge which relies on a simple hierarchy of theoretical entities. They have called these entities 'goals', 'plans', and 'scripts'. At the highest level in their proposed system information is stored about the kinds of goals which we are likely to hold and about how these goals interact.[15] Then there are plans. Information at this level enables us to cope with the variety of situations which confront us daily; and it allows us to make inferences about other people's behaviour.[16] And at the lowest level there are scripts.[17] Scripts organize information about the events and actions through which we fulfil our plans—events and actions which, for the most part, we experience routinely.[18]

[14] See Schank and Abelson, *Scripts*, 3–5, 36–7 (with examples). Schank and Abelson define world knowledge as 'the world of psychological and physical events occupying the mental life of ordinary individuals, which can be understood and expressed in ordinary language' (4). And see Rubin, *Memory*, 24–5.

[15] See Schank and Abelson, *Scripts*, ch. 5. Note that Schank and Abelson locate the origins of an individual's goals in his background 'themes' (on 'themes' in this system, as biological needs or elements of personality, see Schank and Abelson, *Scripts*, ch. 6).

[16] See Schank and Abelson, *Scripts*, ch. 4. Information at the level of plan enables us to cope with mundane problems and to understand what motivates certain behaviour (that is, to infer possible goals for the behaviour we observe in others).

[17] For a comprehensive account of the script, see Schank and Abelson, *Scripts*, ch. 3. And note the definition of the structure itself at 41: 'A script is a structure that describes appropriate sequences of events in a particular context.' Schank and Abelson claim (67–8) that human understanding is heavily script-based. See Rubin, *Memory*, 26–8 for further references.

[18] Notice the sequence: goals > plans > scripts. R. Abelson, 'Psychological Status of the Script Concept', *American Psychologist*, 36 (1981), 715–29, at 719,

I shall be considering this last category in some detail; for there is clear evidence in the Homeric tradition for this particular cognitive entity.

Even from birth, as we experience various event sequences as part of our daily routines, we store these experiences in our memories as sequential units. These episodic memories are what Schank and Abelson have called scripts.[19] Scripted knowledge becomes increasingly important to us as we develop, for it enables us, by a mental process akin to pattern matching, readily to comprehend and to make predictions about what is happening in the real world or in a story world.[20] Because we all have a wide range of experiences in common, we have a large number of scripts in common. It is possible, therefore, that one person can communicate with another simply by making a brief reference to a script. It is not necessary to express all its details, since both parties, it is assumed, already share this information. A speaker need only mention one key action from the scripted sequence and this so-called script-pointer activates the whole script in the mind of his or her listener.[21] When the script of the speaker and that of his audience do not coincide, misunderstandings

argues that just as this rationale underpins the organization of our memories, so it underlies all human behaviour.

[19] See Schank and Abelson, *Scripts*, 17–19. It is important to note that this conviction is not unique to cognitive science or to cognitive psychology: D. Tannen, 'What's in a Frame? Surface Evidence for Underlying Expectations', in R. O. Freedle (ed.), *New Directions in Discourse Processing* (Norwood, NJ: Ablex, 1979), 137–81, offers an excellent survey of this structure (from the different perspectives of linguists, psychologists and anthropologists) and the role it plays in the understanding process. Nor is 'script' the only term used to describe this phenomenon. Tannen examines the current range of terms, which includes 'schemata', 'frames', and 'memory organization packages'.

[20] See my discussion in the Introduction, above; and see Schank and Abelson, *Scripts*, 67: 'The actions of others make sense only insofar as they are part of a stored pattern of actions that have been previously experienced.'

[21] See Schank and Abelson, *Scripts*, 46–50. By expressing what Schank and Abelson call a 'script pointer' (47), a speaker alerts his listeners to the whole episode. For example, if, in conversation (or in writing), we wish to refer to the telephone script (making a call), we do not need to spell out all the details of the procedure: we use a script-pointer. Sentences like 'I shall *ring* home' or 'I shall *make a call*' act as pointers to indicate the entire script in the listener's mind. It is then possible for the listener to make a rational connection between the original statement and subsequent sentences like 'Have you any change?' or 'Does this phone take cards?'.

may occur. For example, children's scripts may not be sufficiently developed to handle certain situations; cultural differences may account for incompatible scripts; or scripts may have changed over time (over decades or over centuries) because of changes in both the physical and the social world.

Scripts encapsulate knowledge about physical and social situations. By reference to the appropriate situational scripts we are able to use public transport systems or libraries; we know what to expect when we go to restaurants, to parties, or to academic conferences; instrumental scripts guide us in handling mechanical operations such as making a cup of tea, lighting a cigarette, or unbolting a door.[22] The interpersonal script holds information about the behaviour of both parties engaged in familiar transactions: borrowing, or making a bargain, an exchange, or a purchase.[23] Knowledge about some aspects of verbal behaviour is also stored in memory. Many of our spoken exchanges are realizations of stored information about speech acts. Think of the way in which we go about refusing an invitation, rebuking a child, or protesting our innocence. We regularly reproduce, almost without forethought, certain predictable sequences of ideas (where the sequence is predictable, rather than the content). Because we frequently hear and practise sequences of this kind, each routine acquires the status of a script in our memories. The speech-act script, like all scripts, is pre-verbal; it is not a store of pre-arranged words and phrases but a sequence of marked slots. To refer to such a sequence I shall use the term 'format'. Each time a speech-act script, or format, is activated, it generates a series of ideas, not the verbal expression of those ideas. Some ideas, indeed, may be expressed in an identical way with each realization; but this is a reflection of individuals' reliance on speech formulas to express certain notions. This more abstract format, or 'series of ideas', which I have mentioned holds the kind of information which I described in the introductory chapter

---

[22] For discussions of situational and instrumental scripts, see Schank and Abelson, *Scripts*, 61–6.

[23] The interpersonal script has been proposed by M. Dyer, *In-Depth Understanding: A Computer Model of Integrated Processing for Narrative Comprehension* (Cambridge, Mass.: MIT Press, 1983), ch. 10.

as 'implicit knowledge': in Rubin's words, it is 'knowing how' rather than 'knowing that'.[24]

COGNITIVE SCRIPTS AND HOMERIC THEMES

According to cognitive research, we all have a store of scripts, which contain information stored in sequential form about routine experiences. I ask, therefore, whether there is a place in this scheme for the Homeric theme. And in response I submit that Homer's narrative patterns, namely those typical scenes or themes noted by Parry and Lord (which replay in more or less detail everyday situations, procedures, and speech acts), may be identified as the expressions of cognitive scripts. I suggest that these so-called themes have been laid down, as scripts, in the memories of aspiring singers long before their apprenticeship. Homer, along with other singers and all the members of their audiences, would have acquired them in the normal course of living, either through his experience of life in the real world, or through listening to the stories of others. These units of knowledge are not peculiar to the repertoire of the singer; they are part of everyone's repertoire. Thus, both poet and audience hold in memory scripts for setting out on a journey, preparing a meal, dressing, preparing a bed, and so on; these are routines which they have often witnessed and performed. On the other hand, not every listener would know by personal experience an arming script. But it is not difficult to acquire this script (through the medium of epic or through stories told in everyday

---

[24] See Rubin, *Memory*, 190–2. This type of script, or format, has not been isolated by Schank and Abelson; they have limited themselves to a study of narrative proper. Linguistic studies and discourse analysis, however, support a concept of formalized speech modes, which I have termed 'formats': see e.g. A. Liddicoat, 'Discourse Routines in Answering Machine Communication in Australia', *Discourse Processes*, 17 (1994), 283–309, esp. at 290–3, on the 'message phase'. Verbal scripts will often occur in clusters of two, three, or four parts. Thus both address and reply taken together make up what Erving Goffman, 'Replies and Responses', *Language in Society*, 5 (1976), 257–323, calls a 'ritual exchange' (266–7); on this see also Liddicoat, 'Discourse Routines'. The story format, which I discuss below, in Ch. 6, is a further example of this kind of script.

conversation), since it is closely related to a dressing script (I shall comment further on tracks of scripts below). A twentieth-century audience, however, may not understand some Homeric sequences with the same ease as an audience of Homer's own time; we must allow for the possibility that some scripts have been altered over time and that others are culture-specific.[25]

In that the cognitive script is a pre-verbal construct, we should recall the work of Michael Nagler, who, in his discussion of the nature and origins of the type-scene anticipated this aspect of cognitive theory. More than twenty years ago Nagler proposed that the expression of the Homeric type-scene is generated by a mental structure, 'an inherited pre-verbal Gestalt', which supplies a 'motif' but does not prescribe its verbal expression.[26] Although Nagler declared that his reconstruction of composition was 'highly speculative', the cognitive research which I describe above offers the necessary theoretical underpinning for his proposals; his pre-verbal Gestalt is no more and no less than the cognitive scientist's script.[27]

Whereas the casual storyteller uses everyday language to express his scripts, the singer in the Homeric tradition uses the poetic language of epic. Although Homer's listeners—or, today, his readers—share most, if not all, of Homer's scripts, very few would have mastered the metrical language through which he has expressed their sequences. It is this skill which the apprentice poet worked so hard to acquire as he listened to experienced traditional storytellers.[28] Like a

---

[25] e.g., when Homer describes the harnessing of horses to a chariot or mules to a wagon (through a script pointer at *Il.* 5. 727–32; at *Il.* 24. 266–78 in more detail), we understand what is happening at a general level, but many of us may have difficulty in visualizing the detailed sequence of actions.

[26] Nagler, *Spontaneity*, 81–2.

[27] Ibid., 22. For another foreshadowing of cognitive theory, see F. Cairns, *Generic Composition in Greek and Roman Poetry* (Edinburgh: Edinburgh University Press, 1972). Cairns uses the term 'genres' to describe conceptual phenomena which represent 'standard responses to standard situations' (34); he claims that the genres which he identifies in ancient literature originate in 'important, recurrent, real-life situations' (70). I suggest that Cairns's genres (universally recognizable verbal routines) may be identified with verbal scripts. I thank Frances Muecke for drawing my attention to this parallel.

[28] This operation is equivalent to learning a first language, as Lord observes, in *Singer*, at 22: '[h]e is like a child learning words, or anyone learning a language

language-learner who receives very limited tutoring, he must have concentrated on taking in the vocabulary of this traditional language, on deducing the rules of combination which underpin it, and on practising singing in his epic language the songs he had chosen for performance.

So what is the point of all this? By recasting our views of the Homeric theme as I have described, we obtain a more plausible and a more realistic view of a poet who composes as he sings. Preparation for composition and composition itself are rationalized, in that the apprentice singer's task is not quite as extraordinary (or as burdensome on the memory) as Lord's account would suggest. To learn a new, poetic, language is not easy, nor is it quickly done.[29] As for what Lord would call the singer's themes, there is little or no need for the kind of learning which he has described: these scripts are already part of the singer's knowledge store. He activates these scripts in the course of a day's activities; when he tells stories casually to friends in the everyday language of his community and when he has the opportunity to sing before an audience in the traditional language of epic. He can sing any of his scripts, provided that his traditional language does not fail him at the moment of performance. Finally, to acquire a repertoire of stories is by no means impossible; many people today, even in a literate culture, can remember the storylines of quite long

without a school method'. Like any language, the metrical poetic language of traditional epic has its own vocabulary and its own rules of combination and production, which must be learnt through a 'process of imitation and of assimilation through listening and much practice on one's own' (Lord, *Singer*, 24). For a valuable discussion of the topic, with comparative evidence from a number of singing traditions, see D. Rubin, 'Learning Poetic Language', in F. S. Kessel (ed.), *The Development of Language and Language Researchers: Essays in Honor of Roger Brown* (Hillsdale, NJ: Lawrence Erlbaum, 1988), 339–51, esp. at 339.

[29] For discussion of what the poet may have known through learning, as opposed to what he considered to be the inspiration of the Muse, see M. Finkelberg, *The Birth of Literary Fiction in Ancient Greece* (Oxford: Clarendon Press, 1998), 48–61. She argues that the storyteller was responsible for acquiring technical skills, such as playing the lyre, and competence in a range of epic subjects and their basic plots. The Muse, on the other hand, gave him the ability to transform a subject into epic—i.e. it was she who 'stirred' him so as to 'elaborate a given story into an epic song' (57). I propose that learning the formulaic language of epic poetry is, like learning to play the lyre, one of the technical skills for which the poet is responsible; but that the poet attributed to the intervention of the Muse his ability to find the words he needed as he performed. See also Ch. 5, below.

and complex tales. We should note, in connection with this, that stories are versatile. When the time comes to tell a tale he has learned from another source, there is no compulsion on the storyteller to reproduce it word for word. He may collapse or expand event sequences, omit details, or incorporate new episodes. He may make any or all of these changes, intentionally or unintentionally; but as long as he leaves undisturbed the causal chain which is at the heart of the narrative, his listeners will recognize it as the same tale.

If, in the light of my discussion above, we abandon Lord's notion that typical scenes are learned specifically for, and are peculiar to, oral performance of this kind, we can give Homer considerably more credit for the story he chooses to tell than Parry and Lord have allowed us. If the singer, as singer, is not obliged first to memorize a number of fixed groupings of ideas and then to reproduce them strung together as narrative, he is considerably freer than was at first suggested—although perhaps not as free as we are when we tell a story, for he is not working in his first language. We should therefore set aside the image of Homer the conformist poet, who is limited in his singing by the scope of his traditional material. Rather, he is a creative poet who can work as he chooses, within the broad guidelines of his inherited stories.[30]

SCRIPTS AND TRACKS OF SCRIPTS: THE CONTEST SCRIPT IN HOMER

I have to this point described the script in general terms, through reference to its nature and its function as an episodic storage system. But there is more to be said concerning the nature of scripts and the ways in which they serve us. Again I shall compare what we know of

[30] For discussion elsewhere of the Homeric compositional process from a cognitive perspective, see E. Bakker, 'Homeric Discourse and Enjambement: A Cognitive Approach', *TAPA* 120 (1990), 1–21; and D. Gary Miller, 'A New Model of Formulaic Composition', in J. Miles Foley (ed.), *Comparative Research on Oral Traditions: A Memorial for Milman Parry* (Columbus, Ohio: Slavica, 1987), 351–93.

script-based memory as proposed by cognitive research with our observations of Homeric practice.

First, we must reconsider the capacity, that is, the scope, of the individual script. If we were to store under a separate code information about every different sequence of events which we encounter in our lives, we would be testing the limits of our memory store; and we would find it difficult to access the scripts which we need at the moment we need them. Schank and Abelson, however, have argued that our storage system is effective because scripts themselves are flexible. They have claimed that of all the scripts which we store only a small number represent an action sequence which is immutable. Most scripts contain general information about a routine along with information about other possible patterns within that routine. That is, each script holds information about what usually happens: it expresses a generalized course of action. But within that general sequence it accommodates a number of paths, or 'tracks', as Schank and Abelson call them, which describe patterns of internal variation.[31] The economy of human memory depends on a system of this kind.

If we turn to Homer, and if we assume that Homer's themes are the expression of scripted material, we can find abundant evidence for this same kind of flexible system, of scripts and tracks, in his narrative. Take, for example, Homer's descriptions of the various formal contests which take place in the course of the *Iliad*. We can recognize in a contest, as Homer describes it, the outline of a cognitive script. Working from these descriptions, I propose that Homer's contest script comprises the following principal events:

> *The prizes are set up*
> *A challenge is announced*
> *Competitors come forward*
> *Preparations for the competition are made by:*
> *   drawing of lots*

---

[31] See Schank and Abelson, *Scripts*, 40–1 (with examples). It is through reference to script and track that in the real world we can cope with different procedures at different libraries or with the transport systems of different cities. We do not need a separate script for each procedure or each system.

taking one's mark
judge/witness appointed
The Contest takes place:
engagement
performance
reaction of spectators
the end of the contest
identification of victor
Collection of prizes

The script includes a number of events at a lower level (including the details of the actions which realize each of the principal events that I have listed above), but Homer has not always chosen to express any of these. It is this contest script which structures the formal duel (such as that of *Il.* 3. 76–461 and *Il.* 7. 54–305), in which two heroes fight to take each other's life. This same script, moreover, underpins both the single combat held in the context of the funeral games for Patroklos (*Il.* 23. 798–825) and all the other contests held on that occasion.[32] I refer here to the succession of contests in *Iliad* 23: chariot-race, 262–652; boxing, 653–99; wrestling, 700–39; footrace, 740–97; single combat, 798–825; throwing the weight, 826–49; archery, 850–83; javelin, 884–97.[33] When we watch any competitive event today, we use a script very close to Homer's contest script. But it is not identical, as I shall demonstrate in my discussion of the chariot race of *Iliad* 23; the script has changed over time.

To sing the succession of contests which make up the funeral games for Patroklos, Homer refers for the most part to the generalized contest script. But when he wishes to refer

---

[32] For discussion of the parallels between games and combat, see J. Redfield, *Nature and Culture in the* Iliad: *The Tragedy of Hector* (Chicago and London: Chicago University Press, 1975), at 206.

[33] Note that the games of the Phaiakians (*Od.* 8. 100–240) follow the same script, with the following variations: there are no prizes (these games are not commemorative games); and all contenders appear to compete in every event. Note also that Homer's expression of the script is less developed: the elements describing the competitions are (with the exception of the foot-race, 120–5, and the discus-contest, 186–240) pared back to script-pointers (e.g. 126) or simple statements concerning the victor in each event (e.g. 128, 129, 130). For commentary on these games, see A. Heubeck, S. West, J. B. Hainsworth, *A Commentary on Homer's* Odyssey, i (Oxford: Clarendon Press, 1988), 353–61.

directly to the performance of whatever skill is in question—running, wrestling, or boxing, for example—he must go beyond the general script, which holds only the broad outline of the contest. He must follow the track which generates the details applicable to the individual sequence; or he may call up another script which will serve him in this context. As we read this episode, we refer to our own contest script and, where necessary, to the relevant track or to an additional script. We do not need to hold seven separate scripts for contests in our minds; neither did Homer, as he sang. A single script with a number of tracks and options to cover internal variations is in every way a more efficient mode of storage.[34]

THE INTERACTIVE NATURE OF SCRIPTS

As I have indicated above, when we are engaged in making sense of what is happening around us in the real world, or when we are processing narrative, we rarely have recourse to one script only. More often we need to refer to several scripts at once. One situational script may be interwoven with another, or with one or more personal scripts, not to mention a number of instrumental scripts or verbal scripts.[35] By way of example, think of the variety of scripts which might underpin real-world events such as an evening spent with friends at a restaurant, international travel, or attendance at a conference. A relevant situational script provides the context for action; and a variety of other scripts will be played out by the actors. Indeed, on many occasions these interwoven scripts, or even chance events, will delay or derail the expected (that is, scripted) course of events—and this is not without its own interest. In narrative, as we shall observe

[34] For tabulation of the contest-script and its various tracks, see Table 1. Other examples of scripts and tracks are the dressing script (e.g. at *Il.* 10. 21–4; *Od.* 13. 434–8) and its track, arming (e.g. at *Il.* 3. 330–8); the journey-script (e.g. at *Il.* 24. 322–9) and its tracks, journey by sea (*Il.* 1. 475–86) and an immortal's journey (e.g. *Il.* 15. 79–85).

[35] On the meshing of scripts, see A. Baddeley, *Human Memory: Theory and Practice* (Hove and London: Lawrence Erlbaum, 1990), at 336–7.

TABLE 1: Expressions of the Contest Script and its Tracks at *Il.* 23. 262–897

Scripted elements	Chariot-race	Boxing	Wrestling	Foot-race	Combat	Throwing	Archery	Javelin
Prizes set up	262–70	653–6	700–5	740–51	798–800	826–9	850–1	884–6
Challenge announced	271–3,[a] 285–6	657–63, 667–75	706–7	752–3	801–10	831–5	855–8	—[b]
Competitors come forward	287–351	664–5, 677–80	708–9	754–6	811–12	836–8	859–60	886–8
Preparations for competition	287–351[c]	683–85	710	—	803, 813	—	—	—
Drawing of lots	352–7[d]	—	—	—	—	—	—	—
Taking one's mark	358[e]	685	710	757	814	839	—	—
Judge/witness	359–61	661	—	—	—	—	861–2	—
Contest	362–533*[f]	686–95*	711–32*	758–77*	814–23*	839–47*	862–81*	—
Spectators	448–98[g]	—	721, 728	784	822–3	840, 847	869, 881	—
End of contest	510	695–98	738–39	779	823	—	—	—
Collection of prizes	510–13,[l] 534–615	666,[h] 669	736–7	778–83, 785–97	824–5[d]	848–9	882–3	889–97[k]

NOTE: Asterisk (*) indicates that this element of the sequence is represented by a track appropriate to the nature of the skill being tested.

a At 274–84 Achilleus announces that in any other circumstances he would compete and win. We recognize here a typically Achillean pattern of assertion and defence (cf. *Il.* 9. 644–55). We are returned to the contest script at 285–6.

b The omission of a *challenge* in this last event and the presentation of the prize to Agamemnon without a contest suggest that the poet is abandoning the contest script in favour of a gift-offer script (cf. 615–24).

c *Preparations* are expressed through references to a harnessing script. Here the poet uses the script-pointer (at 291, for example) rather then expressing more detail (as at *Il.* 5. 720–32). *Harnessing* is a necessary preliminary to the journey (as well as to the chariot-race); we shall observe that the contest itself (the chariot-race *per se*) is represented as a track of the journey script. Therefore, we should not be surprised to hear those words of parting advice (306–48) offered to the chariot-driver Antilochos, like those to a departing traveller (cf. *Il.* 24. 287–98). The advice script is a verbal script (its pattern is set out in the discussion).

d An instrumental script: cf. *Il.* 7. 175–90. *Drawing of lots, taking one's mark, judge/witness* are not relevant to all contests. They are stored as tracks within the contest script. Note that at 839 the contestants for the throwing event are ordered (but Homer does not reveal the guiding principle).

e Another element, *course description*, is included here at 358–9 and 757. This is an element peculiar to events such as the foot-race and the chariot-race.

f Note that the race begins as a journey. Each driver, by mutual agreement, whips up his horses. The journey script maps out the course of this competition. The narrative of the race is realized through the interaction of a number of scripts. We return to a rerun of the journey script in the next-to-last stages of the race.

g This element has been expanded into a narrative in its own right, itself based on the contest script. Achilleus brings the dispute to a close with a rebuke.

h Note Homer's reversal of the expected order of the contest script. Epeios claims the prize (666) before the contest takes place. Here we locate the humour of this particular contest.

i *Collection of prizes* is implied here through Achilleus' instruction to cease fighting.

j Note that the prizes are not *collected*: Achilleus, contrary to practice and contrary to the spectators' inclination *gives* them to Diomedes.

k Prize—or gift. See above, note b.

l *Collection of prizes*, too, can be expanded. And note that the fifth prize becomes a gift.

below, it is the meshing of scripts and the unexpected turn of events which is more interesting than what is predictable in the circumstances.[36]

THE FUNERAL GAMES FOR
PATROKLOS AND THE CONTEST
SCRIPT

To test for the interaction of scripts in Homer, we might look again at the funeral games of *Iliad* 23. Games such as these, as Dunkle notes, are a community strategy which returns heroes to the normal activities of their lives after the death of and funeral rites for one of their fellows.[37] In the contests of the games the heroes are given the opportunity to behave again as heroes: they can now compete for honour and prizes. Although games, by contrast with warfare, are a form of play, Homer's Achaian heroes take this form of play very seriously.[38] The emotional intensity which marks the behaviour and speech of both competitors and spectators is the same as that which we find in accounts of combat on the battlefield.

Dunkle comments on the 'richness and variety of the narrative' of this episode, which, as we noted earlier, is structured by the recycling, seven times, of the contest script.[39] But these replayings are not identical; the seven tales of the seven events differ from each other in interesting ways. In the first place, in describing each event Homer links his contest script with an action sequence which will render the event in question (the chariot-race, for example, or the single combat, or the archery contest). And, secondly, although most of the actors within each narrative share the same goal, to win or, at least, to acquit themselves honourably, the means by which that goal is

---

[36] See Schank and Abelson, *Scripts*, 61–6, especially 65–6.

[37] See J. R. Dunkle, 'Some Notes on the Funeral Games: *Iliad* 23', *Prometheus*, 7 (1981), 11–18, at 12. See also Redfield, *Nature and Culture*, 204–10.

[38] See Dunkle, 'Funeral Games', 12.

[39] J. R. Dunkle, 'Nestor, Odysseus, and the Mêtis–Biê Antithesis: The Funeral Games, *Iliad* 23', *CW* 81 (1987), 1–17, at 1.

achieved, if indeed it is achieved, is different in every case.
Each contest, therefore, is represented by the interplay of a
script which establishes a context—the contest script—with
a number of other scripts, which together individualize the
scene. It is this interaction which shapes each story and
makes it worth our attention.

My aim in the following discussion of several sequences of
the first event in the Funeral Games, the chariot-race (*Il.*
23. 262–652), is to demonstrate how the knowledge structure which I have identified above, and which we call the
contest script, structures the Homeric narrative and guides
our understanding; and how novel developments in the
narrative routine may be achieved when script-based expectations are not met.

THE CHARIOT-RACE: THE EARLY STAGES

The competition commences in conformity with the contest
script, which I have set out above. First, the *prizes are set up*
(262–70). Homer describes five prizes in all. At 262–5 he
describes the prize for first place:

> Ἱππεῦσιν μὲν πρῶτα ποδώκεσιν ἀγλά' ἄεθλα
> θῆκε γυναῖκα ἄγεσθαι ἀμύμονα ἔργα ἰδυῖαν
> καὶ τρίποδ' ὠτώεντα δυωκαιεικοσίμετρον,
> τῷ πρώτῳ·

First of all
he set forth the glorious prizes for speed of foot for the horsemen:
a woman faultless in the work of her hands to lead away
and a tripod with ears and holding twenty-two measures
for the first prize . . .

Achilleus next announces the competition (272–3): this is
the element which we might describe as the *challenge*:

> Ἀτρεΐδη τε καὶ ἄλλοι ἐϋκνήμιδες Ἀχαιοί,
> ἱππῆας τάδ' ἄεθλα δεδεγμένα κεῖτ' ἐν ἀγῶνι.

Son of Atreus and all you other strong-greaved Achaians,
these prizes are in the place of games and wait for the horsemen.

At this point we expect the *competitors to come forward*. Homer follows the script—after a fashion: he allows Achilleus first of all to explain why he will *not* be coming forward. As host of the games in honour of his companion Patroklos, he cannot take the field. And yet it is not possible for Achilleus simply to stand aside while others nominate themselves for, and compete in, an event at which he shines. Being Achilleus, he defends his decision and his honour. His speech (274–86) is true to character, a blend of defence and assertion.[40] He claims at the outset that if he were a contestant he would win the race, for his horses excel all others. His claim (274–5) is a compressed expression of the contest script which structures the whole episode:

εἰ μὲν νῦν ἐπὶ ἄλλῳ ἀεθλεύοιμεν Ἀχαιοί,
ἦ τ' ἂν ἐγὼ τὰ πρῶτα λαβὼν κλισίηνδε φεροίμην.

Now if we Achaians were contending for the sake of some other hero, I myself should take the first prize away to my shelter.

Note that, despite the disparity of circumstance, Achilleus in his self-exclusion is recreating the situation which had developed in the early stages of the *Iliad*. This is the first of the indirect reminiscences in this episode of the great quarrel of *Iliad* 1 between Agamemnon and Achilleus. As Dunkle points out, the problems of *Iliad* 1 are presented in *Iliad* 23 in a new context;[41] what is remarkable is that they will be resolved now in an atmosphere of goodwill.

To return us to the contest script, and to focus our interest again on the competition, Homer has Achilleus repeat his *challenge* (285–6). In response five challengers come forward (287–351): Eumelos (the skilled charioteer); Diomedes (who has the best horses); Menelaos (who has two fine horses, one of his own and one of his brother Agamemnon); Antilochos (whose horses are slowest); and Meriones. The number of prizes on offer in this context appears to prescribe the number of competitors in this event, a fact which may indicate some degree of preparation on the part

---

[40] Cf. Achilleus' words at *Il.* 9. 644–55.
[41] See Dunkle, 'Funeral Games', 12. For further discussion, see below.

of the poet.[42] In our culture, by contrast, we would expect more entrants and relatively fewer prizewinners. Homer's expression of his script therefore implies a cultural difference between the world which he depicts and our own: his script is different from ours.

The poet brings this phase of the contest script to life (*competitors come forward*), as each of his heroes goes about the routine task of harnessing his horses, an element of *preparations for the competition*, which is specific to the chariot-race. The harnessing script, an instrumental script, is referred to briefly through a script-pointer (ὕπαγε ζυγόν, he led under the yoke, or its equivalent, at 291, 294, 300, 301, 351). Note that Homer has rendered his catalogue of contenders not as a list but as narrative: he has built his catalogue around the scripted event *harnessing*, and he has used small stories, or story fragments, to enrich almost every entry.[43]

The drivers continue their *preparations*. They mount (352) and *draw lots* (352–7). To generate this sequence the poet refers to the instrumental script, the drawing-of-lots script, which is covered here in the *depositing of lots* (352); *shaking of lots* (353); *a lot falls out* (353–4, 354, 355, 356, 356–7). This is the type of script which we ourselves as storytellers might not express in any detail. In our own tradition there are some occasions on which we linger over certain scripts; but for the most part we refer to mechanical sequences in a fleeting fashion through a script-pointer (lots were drawn and this was the outcome).[44] Homer, however,

---

[42] See W. Willis, 'Athletic Contests in the Epic', *TAPA* 72 (1941), 392–417, at 410.

[43] Note Homer's inclusion of the stories about the horses: at 291–2 and 295–9; and Nestor's own story-enriched farewell/speech of advice to Antilochos (306–48). On the narrative content of catalogues, see Ch. 2, below.

[44] As storytellers, we do not 'atomize' event sequences as regularly as Homer does, as I have noted above. On 'atomization' see E. Gülich and M. Quasthoff, 'Storytelling in Conversation: Cognitive and Interactive Aspects', *Poetics*, 15 (1986), 217–41, at 223–4, 235–6. Amongst the scripts which we often choose to express more fully in oral (and, indeed, written) storytelling are hospitality/meal scripts (like those of Homer, at *Il.* 9. 193–221; *Od.* 14. 33–110), healing scripts (cf. *Il.* 4. 210–19; 11. 842–8), and scripts for the major social rituals, such as the funeral (cf. *Il.* 24. 707–804). On the other hand, some oral storytellers dwell on scripted details indiscriminately, with no concern for either their story or their audience. As a consequence, the stories they tell are tedious. This is not in the spirit of Homer.

has chosen here, as he so often does, to spell out its principal events, since it is easy for him to visualize its sequence and to find the words to express it.[45] For this reason Homer, when he speaks as narrator, will take advantage of his instrumental scripts, such as preparing a meal or a bed, or dressing, to assist him in maintaining the continuity of his song in performance.[46] But there is a further reason: Homer is a storyteller. He wishes to create suspense and a certain ambience in the tale he is telling. By realizing an instrumental script in detail he is able to create a sense of actuality (in the interests of authenticity and involvement); he is able also to slow the pace of his narrative and to postpone a critical moment (in the interests of suspense, or curiosity).[47] A consequence of scripted elaboration of this kind is that everyday actions become small ceremonies: a pleasing characteristic of epic song.[48]

Finally, the contest begins. The competitors take their marks ($\sigma\tau\grave{\alpha}\nu$ $\delta\grave{\epsilon}$ $\mu\epsilon\tau\alpha\sigma\tauo\iota\chi\acute{\iota}$, 358). This expresses the element *engagement*. Achilleus indicates the turning post (358–9, cf. 757), a scripted event which is peculiar to a race, whether a foot-race or a chariot-race. We might describe it as an element in that track of the contest script which holds information about races. He appoints the adjudicator (*judge/witness*, 359–61). Someone, we assume, must confirm that all contestants have satisfied the terms of the contest. It appears there is no element in the Homeric contest script

---

[45] For discussion of storytelling as a description of events visualized in the cinema of the mind, see Fleischman, *Tense and Narrativity*, 266–74; and see my Introduction, above. Scripted sequences, like stories, will be visualized, fleetingly at least.

[46] See e.g. his accounts in the *Iliad* of the harnessing of horses (24. 266–74), the preparation of meals (1. 458–66; 9. 206–20); dressing for battle (3. 328–38; 11. 15–46). There are some occasions on which the poet refers to familiar sequences in summary, e.g., at *Il*. 1. 315–16 (sacrifice); 3. 339 (arming); *Od*. 15. 186–8 (the hospitality sequence). On the other hand, we rarely find a detailed expansion of scripts (arming, preparing a meal) in the stories which Homer's characters tell each other. The poet is inclined to reserve such expansions for himself, when he speaks as narrator. For further discussion of this point and of Homer's elaboration of scripts, see Epilogue, below.

[47] For discussion, from a psychological perspective, of these factors in the development of a successful story, see Epilogue, below.

[48] In Austin's words, he is able 'to put time into slow motion and to create a ritual out of the moment': see N. Austin, 'The Function of Digressions in the *Iliad*, *GRBS* 7 (1966), 295–312, at 308.

which marks the start of the race; or it may be that Homer does not consider the signal for the start worthy of mention, as we would.[49] Rather, each driver, perhaps by mutual agreement and apparently at the same time (ἅμα, 362), whips up his horses. And the race begins. The account of the race itself is rendered in the first instance through the journey script, a script which refers to goal-directed travel. Since the traveller's goal in this case is not simply to reach his destination, but to reach it first, the pursuit script will be occasionally accessed as well. The desire to win this race, or to perform well, will reveal itself in the ambitious behaviour of the competitors. Homer has divided the field into two separate competitions: one between Diomedes and Eumelos and another between Antilochos and Menelaos. In this way he will make this event more interesting to us, and easier to follow.[50] Meriones, the fifth contestant, with his slow horses and a lack of special skills as a charioteer, is not a contender for a major prize. He will play an insignificant role in the race.

THE CHARIOT-RACE: THE RACE AS A JOURNEY

In realizing the race which is at the heart of this particular contest, Homer (as we would) has exploited the journey script which he has in his memory store. This script, along with the pursuit script (which will render the two chases), stores information about what regularly happens, both in Homer and in the real world, when a race is being run. The journey script is marked in Homer by the following elements:

> *The departure*
> *harnessing of the horses*
> *farewell*
> *mounting the chariot*

[49] The signal to start may, however, have been subsumed in σήμηνε δὲ τέρματ' ([he] showed them the turning post), 358, cf. 757.

[50] By splitting the contest in this way Homer also makes his task easier for himself, as storyteller, and for his listeners, as they follow the tale. For the rationale which lies behind this, see G. Miller, 'The Magical Number Seven, Plus or Minus Two: Some Limits on our Capacity for Processing Information', *Psychological Review*, 63 (1956), 81–97.

taking up whip or reins
whipping up the horses
the horses and/or chariot in motion
accompanying detail
The route:
    a landmark
Arrival.[51]

The harnessing of horses provides a link between the contest script which contextualizes the chariot-race of *Iliad* 23 and the journey script which expresses the nature of this particular competition. In the context of a journey, the preparation of horse and chariot may be followed by some words of farewell addressed to the traveller by his host.[52] Nestor during the harnessing has given his son the parting injunctions which are part of any expedition of importance (306–48). Seizing the moment, he has been as quick-thinking as his son is quick to act;[53] he counsels Antilochos on the tactics appropriate to the course.[54] Nestor's practical advice on the conduct of the race is rendered by reference to the advice format: *address*; *the problem defined* (309–10, 311); *proposal* (in general terms, 313–14); *justification* (315–17, 318–25); *the remedy* (specific advice, 326–48).[55] In the course of the *Iliad*-story he has had frequent recourse to this script; this, along with the exemplars which he includes as *justification*, is a mark of a Nestorian behavioural pattern to which he himself attests.[56] Indeed, it is one of the pleasing aspects of this episode that each member of Homer's cast acts so consistently in

[51] My account of the principal events of Homer's cognitive script corresponds to Arend's account of the typical scene: see W. Arend, *Die typischen Scenen bei Homer* (Berlin: Weidmannische Buchhandlung, 1933), 86–7. For other examples of the expression of this script, see *Il.* 24. 322–447, *Od.* 15. 144–87 (much expanded).

[52] If the *farewell* is rendered as direct speech, it may be realized through the speech-act script, the advice script, which includes final instructions regarding the conduct of the expedition: cf. Hekabe's farewell to Priam, *Il.* 24. 287–98.

[53] For commentary on Antilochos' opportunism, see below.

[54] Cf. *Il.* 11. 782–9.

[55] Compare this expression of the script (*Il.* 23. 306–48) with *Il.* 1. 254–84; 7. 327–43; 9. 96–113; 11. 656–803. Note that despite the length of the speech itself, the scripted pattern (that sequence of marked slots, to which I refer above) is realized.

[56] At *Il.* 4. 318–25. On exemplars, see his use of stories from his own past at *Il.* 1. 259–73; 4. 318–19; and see Dunkle, 'The Mêtis–Biê Antithesis', at 2.

character. Nestor's advice does not, in fact, anticipate the action of the race. But it allows us some insight into the direction of Antilochos' plans. In order to finish creditably, he will be obliged to rely on strategies of his own devising, on μῆτις, rather than on the speed of his horses. This information will assist us in comprehending Antilochos' behaviour at each stage of the race he is to run.[57]

The development of the communal rites for Patroklos into a substantial narrative has allowed Homer to parade before us, on one last occasion, the heroes whom we have come to know.[58] It is not now time to reveal a new side of an actor's character; this is the occasion for repetition and for confirmation of the familiar.[59] We note that Homer makes reference again to those scripts or elements of scripts which we have associated with different characters: for example, we associate the advice format with Nestor; we expect Diomedes to be the hero who wins any contest; we are not surprised at Achilleus' words when he rules himself out of competition. Willcock's comments on Homer's mode of characterization run parallel with what I am describing here in cognitive terms. He describes a 'mental mould' or 'pattern' which 'directs' Homer's invention; he sees a 'mould' where I see patterns of association, between script and actor, to which the poet regularly refers.[60] Nevertheless, we might ask how Homer holds our interest, since so much

---

[57] For an excellent discussion of Nestor's two speeches in this episode, the context in which they are made, and the issues which they address, see Dunkle, 'The Mêtis–Biê Antithesis', esp. at 1–9.

[58] Cf. M. Willcock, 'The Funeral Games of Patroclus', *BICS* 20 (1973), 1–11, at 3. I claim that we know these characters completely because Homer presents them as relatively simple beings, each defined by a limited number of personal qualities. Homer's characters will rarely surprise us; they are flat, not rounded: on these terms, see S. Chatman, *Story and Discourse* (Ithaca: Cornell University Press, 1978), 131–4. The rounded character is a feature of, but not essential to, written storytelling (especially the novel). Only when a storyteller has time to work on the composition of his tale and the reader has time to ponder the action can the greater complexities of open-ended, rounded, characterization be contemplated. Not even Achilleus is a character of this rounded kind. For a contrary view, however, see A. Heubeck, 'Homeric Studies Today', in B. Fenik (ed.), *Homer: Tradition and Invention* (Leiden: E. J. Brill, 1978), 1–17, at 13–14.

[59] As Redfield, *Nature and Culture*, at 209, remarks, the occasion 'serves to reconfirm a pre-existing order as much as to construct a new one'.

[60] See Willcock, 'Funeral Games of Patroclus', 3; and Schank and Abelson, *Scripts*, ch. 6.

of his material is familiar to us. A measure of new material is normally considered essential to the success of any story. In response to his wish at this time to present his characters in a consistent fashion and to his audience's expectations of novel elements, the poet here produces a careful blend of the predictable and the unpredictable.[61] The predictability of each hero's temperament is indeed central to the narrative; but what captures our interest is the problems which arise when selected heroes, who to this point have worked together, are now pitted *against* each other, in competition for the same prizes.

The urgency of the drivers at the beginning of the race is invoked through the regular elements of the journey script; but these have been elaborated to indicate the spirit of the race: *whipping up*, therefore, is accompanied by words of encouragement (362–4, repeated at 371–2); the *details* which indicate motion and pace are the cloud of dust (repeated through simile 365–6, 372) and the streaming manes of the horses (367).

The *landmark* assumes an important role in the narrative of the chariot-race, as it does elsewhere.[62] That the turning post will provide the setting for dramatic events has been foreshadowed already in Nestor's description of the mark and its surrounds (326–33). But certainly, as elsewhere in the epics (*Il.* 14. 433–4, the ford of the river; *Il.* 5. 773–5, the confluence of two streams; *Il.* 24. 349–51, a watering place), the story does not become exciting until a designated landmark has been reached.

THE CHARIOT-RACE AS PURSUIT

The contest of the leaders, Diomedes and Eumelos, is expanded into a pursuit script, the same script which Homer uses to describe Achilleus' pursuit of Hektor

---

[61] See e.g. S. Hidi and W. Baird, 'Interestingness—A Neglected Variable in Discourse Processing', *Cognitive Science*, 10 (1986), 179–94.

[62] Note that Homer will set telling moments in the drama against a realistic backdrop (cf. the recovery of Hektor, *Il.* 14. 433–4, or Hermes' appearance before Priam (*Il.* 24. 349)). The setting may be minimal, but it is a critical element of a persuasive story.

(*Il.* 22. 136–253). This is an interpersonal script, which is active only as long as both participants have the same desire, to be the first to reach their goal. The particular track to which Homer is referring and which is guiding our understanding here is that of overtaking the leader. At this point, Eumelos is ahead (375–6); but Diomedes is close behind (as Homer repeatedly tells us, at 377–81). At 382, however, the poet runs his pursuit script to its end. He tells us what might have happened had Diomedes' horses continued to run so strongly—καί νύ κεν ἢ παρέλασσ' ἢ ἀμφήριστον ἔθηκεν (and now he might have passed him or run to a doubtful decision)—and wakens our desire to learn what actually did occur: does Diomedes pass Eumelos? This segment of the narrative shows how a story can engage its audience. Here we observe a conflict of goals on the part of the heroes. Diomedes and Eumelos have the same goal, to win; and we, the audience, experience a conflict of expectation. For each of the heroes appears to have a claim to first prize: Homer has told us that Eumelos is the best charioteer and his horses are divinely-bred; on the other hand, the poet has depicted Diomedes throughout the *Iliad* as the hero who does not lose a contest.[63]

What actually occurs is an unexpected but not unmotivated interruption of the pursuit script (383–4). As observers, we might have called it an accident. But, as Homer tells it, this is no accident; nor is it the result of the random working of fate. What happens is explained as the work of the gods and is rendered as a track of the divine-interference script. Apollo in anger strikes the whip from Diomedes' hand:[64]

εἰ μὴ Τυδέος υἷϊ κοτέσσατο Φοῖβος Ἀπόλλων,
ὅς ῥά οἱ ἐκ χειρῶν ἔβαλεν μάστιγα φαεινήν.

had not Phoibos Apollo been angry with Diomedes,
Tydeus' son, and dashed the shining whip from his hands

[63] He performs well even against Ares: *Il.* 5. 846–63. For other contests in which he does not lose, see *Il.* 6. 232–6 (the exchange of armour with Glaukos); 23. 802–25 (single combat in the funeral games).

[64] For a possible reason for Apollo's alleged hostility to Diomedes, see 291–2. Apollo, furthermore, had bred the horses which Eumelos was driving (*Il.* 2. 766–7). For brief comment on this event and on Athene's restoration of the whip, see N. Richardson, *The* Iliad: *A Commentary*, vi (Cambridge: Cambridge University Press, 1993), 215.

But Athene has seen all. Her partiality for Diomedes ensures that his anger and frustration (385–7) will not last.[65] At 388–90 she restores Diomedes' whip. Chance plays no part in this. And at 391–3 she inflicts gratuitous damage on Eumelos' chariot and on the hero himself (394–7, a track of the chariot-accident script). This puts him out of the race. With this, Diomedes is able to take the lead: πολλὸν τῶν ἄλλων ἐξάλμενος ([springing] far out in front of the others) (399).

The first pursuit, the contest between Eumelos and Diomedes, has been described through actions and events physical in nature: through tracks of pursuit, divine interference, and chariot-accident. The second contest will not be a repetition of the first. It will be brought to life by the spirited exchanges of Menelaos and Antilochos. Events will, for the moment, be structured by the pursuit script, but our interest will be engaged by the energetic interaction of the participants both in competition and negotiation.

Although Antilochos is a competent charioteer, his horses are slower than those of his competitors. His goal, therefore, is not to win—that distinction, he knows, is reserved for someone else—but to defeat a rival of merit (404–9). Antilochos, therefore, aims to outstrip Menelaos, who is currently in front of him on the track (401). In his first attempt to overtake Menelaos, Antilochos has recourse to a persuasive approach: his appeal to his horses is expressed through the exhortation format: *address* (403); *instruction* (407–8); *reason* (408–9).[66] But exhortation is to no avail (409). Antilochos, therefore, modifies his plan; he selects a more forceful verbal strategy. And he threatens his horses. The threat format which Homer uses may be set out as follows: *address* (409); *the problem defined* (409); *threat* (410–13); *remedy* (414–16).[67]

The violence of Antilochos' threat at 412—ὔμμε κατακτενεῖ ὀξέϊ χαλκῷ (he will slaughter you with the edge of bronze)—may surprise us; it is atypical of the Antilochos whom we

[65] For brief commentary on the role of the gods at this point, see Willcock, 'Funeral Games of Patroclus', at 4.

[66] For exhortation on the battlefield, see *Il.* 5. 601–6, 15. 561–4; for exhortation of one's horses, see *Il.* 8. 185–97.

[67] Cf. *Il.* 2. 246–64; 15. 14–33. Note that Antilochos' threat (409–16) grows out of his exhortation (403–9).

have known from earlier encounters in the *Iliad*. We must read his harsh language as an expression of the intensity of his ambition. More in keeping with our understanding of Antilochos, however, is his next strategy (described at 414–16), by which he proposes to gain advantage over Menelaos. His competitive nature and the recklessness of youth suggest to him a plan of action: to contrive that his horses will pass those of his opponent at a narrow stretch of the course (415–16).[68] To this point of the narrative of the *Iliad*, Antilochos has enjoyed warm relations with Menelaos. His attitude to the older man has been warm, respectful, and protective.[69] And his goodwill and respect have been reciprocated. In the light of this relationship, the encounter which Homer has devised at this point of the narrative cannot fail to interest us. What is to happen between the two?

Meanwhile, Antilochos' violent words to his horses produce results.[70] The horses strive harder. They are now within striking distance of Menelaos' team. At this point Homer returns us to his pursuit script, which includes a specification of the terrain to be covered by pursuer and pursued.[71] The account of the terrain, at 418–21, is intended to explain Antilochos' earlier reference, at 416, to στεινωπῷ . . . ὁδῷ (the narrow place of the way).

Menelaos drives cautiously along the broken track (422). But Antilochos makes a daring move: he pulls out off the course (423–4).[72] He is now pressing hard on Menelaos' chariot, eager to overtake. Antilochos' determination and his readiness to expose not only his own team but that of his opponent to the risks of an accident excite fear in Menelaos. He protests energetically (426–8). The structure of Homer's

---

[68] This decision is entirely in character. We know Antilochos to be alert (*Il.* 5. 561–7; 18. 32–4); quick (*Il.* 13. 545–59; 15. 569–71); and opportunistic (*Il.* 5. 576–89; 13. 394–401). For a discussion of Antilochos' character, and of the role he plays in the *Iliad*, see M. Willcock, 'Antilochos in the *Iliad*', in E. Delebecque, *Mélanges Edouard Delebecque* (Aix-en-Provence: Université de Provence), 1983, 477–85.

[69] See e.g. *Il.* 5. 565–70.

[70] In the Homeric storyworld a threat is taken seriously. The obedience script, rendered through *fear* (ὑποδείσαντες, 417) and *action* (417–18), allows the poet to effect a change in the course of action.

[71] Cf. the course-description at *Il.* 22. 145–56.

[72] I am following Richardson's interpretation of the scene here: see Richardson, *The* Iliad: *A Commentary*, vi, 217–18.

protest format is as follows: *address* (426); *reproach* (426, 428); *problem defined* (427); *counter-proposal* (426).[73] This is the reaction we would expect of Menelaos. He is by temperament far less adventurous and far more attentive to his own safety than his peers.[74] In the Homeric world a protest such as this will rarely go unacknowledged. And yet Menelaos' protest is disregarded—ὡς οὐκ ἀΐοντι ἐοικώς (as if he had never heard him, 430)—by the very person whom we would have expected to be punctilious in his treatment of his elders. Again we understand Antilochos' behaviour, as we understood his threats to his horses (409–16): they are the outcome of his zeal for pre-eminence.

Pressing his advantage now on the broken ground, Antilochos uses the whip; and he draws even with Menelaos (431–3). The two teams run neck and neck for a distance calculated in terms of a young man's discus throw (431–2).[75] And now Menelaos slows his pace (433–4). This action closes down the pursuit script, a script which is active only as long as both participants wish to compete. Menelaos is reluctant to take the risks to which Antilochos has exposed him. To support Menelaos' decision, Homer sets out for us what might have happened if Menelaos had not allowed his horses to slow their pace. The scene at 435–7 is described through the chariot-accident script (the track we are considering here is the collision track): the chariots *collide*; they *overturn*; the drivers are *thrown out*. And yet, although he has given ground, Menelaos' ambition reasserts itself. He threatens Antilochos with retribution (439–41): *address* (439–40); *the problem defined* (440); *threat* (441).[76] Menelaos intends to appeal against Antilochos' placing ahead of him. Despite his decision to pull back, he finds it painful to contemplate defeat. Like a loser in hand-to-hand combat,

[73] For other realizations of the protest format, see *Il.* 4. 25–9, 350–5, 412–18; 14. 83–102.

[74] See *Il.* 4. 150–2; 7. 104–21; 17. 91–105. At *Il.* 7. 104–21 he does not proudly reject his brother's insistence that he withdraw his response to Hektor's challenge (as we would expect a hero to do). Because he values safety over honour, he sees the wisdom of withdrawal (120–1).

[75] Antilochos and the discus-thrower share youth, ambition, and a desire to succeed. For further discussion of similes, see Ch. 4, below.

[76] For the threat format, see above.

he forecasts another more difficult test after the race. It will be a test which Antilochos will not, he implies, be able to pass.[77]

The positions are reversed. Menelaos is behind Antilochos. And now as pursuer, and with the perilous stretch of the course behind him, he urges on his horses. But Menelaos chooses neither exhortation (cf. 403–9) nor threat (cf. 409–16). In his efforts to revive the spirits of his team he uses a milder form of encouragement, which he expresses through reference to the consolation format: *commiseration* (443); *the need for patience/endurance* (443); *practical advice* (444–5); *distraction* (others are worse off than you, 445).[78] Menelaos' horses recognize their master's desire. And with the predictable response, obedience (446–7), the action of the pursuit script is for a moment resumed.

THE CHARIOT-RACE AND ITS SPECTATORS

The narrative of the chase is interrupted by an account of a violent disagreement amongst the spectators (*reaction of the spectators*, 448–98). This element, which acknowledges the heightened emotions of the spectators at the closing stages of a competition, is part of the contest script. Here it has been expanded into an episode within the story. In taking us into the audience, Homer invites us to sense the excitement which the race has aroused: this small element, therefore, serves an evaluative role.[79] In formal terms, the element, *reaction*, is realized here not through an account of actions

[77] This speech-act script, the threat format (cf. above), is the script which expresses both Patroklos' and Hektor's last words before they die (*Il.* 16. 844–54; 22. 356–60). Although they know that they have been defeated, they, like Menelaos, refuse to succumb without a show of defiance: just as they forecast short-lived glory for their victors, so Menelaos promises that Antilochos' triumph will be brief.

[78] Cf. Hektor to Andromache, *Il.* 6. 484–93; Achilles to Priam, *Il.* 24. 516–51. For a comparable outline of the verbal structure, see Nagler, *Spontaneity*, 176.

[79] On internal evaluation (the kind of evaluation which is built into the narrative), see Introduction. For comment on the way in which Homer creates an audience for evaluative purposes, see W. Wyatt, 'Homer in performance: *Iliad* 1. 348–427', *CJ* 83 (1987–8), 289–97, esp. 293.

and events but through a series of speech-act scripts: the announcement format (457–72); the reproach format (474–81); the challenge format (483–7); and the rebuke format (492–8). The escalating hostility of the quarrel amongst the spectators reminds us again of the quarrel which began the story of the *Iliad*. This 'reminding', to use Schank's term, is achieved through the poet's reference, on this occasion as before, to certain scripted speech acts: reproach, challenge, and rebuke.[80] And we observe, too, that violence may erupt suddenly, especially among people who feel the need in all circumstances to defend their integrity. The dignity and restraint of Achilleus' speech as he cools the heated tempers of the spectators characterize a more sympathetic Achilleus, whom we have met only briefly in the *Iliad*, the Achilleus of *Il*. 1. 59–67, 85–91.[81] It will be this Achilleus whom Priam will so admire, when he and his host share a meal (*Il*. 24. 599–672).

THE RACE IS CONCLUDED: THE COLLECTION OF PRIZES

After the interlude with the spectators, we are returned to the race for the *identification of the victor*. We watch Diomedes complete the course in first place (499–510). Again the journey script is invoked, now to realize in summary the next-to-last stages of the race: *whipping up horses*, 499–500; *motion*: the horses' gait, 500–1; *accompanying detail*: the dust, 502; *motion*: the chariot, 503–4; *accompanying detail*, 504–6; the horses' *speed* (a track which marks the urgency of the race, in comparison with a true journey), 506.[82] Note that even here, where he is not striving for

[80] For discussion of 'remindings', see Schank and Abelson, 'Knowledge and Memory', *passim*; for a description of the 'gratuitous insult' of Agamemnon, Achilleus' 'fierce anger', and Nestor's attempt at reconciliation (which, in my terms, is the scripted speech act, rebuke), see Dunkle, 'Funeral Games', 16.

[81] See Dunkle, 'Funeral Games', 16, who points out that Achilleus twice in the course of the chariot-race episode helps bring about a compromise which avoids physical violence and does not lessen the τιμή (honour) of the heroes involved; on Achilleus' 'sympathetic justice', see ibid., 14–15.

[82] For the journey script, see above.

suspense, Homer pauses to take us through the familiar script. He delights in detail, especially in visual and aural information, which cues responses in our long-term visual and auditory memories and assists us in 'seeing' and 'hearing' the event for ourselves. Thus, he is able to arouse a sense of excitement. It is important to our appreciation of his art, therefore, that we follow these scripted paths (499–506):

> . . . Τυδεΐδης δὲ μάλα σχεδὸν ἦλθε διώκων,
> μάστι δ' αἰὲν ἔλαυνε κατωμαδόν· οἱ δέ οἱ ἵπποι
> ὑψόσ' ἀειρέσθην ῥίμφα πρήσσοντε κέλευθον.
> αἰεὶ δ' ἡνίοχον κονίης ῥαθάμιγγες ἔβαλλον,
> ἅρματα δὲ χρυσῷ πεπυκασμένα κασσιτέρῳ τε
> ἵπποις ὠκυπόδεσσιν ἐπέτρεχον· οὐδέ τι πολλὴ
> γίγνετ' ἐπισσώτρων ἁρματροχιὴ κατόπισθεν
> ἐν λεπτῇ κονίῃ· τὼ δὲ σπεύδοντε πετέσθην.

. . . and now Tydeus' son in his rapid course was close on them
and lashed them always with the whipstroke from the shoulder.
His horses
still lifted their feet light and high as they made their swift
passage.
Dust flying splashed always the charioteer, and the chariot
that was overlaid with gold and tin still rolled hard after
the flying feet of the horses, and in their wake there was not much
trace from the running rims of the wheels left in the thin dust.
The horses came in running hard.

The last stage of the journey script, *arrival*, serves to identify the victor. *Arrival* is realized through the following elements: *stopping* (507); *the condition of the horses* (for this particular track of the journey script) (507–8); *dismounting* (509); *unharnessing* (513).[83]

The end of the journey script signals the end of the contest script for Diomedes: στῆ δὲ μέσῳ ἐν ἀγῶνι (he stopped them in the middle of where men were assembled, 507). He lays aside his 'arms'. At 510 he leans his whip against the yoke (κλῖνε δ' ἄρα μάστιγα ποτὶ ζυγόν), a gesture which is included in Homer's contest script to signal its end (cf. *Il.* 22. 112–13). The contest for first place is over. And although the place-getters have yet to arrive, Diomedes promptly *collects* the prize he has won—through Sthenelos, his hench-

---

[83] For other realizations of arrival, see *Il.* 5. 775–7; 24. 448–59 and 469–71.

man (510–13), who supervises the arrangements for the woman and for the tripod:

> οὐδὲ μάτησεν
> ἴφθιμος Σθένελος, ἀλλ' ἐσσυμένως λάβ' ἄεθλον,
> δῶκε δ' ἄγειν ἑτάροισιν ὑπερθύμοισι γυναῖκα
> καὶ τρίποδ' ὠτώεντα φέρειν·

Nor did strong Sthenelos delay, but made haste to take up the prizes, and gave the woman to his high-hearted companions to lead away and the tripod with ears to carry

In Homer's script there appears to be no final presentation ceremony, as we would expect; the competitors take their prizes as they complete the course.[84]

Homer now turns his attention to the other competitors in the race. At 514–15 he tells us the outcome of the contest between Menelaos and Antilochos: Antilochos is the winner. And, then, at 516–27, he reviews the last phase of the race, from the point at which we had left it, when Menelaos, who had been overtaken by Antilochos, had resumed the pursuit. Again the pursuit script is invoked, to describe Menelaos' race to catch the younger man. It is supplemented by an assessment of the distance which separates them (517–23) and by the simile of the discus (523–4), which links this phase of the race to the preceding action (cf. 431–3). Since suspense is out of the question, we must ask what Homer's strategy is, in offering us so much information at this point. His aim is again to focus our attention (through detail and through the repetition which occurs with the simile) on the closeness of the contest—when two contestants, well-matched, have called upon every strategy to achieve their goal.

The arrival of Meriones, in fourth place, and of Eumelos, the favourite, in last place, is duly reported, through reduced reruns of the journey script (528–33) and through

---

[84] Note that one takes one's prize: one claims it as one's due (this is the significance also of Epeios' proprietorial gesture at 664–6). A prize is not a gift (which is presented by the host). On the difference between prizes and gifts in the Homeric world, see L. Gernet, 'Jeux et droit (remarques sur le XXIIIᵉ chant de l'*Iliade*)', *Revue historique de droit français et étranger*, 26 (1948), 177–88, at 178–81, 183–6.

the element *arrival*, now modified (532–3) to express the consequences of his accident:

υἱὸς δ' Ἀδμήτοιο πανύστατος ἤλυθεν ἄλλων,
ἕλκων ἅρματα καλά, ἐλαύνων πρόσσοθεν ἵππους.

Last and behind them all came in the son of Admetos
dragging his fine chariot and driving his horses before him

In the normal course of events each competitor would claim the prize to which he was entitled. But the predictable sequence is interrupted: Achilleus suggests that the routine of prize collection should be suspended and that the second prize should be given to Eumelos (536–8). Achilleus feels pity for Eumelos; he wishes to compensate him for this unexpected blow to his prestige, and to reassure him that his standing amongst his peers is almost undiminished.[85] His proposal is expressed through the scripted proposal format: *reason* (536); *proposal* (537–38).[86] His suggestion, which initiates a further negotiation pattern within the narrative, is received with the general approval (539) which endorses an appropriate and convincing resolution. The suggestion interests us, too, as will any interruption of a scripted sequence, through its very unexpectedness. As Schank points out, if a story conforms to a script, then we do not need to track it in a serious way, since all events are predictable.[87] We would deem such a story uninteresting. It is the unpredictable element and the working out of its consequences that catch our interest.

Antilochos, however, who has won the right to second prize, challenges Achilleus' suggestion. He, of course, wishes the scripted element, *collection of prizes*, to be reinstated. Eumelos' failure, Antilochos points out, was due to bad management rather than bad luck (546–7). Achilleus may give him the prize if he wishes, but not the

---

[85] Notice that he makes no attempt to take the prize from Diomedes. Eumelos may be the better charioteer (536); but Diomedes can never be seen to lose.

[86] For expressions of the proposal format, see *Il.* 9. 17–28; 22. 168–76. Note that Achilleus proposes to *give* the mare to Eumelos; it will lose its status as a prize.

[87] See R. Schank, 'Interestingness: Controlling Inferences', *Artificial Intelligence*, 12 (1979), 273–97, at 290–1, who notes, however, that some scripts are inherently more interesting to us than others; see also Hidi and Baird, 'Interestingness'.

prize originally designated for the second place-getter. The speech-act script which realizes Antilochos' intention—to recover the prize due to him—and which shapes his speech, is the protest format (track: resolute resistance): *address* (543); *promise* (543); *the problem defined* (544–6); *counter-argument* (546–7); *counter-proposal* (548–52).[88] The element which conveys Antilochos' resolute stance is his *rejection*, an emphatic statement of defiance, 553–4:

> τὴν δ' ἐγὼ οὐ δώσω· περὶ δ' αὐτῆς πειρηθήτω
> ἀνδρῶν ὅς κ' ἐθέλῃσιν ἐμοὶ χείρεσσι μάχεσθαι.

But the mare I will not give up, and the man who wants her must fight me for her with his hands before he can take her.

Antilochos' protest runs in accordance with the format. He conducts his case with characteristic courage and forthrightness. Yet, even as he protests against the proposed award to Eumelos, he is not mean-spirited, as his counter-proposal confirms (551). Nor does he direct any reproach to Achilleus. It is this element, *reproach*, which in other interactions in the Homeric epics (for example, *Il.* 1. 122–9 and 149–71), and in everyday interactions in the real world, can strike a sharp, even a strident note; in such cases, a protest will be read as a personal challenge.[89] But note that Antilochos has modified his reproach for Achilleus; it is a *promise* of anger, not anger itself. The young hero shows us again, through his modification of a familiar speech act, how well he understands Achilleus' temperament.[90] Achilleus, as Antilochos knows, resists and resents any challenge to his integrity. Antilochos, therefore, carefully avoids confrontation. He diverts his criticism to Eumelos. Such sensitivity on Antilochos' part bears fruit. The grounds for his protest will be recognized; his *counter-proposal* (548–52) will be accepted by Achilleus (558–9):

---

[88] For other realizations of the protest script, see above.

[89] For commentary on this moment, see O. Taplin, *Homeric Soundings: The Shaping of the* Iliad (Oxford: Clarendon Press, 1992), at 255–6; Dunkle, 'Funeral Games', 14.

[90] We have already seen evidence of Antilochos' sensitivity to Achilleus' needs: see *Il.* 18. 1–34. Redfield, *Nature and Culture*, at 208, speaks of Antilochos' 'delicate mixture of bravado and compliments'.

'Ἀντίλοχ', εἰ μὲν δή με κελεύεις οἴκοθεν ἄλλο
Εὐμήλῳ ἐπιδοῦναι, ἐγὼ δέ κε καὶ τὸ τελέσσω.

Antilochos,
if you would have me bring some other thing out of my dwelling
as a special gift for Eumelos, then for your sake I will do it.

Antilochos' stout defence of his right to take the second prize does not in itself seem sufficient motivation for Achilleus' gentle and affectionate response (the verbal script, the agreement format, is qualified by a rare smile [555]). But Homer reminds us that Antilochos already stands high in Achilleus' affections: he is his φίλος . . . ἑταῖρος (his beloved companion, 556).[91] The host of the games, therefore, readily responds to the logic of his friend's proposal. His agreement generates a sketchy realization of the gift-presentation script: *orders to fetch gift* (563–4); *fetching of gift* (564); *presentation* (565); *acceptance with pleasure* (565). This script will be reactivated with Antilochos' gift to Menelaos (591–5) and with Achilleus' gift to Nestor (616–24).

Antilochos has defended his prize successfully against Achilleus' impulse to grant it to Eumelos. But a new obstacle is thrown into his path. At 441 and 527 we were warned that after the race a protest would be registered by Menelaos. At 570–85 Antilochos is called upon to defend not the prize but the way in which he won it. This second and more substantial detour from the expected sequences of *collection of prizes* is, typically, much more complex in its action and interaction than the first. In a sense, Homer has 'primed' us cognitively for the more complex events of the ensuing scene.[92] In outline, this sequence (566–611) is initiated by Menelaos' accusation, realized through reference to a rebuke format: *reproach* (570); *behaviour at issue* (571–2); *proposal* (573–8, 579–85).[93]

The next phase of action is a model of amicable dispute-settlement. Antilochos—who is given at 586 the epithet

---

[91] For further confirmation of Achilleus' affection, see *Il.* 23. 785–96 (Antilochos earns from Achilleus a supplementary prize in the foot-race).

[92] For a discussion of this phenomenon in cognitive science, as a device which assists both production and comprehension of discourse, see P. Thorndyke and F. Yekovich, 'A Critique of Schema-Based Theories of Human Story Memory', *Poetics*, 9 (1980), 23–49, at 38.

[93] Cf. realizations of the rebuke format at *Il.* 3. 39–57; 4. 338–48; 23. 492–8.

πεπνυμένος (discreet)—accepts the blame for what happened and offers to make amends.[94] His proposal to return the mare (through reference to a gift-offer format: *offer* (591–4); *reason* (594–5)) is designed to compensate for Menelaos' loss of prestige; the offer of gifts in addition is intended to buy back his goodwill.

This is an important moment in the *Iliad*. The contest between the two men has provoked bitterness and recrimination; yet, without mediation and without divine intervention, Antilochos and Menelaos have been able to resolve their differences. Even as he reminds us again, through reference to the scripted speech act, rebuke, of the quarrel of *Iliad* 1, Homer shows us that a dispute can be resolved to the satisfaction and credit of both parties, provided that each party is prepared to make a concession to the other. Antilochos' deference, his generous offer of reparation, and his prompt presentation of the mare (596–7) earn a positive reaction (597–600) and a favourable response from Menelaos (602–11). For Menelaos formally renounces his anger. His renunciation is expressed through reference to the renunciation script: *renunciation* (602–3); *reason* (603–6, 607–9). Within his explanation of his softened stance, Menelaos' tone changes (606). His words, apparently still a realization of *reason*, effect a neat transition to a new script, through which the old man acknowledges publicly his debt to Nestor and his sons, who have done so much on his behalf. He pays off his debt both in words and through the gift of the mare. This offer is expressed through the gift-offer format, more developed now than before: *address* (607–8); *reason* (607–8; 610–11); *offer* (609–10). With this gesture and with these words Homer is able to resolve a question which has troubled us with regard to the characterization of Menelaos. Why is he so well-loved by the Achaians? Why is his welfare always of such concern to his fellows? In this final speech we can see the answer. His appreciation of the efforts on his behalf of other, more capable, men and his readiness to acknowledge in public his gratitude, strength-

---

[94] His response to Menelaos' anger is expressed through the conciliation script: *request for understanding/patience* (587–8, 591); *reason for behaviour* (589–90); *suggestion for amends* (591–2).

ens the bond of affection between himself and the Achaian princes.[95]

At this point the detour from the element *collection of prizes* comes to a close. The remaining prize-getters collect their prizes: Menelaos takes third prize (613); Meriones the fourth (614–15). But the fifth prize lies unclaimed, since Eumelos has been awarded a supplementary prize. The unclaimed bowl is available for another purpose. It will serve not as a token of a recent triumph in a contest; rather, it will become an extraordinary gift, a souvenir of Patroklos, for Nestor, the old charioteer (616–17). As Achilleus says at 620–1: δίδωμι δέ τοι τόδ' ἄεθλον αὔτως (I give you this prize for the giving). The hero uses the unclaimed prize as a token of sympathy and respect for the old man who can no longer compete as he once had and as a means of drawing him into the public ritual of commemoration. Nestor, therefore, is no longer a spectator; he is a participant. All this is achieved through reference again to the gift-offer format: *address* (618); *reason* (618–20, 621–3); *offer* (620–1).

Expressions of gratitude for gifts given are realized in Homer only on extraordinary occasions. In this case Nestor's thanks are expressed in accordance with the acceptance format: *acceptance* (624); *confirmation of reasons offered* (626–8); *joy* (646–9); *benediction* (650). He interrupts his thanks with the story of his performance in the funeral games of Amarygkeus, a story which he begins in characteristic vein (629–30):

εἴθ᾽ ὣς ἡβώοιμι βίη τέ μοι ἔμπεδος εἴη
ὡς ὁπότε . . .

I wish I were young again and the strength still unshaken within me, as once . . .[96]

The old man, who has no triumphs to enjoy in the present, returns to the past in order to relive the pleasure of success. In doing so he refers to the contest script, the same script as that which structures the larger tale. Restating his *confirmation*

---

[95] Hohendahl-Zoetelief, however, finds the scene unconvincing: Menelaos, he feels, despite his respect for public opinion, makes a bad impression (I. Hohendahl-Zoetelief, *Manners in the Homeric Epic* (Leiden: E. J. Brill, 1980), 143–4).

[96] Cf. *Il.* 7. 157; 11. 670–1; and 1. 260–1 (a variant on the same theme).

(626–8, 645), Nestor returns to the acceptance format. In his expression of the old man's delight, and of his benediction, Homer makes explicit what we have suspected through the *Iliad*, that Nestor's greatest fear is that he and his deeds should be forgotten. In Achilleus' gift he finds the proof he needs that he is honoured, and that he will be remembered.[97]

Cognitive research, following the lead of Frederick Bartlett, has enabled us to clarify some previously unexplained aspects of the composition of the Homeric epics. In studying this long segment from Homer's account of the games for Patroklos, we have discovered that the Homeric story is not found in the strings of so-called 'themes' (I use the term here in the Parry and Lord sense), which have been the focus of research in the last fifty years. Rather, we rediscover what we have always suspected, that the lively stories which Homer tells are the products of the creative mind. As I have shown, Homer's narrative is for the most part founded on and generated by cognitive structures which organize the memory storage not only of singers, like Homer, in an oral tradition, but of all individuals. Such structures include information about the kind of goals which people are likely to hold, the kind of strategies which they are likely to use to satisfy those goals, and, as well, the routine actions, physical or verbal, which they actually carry out. I have used the term 'script' to refer to the knowledge structure which encodes information about actions of this routine kind.

What surprises us as readers of the Homeric epics is that the poet spells out the details of so many of his situational and instrumental scripts, by contrast with our own practice, which is far more compressed. The Parry–Lord hypothesis has suggested that Homer's motive in doing so was convenience in composition. Certainly, Homer, as an oral singer, recognized the practical value of this habit; but his

---

[97] On Nestor's delight, see Dunkle, 'Funeral Games', at 17. Hohendahl-Zoetelief, *Manners*, 114–16, finds Nestor's gratitude excessive. But if we read Nestor's concerns as I have, above, then the depth of his gratitude is as we would expect. For a more sympathetic account of Nestor, in terms of the 'weakened self-image' of the old, see C. Querbach, 'Conflicts between Young and Old in Homer's *Iliad*', in S. Bertman (ed.), *The Conflict of Generations in Ancient Greece and Rome* (Amsterdam: B. Grüner, 1976), 55–65, esp. at 56.

motives were far more complex than Parry suggests. As we shall observe in later chapters, the poet took advantage of a number of memory-based strategies which assisted him in the preparation of his song and at the moment of performance: for example, his exploitation of rhyme and rhythm in list-making, and of visual imagery in the construction of similes. But he saw their aesthetic merits also: in incorporating his strategies for recall into his song, he knew that they in some way gave particular pleasure to his listeners. The poet's reasons for spelling out his scripts in some detail relate, therefore, not only to the practicalities of performance; he is concerned as well with the effects he can achieve in his song and the impact of his song on his audience. As we observed at various points in my discussion of the chariot-race of *Iliad* 23, the poet chooses to express the details of scripted sequences in order to regulate the pace of his story, in order to accommodate it to the needs of his listeners, and to arouse their suspense and curiosity. He uses such sequences to create the semblance of reality, for scripted details are reassuringly familiar and in this respect persuasive. He uses them also, on the other hand, to evoke a certain distinctive ambience. This epic world is a world apart. It is a world which he characterizes through unhurried accounts of deliberate action and solemn ritual;[98] it is a world of tradition, created by his mode of presentation.[99] This practice, whereby the singer chooses to verbalize so much of any script, is a stylistic practice. The expression of what is familiar to us all is a recognizable and pleasing characteristic of oral epic.[100] The singer knows this; and he accommodates his presentation to his listeners' preference.

[98] Cf. Austin, 'Digressions', at 307–10; J. Russo, 'Homer against his Tradition', *Arion*, 7 (1968), 275–95, at 280; C. Segal, 'Transition and Ritual in Odysseus' Return', *La Parola del Passato*, 22 (1967), 321–42, at 342.

[99] For comment on the interplay of form and tradition in the process of traditionalization, see E. Bakker, 'Noun-Epithet Formulas, Milman Parry, and the Grammar of Poetry', in J. P. Crielaard (ed.), *Homeric Questions* (Amsterdam: J. C. Gieben, 1995), 96–125, at 104–6.

[100] On the use of detail in narrative, and its contribution to storytelling in terms of understanding and involvement, see D. Tannen, *Talking Voices: Repetition, Dialogue, and Imagery in Conversational Discourse* (Cambridge and New York: Cambridge University Press, 1989), ch. 5. For further discussion, see Epilogue, below.

In summary it is possible to reconcile what we understand of Homeric practice with current theories in the cognitive sciences regarding the storage of knowledge. Parry and Lord's themes, as they are expressed in Homer, are fundamentally a cognitive phenomenon. If we regard them thus, as cognitive entities shared by the singer and all members of his audience, the way is open to us again to think of Homer—as Aristotle did (*Poetics* 1459a–1460a)—as a creative poet who takes a traditional story and makes it his own.

2

On Working under Pressure: The Performance of Lists and Catalogues

The various lists and catalogues which are to be found in the Homeric epics have, over recent years, been subject to careful scrutiny. But although they have been studied individually in terms of both form and content, there has been no real discussion of the activity itself—the activity of listing and cataloguing—in traditional oral epic.[1] Although scholars recognize that Homer's lists and catalogues, like his narrative, are the products of an oral tradition (indeed, lists of a certain kind may be considered to be a defining feature of the oral genre), they have not yet considered them in the context of oral performance.[2] There has been no sustained

---

[1] Much scholarly attention has been devoted to the catalogues of *Il.* 2, and to the historical and geographical information which they may store. For studies dealing with the content of the Catalogue of Ships, see e.g. G. Jachmann, *Der homerische Schiffskatalog und die* Ilias (Köln: Westdeutscher Verlag, 1958); D. L. Page, *History and the Homeric* Iliad (Berkeley: University of California Press, 1959), ch. 4; R. Hope Simpson and J. F. Lazenby, *The Catalogue of Ships in Homer's* Iliad (Oxford: Clarendon Press, 1970); G. S. Kirk, *The* Iliad*: A Commentary*, i (Cambridge: Cambridge University Press, 1985), 166–240. On the structural patterns which underpin individual entries of the Catalogue: see C. R. Beye, 'Homeric Battle Narrative and Catalogues', *HSCP* 68 (1964), 345–73; B. Powell, 'Word Patterns in the Catalogue of Ships (B494–709): A Structural Analysis of Homeric Language', *Hermes*, 106 (1978), 255–64; M. Edwards, 'The Structure of Homeric Catalogues', *TAPA* 110 (1980), 81–105. For an examination of form and content together, see K. Stanley, *The Shield of Homer: Narrative Structure in the* Iliad (Princeton: Princeton University Press, 1993), 13–26. Homer's other lists have not excited quite the same interest. See Beye, 'Homeric Battle Narrative and Catalogues'; Edwards, 'Structure of Homeric Catalogues'; W. Minton, 'Invocation and Catalogue in Hesiod and Homer', *TAPA* 93 (1962), 188–212; J. Butterworth, 'Homer and Hesiod', in J. H. Betts, J. T. Hooker, J. R. Green (eds.), *Studies in Honour of T. B. L. Webster*, i (Bristol: Bristol Classical Press, 1986), 33–45 (on Homer's lists at *Il.* 12. 20–3 and 18. 39–48).

[2] Like the narrative stretches of epic, Homer's lists and his catalogues are

attempt to explain why a poet might include lists and catalogues in his composition; how he may have prepared them for performance; and how his lists may have appealed to his audience of listeners.

This chapter is a study of Homer's lists and catalogues as a genre of their own which plays a special role in oral art. I shall consider them, in all their variety, not in the guise in which we meet them today in Homer—that is, in print, on the page—but as units of discourse developed with performance, and a live audience, in mind. My discussion will have a dual focus: on the singer and his preparation of catalogue-songs, and on the audience and its response. My point of reference throughout will be our own experience, as singers and as listeners, of list-songs. For a contemporary perspective on list-singing I have drawn on the experiences of an Australian folk-singer, Karen Ottley, who has given me first-hand information on a singer's preparation for list-singing and on audience response to list-songs. In the course of the discussion I shall refer to the hypothesis which I outlined in my Introduction: that there is an intimate relationship between the poet's resources of memory and the way in which he has shaped his song.

LISTS AND CATALOGUES DEFINED

A study of this kind demands a definition of terms. For my purposes, the term 'list' will refer to those passages in Homer where the poet presents a sequence of four or more place names, personal names, or items, all modified by little or no descriptive material. The minimum figure of four is arbitrary. But, in that the sequential presentation of fewer than four items poses little challenge to memory or to performat

expressed in a formulaic language which is the mark of an oral tradition. This observation is all-important when we analyse the composition of catalogue entries or when we discuss the transmission of traditional information. For discussion of the Catalogue of Ships and the oral tradition, see Page, *History*, ch. 4; Kirk, *The Iliad: A Commentary*, i, 168–77. On the place and the nature of the list in oral epic, see W. Ong, *Orality and Literacy: The Technologizing of the Word* (London and New York: Methuen, 1982), 96–101, at 99; on lists in early poetry, see C. M. Bowra, *Homer* (London: Duckworth, 1972), 89–93, at 90–1.

ive skills, I shall not identify smaller collections as lists. An example of a list, in my terms, is the string of names of Greek heroes whom Hektor killed in battle, at *Il.* 11. 301–3:

> Ἀσαῖον μὲν πρῶτα καὶ Αὐτόνοον καὶ Ὀπίτην,
> καὶ Δόλοπα Κλυτίδην καὶ Ὀφέλτιον ἠδ' Ἀγέλαον,
> Αἴσυμνόν τ' Ὠρόν τε καὶ Ἱππόνοον μενεχάρμην.[3]

Asaios first, and then Autonoös and Opites,
And Dolops, Klytios' son, Opheltios and Agelaos,
and Aisymnos, and Oros, and Hipponoös stubborn in battle.

I draw attention here also to a few lists which are, as it were, double-sided. In that both subject and object of the key verb are changed with each entry, these double-sided lists in Homer reflect the nature of combat on the battlefield. Here Homer begins his account of Odysseus' attack on the suitors in his palace (*Od.* 22. 265–8):

> Ὣς ἔφατ', οἱ δ' ἄρα πάντες ἀκόντισαν ὀξέα δοῦρα
> ἄντα τιτυσκόμενοι· Δημοπτόλεμον μὲν Ὀδυσσεύς,
> Εὐρυάδην δ' ἄρα Τηλέμαχος, Ἔλατον δὲ συβώτης,
> Πείσανδρον δ' ἄρ' ἔπεφνε βοῶν ἐπιβουκόλος ἀνήρ.[4]

So he spoke, and they all aimed their sharp spears and threw them
straight ahead. Demoptolemos was killed by Odysseus,
Euryades by Telemachos, Elatos by the swineherd,
Peisandros by Philoitios, the herdsman of oxen.

A catalogue, on the other hand, is equally a list, but one in which some items are supplemented with enlivening description or comment, often rendered through narrative. The most notable amongst Homer's catalogues is his Catalogue of Ships (*Il.* 2. 494–759).[5] Catalogues may well contain fewer entries than lists; they gain their substance, however, from the elaboration of individual items. Some lists develop into catalogues: the singer begins his presenta-

---

[3] For other strings of Greek heroes see *Il.* 7. 162–8; 8. 261–7; 23. 836–8; for the strings of Trojans see *Il.* 5. 677–8, 705–10; 11. 56–60; 13. 789–94; 16. 694–6; 17. 215–18; 21. 209–10; 24. 248–51; for rivers see *Il.* 12. 19–23; for Nereids see *Il.* 18. 39–49; for citadels, *Il.* 9. 149–52; for plunder, *Il.* 11. 677–81; for the Phaiakian volunteers, *Od.* 8. 111–19; and for the suitors, *Od.* 22. 241–3.

[4] See also *Il.* 15. 328–42; *Od.* 22. 283–6.

[5] See also *Il.* 2. 816–77; 14. 315–28; 23. 288–351; *Od.* 11. 235–327. For a catalogue of items rather than personal names, note Agamemnon's gift offers to Achilleus: *Il.* 9. 121–56 (cf. 264–98); 19. 243–8.

tion by listing but, as the song proceeds, he chooses to
elaborate on individual entries. We observe behaviour of
this kind in *Il.* 13. 685–700; 14. 511–22; 15. 328–42. For the
reverse movement, where a catalogue is reduced to a list, see
Il. 16. 399–418.

On the face of it, a list is nothing more than a dry
enumeration of names, or places, or objects which interrupts
the narrative line. More precisely, it erupts from it, given
that each entry in the list is, strictly speaking, part of the
narrative; this relationship is made explicit in the grammar
of the passage.[6] As a list grows longer, however, its link with
its context seems to grow more tenuous. And yet even an
extended list in Homer—for example, the Catalogue of
Ships or the list of the Nereids (*Il.* 18. 39–49)—does not
exist for itself alone. I shall discuss below the role the great
catalogue and the Nereid-list play in Homer's version of the
story of Achilleus.

LISTS AND THEIR AUDIENCES

On the printed page lists and catalogues hold little attraction
for most readers: a quick survey, for example, of first-time
readers of the *Iliad* will reveal their impatience with
Homer's great catalogues or with his pure lists. Although
some readers may admire a list on the printed page for its
antiquarian interest, for its completeness, for its wit, or its
beauty, others, who read stories for the pleasure of narrative,
will find a list tedious.[7] But to hear a list-song is, it seems, a
very different experience. A listening audience will respond
to this kind of itemization with silent attention; and when
the list is completed, the performance will often be acknowledged with applause, often louder or more enthusiastic than
at any point during the narrative.[8] Radlov's descriptions of

---

[6] Note the case relationships of *Il.* 14. 315–28 (where the genitive case of 317,
319, 321, 323, 326, 327 ties each item to the declaration of 315–16); and of *Il.*
11. 56–60 (where it is the accusative case which gives coherence to the list).

[7] Creative writers in recent times (with the conspicuous exception of James
Joyce) are reluctant to use the list-mode with the same frequency as does Homer.
On the creative use of lists in contemporary fiction, see D. Lodge, *The Art of
Fiction* (London: Secker & Warburg, 1992), 61–5.

the enthusiastic reaction of a Kirghiz audience to catalogue-singing are confirmed by singers today. A list-song—even in our literate society—holds an audience's attention in a special way. If the singer reaches the end of his list without breakdown (a flawless performance is essential to success), it will be received with generous applause. This observation raises the question which is at the heart of my enquiry: why is it that a list performed should be received with such enthusiasm?

WORKING WITH MEMORY: THE RECALL OF NARRATIVE

With this question in mind, I propose to contrast list-making and narrative as modes of discourse and as perform-ance pieces, although at first glance it might appear that there is little difference between the genres. When a poet in an oral tradition performs (whether he tells a story or sings a list-song), he faces challenges at two levels. Not only must he call up his material from memory at the moment he requires it, but he must also be able to deliver it effectively. The success of his song will depend, therefore, on both his memory and his performance skills. It is, however, in these very respects that lists also differ from narrative. They differ in the demands which they make on memory and in their style of delivery.

The first requirement of a singer as he prepares to sing an epic tale is that he should be able to recall the gist of the tale he wishes to tell: that is, its sequence of states and actions and of causes and effects.[9] The ability to do this is not exceptional in itself: to remember event-sequences is a natural activity.[10] Given that the principal system for the organization of human memory is thought to be episodic,

---

[8] See e.g. the comments of W. Radlov, reported in H. M. and N. K. Chadwick, *The Growth of Literature*, iii (Cambridge: Cambridge University Press, 1940), 185, and the Chadwicks' discussion.   [9] For discussion, see Introduction, above.
[10] For experimental observations of the recall of stories, see F. Bartlett, 'Experi-ments on Remembering', in *Remembering: A Study in Experimental and Social Psychology* (Cambridge: Cambridge University Press, 1932; reprint edn., 1950), 47–185; for discussion, see Introduction, above.

Lists and Catalogues

the sequential nature of narrative as we know it is reflected in the way in which we organize our memory store.[11] Because narrative is connected discourse—a song-path (Homer's οἴμη: see *Od.* 8. 481)—its sequence of cause and effect lends itself to memorization and recall. And when it comes to fleshing out the events of the narrative chain with details of routine activity, this is likewise a relatively simple matter. We all store in memory (as cognitive scripts) information about activities such as dressing, preparing meals, uttering rebukes, or protests; and we can, if we choose, express these scripts in considerable detail. At these levels, therefore, the poet's ability to generate narrative can be matched by any member of his audience. With little more effort than that of attending to a story, a conscientious listener may learn—and therefore be able to reproduce—its broad outlines; and in retelling it he might, like the oral poet himself, give full expression to the detail of any of the scripts to which he refers. We should bear in mind, too, that there is another factor which works in the favour of a storyteller, whether bard or amateur. As I observed in Chapter 1, a storyteller generally feels no compulsion to reproduce word for word a story which he has heard from another source. It is not always necessary, for example, that he adhere to the same order of presentation and the same style of storytelling, or make the same lexical choices or use the same syntactical structures.[12] If the causal chain of the story he tells is the same as that of the story he originally heard, it will be judged to be the same story.

---

[11] For discussion, see Introduction and Ch. 1, above.

[12] A. B. Lord, *The Singer of Tales* (Harvard: Harvard University Press, 1960; New York: Atheneum edn., 1965), at 95, comments: '[t]o the singer . . . the song has a specific though flexible content'. On recall for a traditional ballad, see W. Wallace and D. Rubin, ' "The Wreck of the Old 97": A Real Event Remembered in Song', in U. Neisser and E. Winograd (eds.), *Remembering Reconsidered* (Cambridge: Cambridge University Press, 1988), 283–310. They conclude (at 303): '[t]he memory for the ballad is not the exact song, nor is it a collection of words; rather, it is a collection of rules and constraints'. Cf. R. Finnegan, *Oral Poetry: Its Nature, Significance and Social Context* (Cambridge: Cambridge University Press, 1977), 133.

WORKING WITH MEMORY: LISTS AND CATALOGUES

The activity of list-making and list-singing requires, by contrast, a different orientation of cognitive skills and a more concentrated application of memory than does narration. There is more emphasis in a list-song on memorization and near word for word reproduction and less scope (than in other oral genres) for innovation.[13]

A list is not a connected sequence of events in the way that narrative is. It is simply a series of 'replayings' of a single event or action. What is being repeated is either one of the events from within an event-sequence (or type-scene) or the type-scene itself, perhaps in compressed form.[14] For examples of repetition of this kind, see *Il.* 14. 315–28 (the series of women whom Zeus has seduced); *Il.* 11. 56–60 (the list of Trojan leaders around whom the Trojans gathered). Because of the very density of the information which a list conveys, a list-song cannot be a spontaneous creation, composed at the moment of performance. It must be prepared in advance.[15] Anyone who has tried, without preparation, to put together a rhythmic list, even of seven or eight items, can testify to this. If the list represents a collection of traditional material, the poet's version will be measured against a fixed standard: this is material which the audience itself will probably have heard before and perhaps knows well. The Catalogue of Ships is such a list. Unlike narrative, where a certain flexibility in presentation is always possible, a traditional list does not permit alteration. No

[13] Cf. Finnegan, *Oral Poetry*, 73 and 84. This is not to say that a singer may not exercise a creative spirit in composing a list, nor do I imply that singers do not rehearse narrative; for they do: Lord, *Singer*, 21–9.

[14] Cf. Edwards, 'Homeric Catalogues', 101.

[15] For evidence from within the text which suggests advance preparation, note Homer's use of numbers in association with lists: εἴνατος, ninth (*Il.* 8. 266); ἑπτά, seven; (*Il.* 9. 149); ἐννέα, nine (*Il.* 24. 252). Second, observe that he often does not take advantage of the formulaic epithets which would promote fluent composition: he constructs his list from nouns alone (e.g., at *Il.* 5. 677–8; 11. 301–3; 16. 415–18; 17. 215–18; 18. 39–49). Finally, on the occasions on which Homer has cause to offer a similar list (*Il.* 7. 162–8 and 8. 261–7; 9. 121–56 and 262–99), the lists are essentially the same and preserve the same order. I thank Mark Edwards for reminding me to include the gift-lists from *Iliad* 9.

name may be omitted; and no wrong attributions can be made. The singer is aware that individual members of his audience are monitoring the list, in expectation of reference to their own family, a family connection, a popular figure, their own region, or, indeed, their own town: the naming of names which are dear to them is a source of pleasure and pride. This kind of list, therefore, must be committed to memory with care.

But not all lists are traditional. Some are fictitious; and some are the original composition of the poet. In these latter cases there is a certain scope for internal variation. A list of this kind may be abbreviated; and names which are metrically equivalent may be substituted or interchanged. Notable examples of this kind of list are the list of the Nereids of *Il.* 18. 39–49 and that of the Phaiakian nobles of *Od.* 8. 111–19.[16] In terms of tradition and invention alone, therefore, there are lists of different kinds. But whatever the case, the performance of a list requires preparation and imposes its own, often exacting, demands on memory.

Narrative, as I noted above, is connected discourse, which lends itself, simply and naturally, to learning and recall. Lists are clusters of elements which are not obviously linked in this sequential way. How, then, does the learning of a list differ from the processing and recall of narrative? How does an oral poet overcome the very real limitations of memory for non-sequential data?[17] What are the factors which assist him in learning and retrieval? How, in short, does he cope with a task which most of his listeners do not willingly attempt? I believe that the discussion which follows will throw some light on the poetic craft of list-making both as it occurred within the Homeric epics and as it continues to be practised today in oral contexts.

---

[16] For comparison of Homer's Nereid-list with that of Hesiod (*Theogony*, 233–64), see Butterworth, 'Homer and Hesiod', at 39–44. For other invented lists, see *Il.* 5. 677–8 (the Lykians killed by Odysseus); 11. 301–3 (the men slain by Hektor); 16. 415–18 (the heroes killed by Patroklos). For further discussion, see below.

[17] The standard text on the limitations of memory is G. Miller, 'The Magical Number Seven, Plus or Minus Two: Some Limits on our Capacity for Processing Information', *Psychological Review*, 63 (1956), 81–97.

THE KEY TO SUCCESSFUL RECALL: THE ORGANIZATION OF MATERIAL

The learning of a list of any kind requires some effort, for all except those few people who have a peculiar talent for this kind of memorization. It has been proposed over the years (and is popularly accepted) that illiterate people have better memories for all kinds of material than people in literate cultures, because they cannot rely on written systems for the storage of data. Certainly, in the ancient world, in societies which were by no means universally literate, more was expected of memory: for example, in the assembly and in the law courts of classical Athens, and in connection with dramatic performance.[18] But were the people of the time better at memorizing because they were illiterate? The very fact that people in the ancient world speak with admiration of various feats of memory suggests that the task of remembering and reproducing large quantities of data was indeed considered difficult—as does the existence of texts which discuss training in artificial memory (through complex mnemonic systems).[19] Furthermore, twentieth-century cross-cultural studies find no direct relation between illiteracy and memory; rather, they indicate that it is particular cultural institutions which promote the skills of memory.[20] So, with regard to the memorization of lists and catalogues, it was the oral tradition which provided a stimulus as well as a context in which its practitioners from the time of their apprenticeship could develop and display their powers.

The critical factor for memorization is organization. If a

[18] For further discussion, see R. Thomas, *Oral Tradition and Written Record in Classical Athens* (Cambridge: Cambridge University Press, 1992), Ch. 1.

[19] For feats of memory, see Pliny, *NH* 7. 88; Seneca, *Controversiae* 1, praefatio 19; Cicero, *Brutus* 88, 301, on Hortensius' memory. As an indication of the ancients' deep interest in memory-training through association, see e.g. *Ad Herennium*; Cicero, *de Or.* 2. 86–8; and Quintilian, *Institutio oratoria* 11. 2. 17–22. For valuable discussion see F. Yates, *The Art of Memory* (London: Routledge & Kegan Paul, 1966), chs. 1 and 2.

[20] Neisser, for example, claims that there is a positive relation between schooling and memory: see U. Neisser, 'Literacy and Memory', in U. Neisser (ed.), *Memory Observed: Remembering in Natural Contexts* (San Francisco: W. H. Freeman, 1982), 241–2 and n. 1; see also S. Scribner and M. Cole, *The Psychology of Literacy* (Cambridge, Mass.: Harvard University Press, 1981), chs. 1, 13.

list comprises items which are completely unconnected and do not lend themselves to categorization or organization, it cannot readily be memorized and requires learning by rote. This demands the time and patience of any list-learner, literate or pre-literate.[21] Most of the lists which we construct for ourselves in everyday life, however, are connected by some thread of association. Because all entries in these lists are related, our range of choice is significantly narrowed (in that all items have something in common); and we expend less effort in learning and recall. The 'learning' of this kind of list, therefore, is less taxing than is the task of rote memorization.[22] All the lists which Homer sings are of this kind: they are 'meaningful' lists.[23] Amongst the easiest to compose, learn, and reproduce would be the strings of named heroes who play a significant role in the narrative. The list of Achaian heroes who respond to Nestor's challenge at *Il.* 7. 161–9 is simply a list of those heroes who play a conspicuous role in the continuing narrative (Agamemnon, Diomedes, the Aiantes, Idomeneus, Meriones, Eurypylos, Thoas, and Odysseus); the list of Trojans who lead their men into battle (*Il.* 12. 88–104) is a register of the principal Trojan actors in the epic; the suitors of *Od.* 22. 241–3 appear elsewhere in the story. For a singer who knows his story, it is possible to assemble such lists simply by reconsidering the gist of the narrative, calling to mind the leading actors across the tale, and allowing the hexameter rhythm of traditional epic to keep them in order.

The singer also includes in his performance lists of invented names. Because these names cannot be retrieved from the narrative proper, the singer has developed other

---

[21] Rote learning is necessary when material cannot be organized or categorized according to any associative, semantic, or syntactic scheme. See G. Mandler, 'Organization and Memory', in K. W. and J. T. Spence (eds.), *The Psychology of Learning and Motivation*, i (New York: Academic Press, 1967), 327–72, at 335. Telephone numbers, for example, and those other personal codes which we must memorize for survival today, are generally learned by rote.

[22] On mnemonic strategies, see A. Baddeley, *Human Memory: Theory and Practice* (Hove and London: Lawrence Erlbaum, 1990), Ch. 8.

[23] For a definition of the term as used by psychologists, see Mandler, 'Organization', 329. For discussion of associative networks, see D. Rubin, *Memory in Oral Traditions: The Cognitive Psychology of Epic, Ballads, and Counting-out Rhymes* (New York and Oxford: Oxford University Press, 1995), 31–5.

techniques of accessing them. These techniques are revealed in the names themselves. Take as an illustration the invented lists of Achaian or Trojan heroes about to die in battle at the hands of one or another of the great fighters. In these lists some names appear several times, sometimes applied to a Trojan hero, sometimes to an Achaian: names such as Chromios, Alastor, Noëmon, and Erymas, all of which are used more than once in the narrative to identify victims of the greater heroes. It seems that Homer collected in memory a store of names which could be readily called to mind and combined in song. It is likely that he used a number of associative cues and semantic stratagems for selecting names for his repertoire and for recalling them as he needed them. Some of these names, at least, are connected by associations of heroic kinship. For example, it is significant that the names Tros and Dardanos occur within a few lines of each other, having been introduced quite casually into the lists of the slain (Dardanos, son of Bias, *Il.* 20. 460; Tros, son of Alastor, *Il.* 20. 463). Other names derive from the names of peoples, as Bowra has already observed.[24] And other names, like Alastor (Avenger: *Il.* 4. 295; 5. 677; 20. 463) and Erymas (Bulwark: *Il.* 16. 345; 415), would be stock names so appropriate to the battlefield that the context alone might generate them. Indeed, in two of Homer's most delightful lists we find clear evidence of his pragmatic approach to list-making in general and the invention of names in particular. The Nereid-list of *Il.* 18. 39–49 comprises a series of invented but meaningful names, most of which remind us of the divinity of the nymphs or of their relation to the sea. Let us take the first three lines (39–41):

> ἔνθ' ἄρ' ἔην Γλαύκη τε Θάλειά τε Κυμοδόκη τε,
> Νησαίη Σπειώ τε Θόη θ' Ἁλίη τε βοῶπις,
> Κυμοθόη τε καὶ Ἀκταίη καὶ Λιμνώρεια

For Glauke was there, Kymodoke and Thaleia,
Nesaie and Speio and Thoë; and ox-eyed Haliä,
Kymothoë was there, Aktaia and Limnoreia

---

[24] See C. M. Bowra, *Tradition and Design in the* Iliad (Oxford: Clarendon Press, 1930), 77–9.

The learning and recall of this list would certainly be facilitated by the rich semantic associations of names such as Glauke (Grey-green), Kymodoke (Wave-receiver), Speio (Grotto), Halia (Belonging to the sea), and Aktaia (Coast-land).[25] Semantic associations hold together also all the names in Homer's list of the Phaiakian nobles (*Od.* 8. 111–19), each one being related to ships or to the sea. Here I cite some of Fitzgerald's renderings: Akroneos (Tip-mast), Okyalos (Tide-race), Nauteus (Hull-man), Ponteus (Blue-water), Euryalos (Sea-reach).[26] The charm of such a list for the listener—its wit and its whimsy—conceals the expedience of thematic association for the singer. Lists of this kind demonstrate both the great value of contextual association for list-construction and list-learning and the extent to which Homer exploited these cues.[27] They would not, however, have allowed him to dispense with the need to prepare and to rehearse. I return to this point below.

THE CATALOGUE OF SHIPS: ORGANIZATION AND RETRIEVAL

To move to a more ambitious example of the genre, let us consider the Catalogue of Ships. This catalogue, an orderly description of the Achaian force, contingent by contingent, offers a combined geographical and demographical account of the Greek mainland and most of the islands nearby. Systematically it links regions and localities with specific heroes and their people. But this is no mere muster list. Through additional narrative material (for example, about Tlepolemos, *Il.* 2. 653–70) and passages of description (for example, of Nireus, *Il.* 2. 671–5), Homer individualizes a number of heroes and makes them memorable.[28] It is this

---

[25] On the list of the Nereids, see Butterworth, 'Homer and Hesiod', 39–44, at 40–1.

[26] R. Fitzgerald, *Homer:* The Odyssey (Garden City, NY: Anchor Books, 1963).

[27] On the 'evocative power' of names chosen for lists written and oral, see R. Lamberton, *Hesiod* (New Haven and London: Yale University Press, 1988), 83; and, in the case of Homer, see A. Heubeck, S. West, J. B. Hainsworth, *A Commentary on Homer's* Odyssey, i (Oxford: Clarendon Press, 1988), 353.

[28] Because most of the heroes of the Catalogue are destined to play major roles in

supplementary information which breaks up the list, enriches it, and gives it substance. In the Catalogue of Ships, as in other catalogues (that of Zeus' loves [*Il.* 14. 315–28] or the the Catalogue of Heroines [*Od.* 11. 235–327]) the narrative mode is used to a greater extent than pure description. That Homer selects narrative so often in preference to description, by way of passing on information about a person, suggests that he is more comfortable with the narrative mode. Stories spring to mind more readily than does evaluative terminology; and they involve the audience in a way that description does not.[29]

In its celebration of the wider region and its resources, the Catalogue of Ships is to be a splendid creation in its own right. The poet, indeed, leaves his listeners in no doubt as to how they are to respond to it. When, at *Il.* 2. 484–93, he speaks of the contribution which the Muses will be making to his song, he uses his invocation to inform his audience that this will be no ordinary performance.[30] To sing this catalogue-song, he says, would be beyond the resources of an ordinary mortal: it would exhaust his powers of memory and even his voice. With the Muses' support, however, the Catalogue of Ships will repay his listeners' attention.

Although this catalogue is long and detailed, it is not difficult to deduce the singer's overall strategy for retrieving it from memory. It resembles all Homer's lists in that it is constructed from material which is connected thematically. But what is more important in this case is that the material is also spatially connected: the catalogue is organized and presented as a kind of circuit around Greece and the islands, broken only at *Il.* 2. 645–80 to include Crete, Rhodes, and the islands close by.

This arrangement is not the result of happy chance. The content of the catalogue had long been structured in this way,

---

the story, Homer is not inclined to single them out at this point. The stories of the catalogue concern a few minor heroes (Askalaphos and Ialmenos, Polypoites, and Tlepolemos) and those heroes who cannot appear in the later narrative: Protesilaos, Philoktetes.

[29] For further discussion of the poet's preference for narrative over the descriptive mode, see Ch. 3, below.

[30] For discussion of invocations, see Ch. 5, below.

formatted in the bard's memory as a 'cognitive map', a kind of schema which preserves information about places and the relationships between them.[31] The sequential order of the 'map' directs search in memory. It assists in the recall of the principal regions and the peoples who dwelt there. It acts as a kind of check: it attempts to guard against the unintentional omission of items (as indeed may have happened in this case, because the Cycladic group of islands is, by accident or design, omitted from the catalogue). This is the first level of organization within the structure of the catalogue. Within the broad categories at this first level further information has been nested: individual entries at each level hold further memories at a lower level.[32] Thus higher-order spatial cues prompt other associations. We all know from experience that to return to a place, or to think of a place, even one which we have not visited, will trigger associations in memory. The major geographical or demographical headings of the catalogue (such as the Phokians, the Lokrians, Euboia, or Athens), therefore, cue further lower-order place-names. These are often found in combination with traditional epithets, which sometimes provide strong visual and, therefore, memorable images of towns and settlements, and in this way assist in fixing the names of individual locations: Eteonos with its many mountain spurs (497); spacious Mykalessos (498); Thisbe abounding in doves (502); grassy Haliartos (503); Arne rich in grapes (507).[33] Many of the place-names

---

[31] For a survey discussion of our memory for spatial imagery, see Rubin, *Memory*, at 57–9. He notes, at 59, that 'oral traditions appear to be remarkably spatial'. On the notion of the 'cognitive map', an organizational schema (and not necessarily a mental display to be consulted) which may operate as a memory system in itself, see U. Neisser, 'Domains of Memory', in P. Solomon, G. Goethals, C. Kelley, B. Stephens (eds.), *Memory: Interdisciplinary Approaches* (New York and Berlin: Springer-Verlag, 1988), 67–83, at 76–7. The value of a cognitive 'map' appears to have been recognized from early times: see Yates, *The Art of Memory*, 21–6. This systematized presentation of the catalogue indicates that the singer has some understanding of the geography of the region. See Kirk, *The* Iliad*: A Commentary*, i. 183–7, esp. 185–6, for a suggestion that the routes of the catalogue are the routes which a traveller of the time would have taken.

[32] On the hierarchical structure of memory see Mandler, 'Organization', 366. On 'nesting', see U. Neisser, 'What is Ordinary Memory the Memory Of?' in Neisser and Winograd, *Remembering Reconsidered*, 356–73, at 369–70.

[33] On the several ways in which visual imagery supports memory, and on the dual coding theory proposed by Paivio, see Introduction.

themselves signify some remarkable attribute of a site, which may serve as a further mnemonic cue. Homer includes in his catalogue Arne (507, cf. ἀρνός; lamb), Araithyreia (571, cf. ἀραιός; narrow), Bessa (532, cf. βῆσσα; wooded glen), Helike (575, cf. ἕλιξ; winding), Kerinthos (538, cf. κηρός; wax), Orneai (571, cf. ὄρνις; bird), Orthe (739, cf. ὀρθός; straight), Pteleon (594, 697, cf. πτελέα; elm).[34] These place-names in turn prompt non-visual material, such as the names of the individual heroes and their stories.[35] Thus the names of less memorable heroes, such as Nireus, Pheidippos, Podarkes, or Gouneus, may be triggered first by spatial and then by visual information. In the light of the mnemonic aids I have noted above (the 'cognitive map', 'nesting', and the visual cues built into the list itself), we see that the catalogue was structured in ways most favourable to learning and that it would have been possible for a poet who works towards performance to learn such a catalogue and to reproduce its crucial information accurately.[36] Since spatial memory is so powerful, so dependable and so enduring, the preservation of the Catalogue of Ships as an entity has been promoted by the very organization of its material for ready recall.[37]

---

[34] On these and other names, see W. A. McDonald, 'Early Greek Attitudes toward Environment', *Names*, 6 (1958), 208–16, at 213–15. On visual images as aids to learning, see Baddeley, *Human Memory*, 106–9 and 188–90, and on ancient recognition of the importance to memory of visual imagery, see Yates, *The Art of Memory*, chs. 1 and 2. The distinctive epithets of oral epic would appear to have been of some assistance to the singer and not an additional burden, as suggested by Minton, 'Invocation and Catalogue', 206.

[35] See Neisser, 'Domains', 75–81.

[36] M. Wood, *In Search of the Trojan War* (London: BBC Books, 1985), 133, records instances of twentieth-century engagement with the Catalogue of Ships.

[37] On this, see Neisser, 'Domains', 77. Neisser, 'Ordinary Memory', 369, suggests that we recall spatial information in considerable detail and for long periods of time. This observation from another field may well provide support (but not, of course, confirmation) for those who argue that the Catalogue of Ships preserves accurate memories of a Mycenaean past. On the other hand it is clear that Homer adapted the catalogue to his own narrative. For discussion see Hope Simpson and Lazenby, *The Catalogue of Ships*, 153–71, esp. 158–9 and 169–70; Kirk, *The Iliad: A Commentary*, i, 195, 198, 231 and 233. Spatial memory may have played a comparable role in the learning and recall of the Catalogue of Heroines (*Od.* 11. 235–327).

THE CONTRIBUTION OF AUDITORY MEMORY

The connectedness of his material at associative and semantic levels would have been of considerable assistance to Homer as he prepared and as he sang his lists and catalogues. This is not, however, the only form of assistance. The surface features of epic song, and of lists and catalogues in particular, such as rhythm, alliteration, assonance, and the formulaic nature of the epic dialect also favour learning and prompt memory.[38] Such phonological patterns, whether they manifest themselves in the quantitative rhythm of epic song or in small-scale repetitions such as we find in the Nereid-list, limit possible choices for word or phrase and reduce the load on memory. Together with the recurrent features of list or catalogue entries, which give the passage a rhythmic 'swing', these patterns of sound promote the recall and production of this kind of enumerative song.[39] Observe, for example, the repeated sound-patterns in the Nereid-list at *Il.* 18. 43–45:

> Δωτώ τε Πρωτώ τε Φέρουσά τε Δυναμένη τε,
> Δεξαμένη τε καὶ Ἀμφινόμη καὶ Καλλιάνειρα,
> Δωρὶς καὶ Πανόπη καὶ ἀγακλειτὴ Γαλάτεια

Doto and Proto, Dynamene and Pherousa,
Dexamene and Amphinome and Kallianeira;
Doris and Panope and glorious Galateia

We see similar sound-play in the list of Phaiakians of *Od.* 8. 111–14:

---

[38] Rhyming or rhythmic couplets in English, for example, help us remember the number of days in each month of the year, or dates of events in history: cf. Baddeley, *Human Memory*, 186–8. On the significance of poetic ties, and on rhythm, see Wallace and Rubin, 'The Old 97', 294–7 and 301–3. For further discussion, see Rubin, *Memory*, ch. 4, and ch. 5, at 101–20.

[39] On Homer's clustering of the names of the Nereid-list according to principles of alliteration and assonance, see Butterworth, 'Homer and Hesiod', 40–1, with examples. He notes Homer's 'cumulative dynamic assonance', by way of comparison with Hesiod's 'localized repetition' of initial or final syllables. On the importance, for the recall of catalogue entries, of balance, see Ong, *Orality and Literacy*, at 99: here he observes that the recurrent patterns of subject–predicate–object observable in so many of Homer's catalogues produce a rhythmic 'swing' which aids recall (and which a mere list of names would lack).

ὦρτο μὲν ᾿Ακρόνεώς τε καὶ ᾿Ωκύαλος καὶ ᾿Ελατρεὺς
Ναυτεύς τε Πρυμνεύς τε καὶ ᾿Αγχίαλος καὶ ᾿Ερετμεὺς
Ποντεύς τε Πρωρεύς τε, Θόων ᾿Αναβησίνεώς τε
᾿Αμφίαλός θ᾿, υἱὸς Πολυνήου Τεκτονίδαο·[40]

Akroneus stood up, and Okyalos and Elatreus,
Nauteus and Prymneus, Anchialos and Eretmeus,
Ponteus and Proreus, Thoön and Anabesineos,
Amphialos, son of Polyneos, the son of Tekton

There is today a recognized discipline of list-learning, to which the hexameter of traditional epic, in which words are grouped in metrical units, would readily accommodate itself. This technique, called 'incremental recall', requires the learner to develop a chunk of material and rehearse it until it is memorized; a second chunk is learned, then combined with the first, and this sequence is repeated until the list is assembled.[41] Once a list is learned, and providing that it is actively maintained, it can be reproduced with ease.[42] This technique is used by Karen Ottley in her preparation of songs of all kinds. I suggest that all traditional poets, including Homer, would have practised and learned their list-songs in this way.

Since the content of these lists and catalogues and its surface expression provide various associative, semantic, and phonological prompts for the poet as he sings, the task of memorization is made somewhat easier than it may at first appear; at the least, he will not have to resort to rote memorization in the preparation of a list-song.[43] I do not

---

[40] Cf. also sound-patterns in lists of heroes: *Il.* 5. 677–8 (Alastor, Alkandros), 705–7 (Orestes, Oresibios; Oinomaos, Oinops); 8. 274 (Orsilochos, Ormenos, Ophelestes); 11. 301–3 (Opites, Dolops; Opheltios, Oros); 14. 511–15 (Mermeros, Meriones, Morus); and the river-list of 12. 19–23 (Rhesos, Karesos, Rhodios; Skamandros, Simoeis). On the role of phonological and other constraints (music and narrative structure) in keeping an oral tradition stable over time, see Wallace and Rubin, 'The Old 97', 285.

[41] On 'chunks' as integrated pieces of information and on incremental recall and its merits, see Baddeley, *Human Memory*, 40–2 and 156–8. This is a technique which lends itself to oral recall of both oral discourse and written texts as well as to the learning of lists: see G. Mandler and P. Dean, 'Seriation: Development of Serial Order in Free Recall', *Journal of Experimental Psychology*, 81 (1969), 207–15.

[42] On 'maintenance rehearsal', see Baddeley, *Human Memory*, 161.

[43] For comparable feats of memory (specifically, memory for names) in another pre-literate culture, all achieved by means other than rote memorization, see G. Bateson, 'Totemic Knowledge in New Guinea', in Neisser (ed.), *Memory*

wish, however, to diminish the effort involved. If a poet is to sing a list or catalogue successfully, he must spend time in preparation and practice; and he will apply himself more intensively to this task than he would to recalling the gist of a story.

PERFORMING THE LIST-SONG

The point of a list-performance is that it should be flawless. Because almost every word is critical, a list-performance makes as many demands on the singer's vocal technique and his performance skills as on his memory. Any small slip will mar the whole song. The singer will, therefore, spend considerable time before performance in practising his song, so that memory and performative skills come together.

When a singer performs a narrative passage he will take pains with enunciation and expression, so that his words may be clearly heard and his meaning taken. But because he is reproducing the natural structures and patterns of sequential discourse, which contain a certain amount of predictable material, he will not give all words the same emphasis. By contrast, when he prepares a list the singer works in the knowledge that all elements have equal weight and that every word is important; and, as he begins to perform his list-song, his diction will become even more studied and precise. For the singer knows that a word lost cannot be recuperated. When the singer begins to sing a list, therefore, every member of his audience is immediately aware that something has changed. Indeed, Homer, as we noted above, sometimes prefaces his performance of a list-song with an address to his Muse, to seek her support in this new enterprise and to indicate to his audience that he is

Observed, 269–73. Bateson observes that the names to be remembered are meaningful, and that paired names are connected by semantic association and/or sound patterns—features which I have identified as crucial to the success of the poet in the Homeric tradition. Ruth Finnegan, *Oral Poetry: Its Nature, Significance and Social Context* (Cambridge: Cambridge University Press, 1977), 73–86, at 73, observes that there is a role for rote-memory in oral poetry: 'memorisation and near word-for-word reproduction sometimes *are* important'. I suggest, however, that the poet rehearses using the resources of memory wherever possible; and that these become the cues for song.

about to undertake a more demanding passage.[44] But, even in the absence of an invocation, the poet's uniform and clear diction, his evenly distributed emphases, his concentration of energy mental and physical—in short, his firmly emphatic delivery—draw attention to his list-song, as does the relentless repetition of sentence structure and grammatical signal. And yet gains in clarity and precision are counterbalanced by a loss of expressiveness, because the material is structurally uniform. For the same reason it is possible that the pace of delivery will be faster. This is a singer's instinctive response to the particular task of recall: the word-for-word reproduction of prepared material.[45] Karen Ottley explains that from her point of view she is 'on automatic' when she performs a list song; if she slows her pace of delivery to the point where she can think about what she is doing, she begins to make mistakes. That is, at a slower pace, her performance would be in some way flawed or, at least, undistinguished.

At the level of performance, as we have seen, the list introduces a change of style and a change of pace. For the audience, therefore, even a brief list of six or seven entries will serve a practical function—as diversion from the task of tracking the narrative. A longer list will do more; it offers listeners the pleasure of listening for the sake of listening. The surface features of the text—its recurrent structural patterns and the phonological qualities of rhythm, alliteration, and assonance—catch their attention and delight their ears. It is significant that these features of list-singing, which constitute a series of mnemonic cues for the singer, are simultaneously a source of pleasure to the listener. Like the associative or semantic cues which I discussed above, the surface features of the song act not only as constraints but also as opportunities.

As a list-song is performed, the audience's response is one of quiet attention and even, in the case of sustained lists and

---

[44] For such invocations see *Il.* 2. 484–93, 761–62; 11. 218–20; 14. 508–10. For discussion see Ch. 5, below.

[45] For a parallel case, in which rhythm, pace, and efficiency of recall are interlinked, see Baddeley, *Human Memory*, 40–1. Butterworth, 'Homer and Hesiod', 40, comments on the 'speed' of the Nereid-passage (due to Homer's economy of epithet).

catalogues, a subdued excitement. This excitement relates in part to the content of the list but also to its delivery. Both the singer and his listeners are anxious that the performance will be a success. Should the singer reach his list's end triumphantly—without faltering and without confusion— the audience's suspense is resolved. The longer the list, the greater will be the relief and delight of the audience once the end is reached. The singing of a longer list or catalogue, therefore, becomes a performance within a performance.

THE LIST IN THE CONTEXT OF EPIC SONG

What does a singer hope to achieve when he includes a list or a catalogue in his performance of epic song? As I have shown above, in respect of content and delivery, lists and catalogues offer a different kind of experience to the listener. They are undoubtedly included as a special feature of the entertainment. But a list or a catalogue can also make a contribution to the story itself. Even as it holds back the onward flow of narrative, a list can arouse in the audience a sense of urgency and of accelerating action. Homer takes advantage of that excitement which I described above and which relates to the performance of the list to arouse suspense in connection with the action of the narrative. He may use a list to express directly the gathering pace and intensity of events or to herald a climax. A number of examples will demonstrate what I mean.

Many of Homer's lists convey the urgency of the battle-field in a way that detailed narrative cannot. When Homer wishes to suggest the eager response of heroes to the prospect of battle or of a contest, he often uses a list. The four-item list of *Il.* 23. 836–8 is a brief example:

> Ὣς ἔφατ᾽, ὦρτο δ᾽ ἔπειτα μενεπτόλεμος Πολυποίτης,
> ἂν δὲ Λεοντῆος κρατερὸν μένος ἀντιθέοιο,
> ἂν δ᾽ Αἴας Τελαμωνιάδης καὶ δῖος Ἐπειός.[46]

[46] For other lists used in this way, see *Il.* 7. 162–8; 8. 261–7; 12. 88–104; 23. 288– 351, 754–6; *Od.* 8. 111–19.

So he spoke, and up stood Polypoites the stubborn in battle,
and Leonteus in his great strength, a godlike man, and there rose up
Aias, the son of Telamon, and brilliant Epeios.

When he wishes to suggest fierce activity across the battle-field, he will list a number of combatants, and sometimes their opponents as well. That this is a favoured method of conveying such impressions quickly and efficiently is evident from the number of lists in the battle narrative of the *Iliad*. Homer sings such a list at *Il*. 5. 677–8:

> ἔνθ᾽ ὅ γε Κοίρανον εἷλεν ᾽Αλάστορά τε Χρομίον τε
> ᾽Αλκανδρόν θ᾽ ῞Αλιόν τε Νοήμονά τε Πρύτανίν τε.[47]

And there he killed Koiranos, and Chromios, and Alastor,
Halios and Alkandros, and Prytanis and Noemon.

Lists of this kind, and the double-sided list, appear also in the fighting of the *Odyssey*, where otherwise lists have been used sparingly (*Od*. 22. 241–3, 265–8, 283–91). Some lists summarize sequential action (see *Il*. 5. 677–8); others, such as that at *Il*. 14. 511–18, provide an overview of simultaneous events:

> Αἴας ῥα πρῶτος Τελαμώνιος ῞Υρτιον οὖτα
> Γυρτιάδην, Μυσῶν ἡγήτορα καρτεροθύμων·
> Φάλκην δ᾽ ᾽Αντίλοχος καὶ Μέρμερον ἐξενάριξε·
> Μηριόνης δὲ Μόρυν τε καὶ ῾Ιπποτίωνα κατέκτα,
> Τεῦκρος δὲ Προθόωνά τ᾽ ἐνήρατο καὶ Περιφήτην·
> ᾽Ατρείδης δ᾽ ἄρ᾽ ἔπειθ᾽ ῾Υπερήνορα, ποιμένα λαῶν,
> οὖτα κατὰ λαπάρην, διὰ δ᾽ ἔντερα χαλκὸς ἄφυσσε
> δῃώσας.

First Telamonian Aias cut down Hyrtios, he who
was son to Gyrtios, and lord over the strong-hearted Mysians.
Antilochos slaughtered Phalkes and Mermeros. Morys
and Hippotion were killed by Meriones. Teukros cut down
Periphetes and Prothoön. Next the son of Atreus,
Menelaos, stabbed Hyperenor, shepherd of the people,
in the flank so the bronze head let gush out the entrails
through the torn side.

Through a list, even a bare list of heroes' names, a poet can multiply a single image, or a single action, a number of

---

[47] See also *Il*. 16. 415–19; 21. 209–10.

times—and with great economy. A list, therefore, can evoke the turmoil of battle, the frenzy, and the scramble. And, because it puts names to faces, it individualizes the actors: these heroes are people.

The Nereid-list, likewise, looks ahead to a climactic moment: Achilleus' decision to return to the fighting, and to die. Thetis cries out (*Il.* 18. 35–7), grieving with Achilleus and at the same time mourning his approaching death. Her sister-nymphs gather to weep with her. And Homer holds back his narrative to name these nymphs of the sea. His steady accumulation of Nereid-mourners, whom he presents one by one, insists on the intensity of double sorrow, the present sorrow and the sorrow to come. Thetis' sorrow, and that of her sisters, is the sorrow of sympathy for Achilleus in his grief. More to the point, it is the sorrow of anticipation; for Thetis knows that he will not return to his home (18. 59–60). The Nereid-list is not, as the Chadwicks claim, an inappropriate interpolation of learned material.[48] Rather, in looking ahead to Achilleus' death, beyond the scope of the *Iliad*, this scene and the list it includes mark a significant point in the story. The catalogue will give us a new perspective on the action of the last books of the epic. The beauty of the list, which resides largely in the phonological and semantic qualities which I have discussed above, serves to highlight its pathos.

The list of Priam's sons (*Il.* 24. 248–51) looks to the future even as it shows us something of Priam's present pain. In these lines, in which the words of the narrator and Priam are fused, we hear that the old king inveighs against nine of his sons, all of whom he will describe as worthless:

> ὁ δ' υἱάσιν οἷσιν ὁμόκλα,
> νεικείων Ἕλενόν τε Πάριν τ' Ἀγάθωνά τε δῖον
> Πάμμονά τ' Ἀντίφονόν τε βοὴν ἀγαθόν τε Πολίτην
> Δηΐφοβόν τε καὶ Ἱππόθοον καὶ Δῖον ἀγανόν.[49]

> He was scolding his children
> and cursing Helenos, and Paris, Agathon the brilliant,
> Pammon and Antiphonos, Polites of the great war cry,
> Deïphobos and Hippothoös and proud Dios.

---

[48] See Chadwick and Chadwick, *Growth of Literature*, i. 276, 510.

[49] I read Δῖον here rather than the Oxford text's δῖον.

He will contrast these with the courageous warrior sons whom he has fathered (255), all now dead (*Il.* 24. 257–9):

Μήστορά τ' ἀντίθεον καὶ Τρωΐλον ἱππιοχάρμην
Ἕκτορά θ', ὃς θεὸς ἔσκε μετ' ἀνδράσιν, οὐδὲ ἐῴκει
ἀνδρός γε θνητοῦ πάϊς ἔμμεναι, ἀλλὰ θεοῖο.

Mestor like a god and Troilos whose delight was in horses,
and Hektor, who was a god among men, for he did not seem like
one who was child of mortal man, but of a god.

This list catches the pathos of the moment; none of these sons can replace the son unnamed, Hektor, who is at the forefront of Priam's mind and ours.[50] And yet, through its quickening pace, the list indicates Priam's renewed energy and looks ahead to the great moment of the epic: Priam's desperate but courageous journey through enemy lines to supplicate Achilleus for the return of Hektor's body.

Turning now to Homer's catalogues, I have selected two for further discussion: the catalogue of Zeus' liaisons and the Catalogue of Ships. Zeus' catalogue, at *Il.* 14. 315–28, functions in the same way as any of the lists above. But, perhaps for the very reason that this catalogue is offered by Zeus to his wife, it has an amusing edge. Zeus, so often the seducer, has on this occasion been seduced by Hera herself. The humour, however, extends further than this. To convey the urgency and intensity of his desire, Zeus asserts that on no other occasion has he felt such powerful love for a woman. He promptly proceeds to compare the strength of his feelings at this moment with passions stirred on a number of earlier occasions—by women other than his wife. He names names; and he proudly refers to offspring of various liaisons. If in any other circumstances Zeus had offered his wife such a catalogue, his indiscretion would have been disastrous. At this point of the narrative, how-ever, it allows us to measure Hera's determination not to be angered, despite her husband's inept, and certainly provoc-ative, declaration.

Finally, I look again at the Catalogue of Ships. When Homer, near the beginning of the *Iliad*, introduced the

---

[50] For a list delivered to achieve a similar purpose, to give emphasis to a point at issue through contrast, see *Il.* 13. 770–2.

leaders of the Achaians and the Trojan allies who came to Troy, it was natural—given the numbers involved—that he should do so in list-form. If we try to approach the catalogue as Homer's audience must have done (as listeners rather than readers, and with a prior knowledge of regional names and places) we will notice that the catalogue is constructed so as to engage his audience through the creation of suspense. We see the development of suspense relating to content in the singer's postponement of 'big' names; in the structure of his individual entries; and in the mutual desire for comprehensiveness.

Scholars have asked why the Boiotian contingent has been given first place in the catalogue, when the Boiotians play a less than significant role in the rest of the tale.[51] I ask instead why the Boiotians should not be named first. They are, indeed, a suitable contingent to lead off such a catalogue, if—as appears to be the case—the singer wished to delay the naming of the greater heroes until later points of his list: Agamemnon, for example, appears at 569–80; Odysseus at 631–7; Achilleus at 681–94. The purpose of such a delay is suspense: the poet's aim is to hold the interest of his listeners. Thus the great heroes' names (ordered in accordance with his cognitive map) have been held in reserve and appear later in the list rather than at its head.

Kirk distinguishes three different list-modes in the catalogue.[52] The most common of these is the singer's practice of naming the towns held by a particular leader before he names the leader, as at 2. 581–7, in the case of Menelaos:

οἳ δ' εἶχον κοίλην Λακεδαίμονα κητώεσσαν,
Φᾶρίν τε Σπάρτην τε πολυτρήρωνά τε Μέσσην,
Βρυσειάς τ' ἐνέμοντο καὶ Αὐγειὰς ἐρατεινάς,
οἵ τ' ἄρ' Ἀμύκλας εἶχον Ἕλος τ', ἔφαλον πτολίεθρον,
οἵ τε Λάαν εἶχον ἠδ' Οἴτυλον ἀμφενέμοντο,
τῶν οἱ ἀδελφεὸς ἦρχε, βοὴν ἀγαθὸς Μενέλαος,
ἑξήκοντα νεῶν.

They who held the swarming hollow of Lakedaimon,
Pharis, and Sparta, and Messe of the dove-cotes,

---

[51] See Kirk, *The* Iliad: *A Commentary*, i, 178–9, 185–6. Certainly the point he makes, that Boiotia is an appropriate place to begin a catalogue, given that the fleet assembled at Aulis before sailing to Troy, is valid.   [52] Ibid., 170–1.

they who dwelt in Bryseiai and lovely Augeiai,
they who held Amyklai and the seaward city of Helos,
they who held Laas, and they who dwelt about Oitylos,
of these his brother Menelaos of the great war cry
was leader, with sixty ships

This is the practice he follows in the cases of the universally recognized heroes, Diomedes, Agamemnon, Nestor, and Achilleus, as well as a number of others. As he sings, therefore, his listeners do not listen idly; they may well try to guess the name of the leader on the basis of the information the singer presents to them (the names of the towns he rules). By prolonging his list of subject towns, the singer prolongs the suspense of the listener who has identified the leader and awaits confirmation.[53]

The singer and his audience are concerned that the list-song should be complete. Individual listeners wait to hear those names which they believe are essential to such a list; this desire for completeness keeps them attentive. But the audience is anxious on another account. They are anxious that the singer should not break down. The subdued excitement, or suspense, which they feel, is sustained through the length of the catalogue-song; the more sustained the song, the more sustained the suspense. This suspense guides their expectations of the story to come. The Catalogue of Ships, by virtue of its comprehensiveness and its duration, clearly presages events on a grand scale. It is designed, that is, not only to make a statement about the mass of troops assembled, nor simply to gratify the pride of his listeners or to provide an entertaining interlude in the evening's performance. This catalogue and the Trojan catalogue together, through their scope and their elaboration, point to the scale and significance of all events and outcomes in the *Iliad*: they are designed to arouse in the audience expectations of a great story.

What is it about a list or a catalogue in the context of epic which can engage its audience so thoroughly? First, if it is a traditional list, it may appeal to an audience because of its

---

[53] Note that Odysseus' name is not postponed (2. 631). His entry is one of the least common catalogue-patterns: see Kirk, *The* Iliad*: A Commentary*, i, 170.

integrity and relevance. Second, if it is an invented list, and if its presentation is imaginative, we are struck by its novelty, its wit, or the beauty of its imagery. Third, it may in some way contribute to or evaluate the ongoing narrative. These first three factors apply to all lists, oral and written; the following three will be the qualities which make direct appeal to a live audience. These are the qualities which distinguish the list performed from the list on the printed page. I draw attention, first, to the critical importance of style, under which heading I include all aspects of presentation, including pace, diction, and poetics. I do not mean to imply that written lists are compiled without attention to stylistic qualities; where the list-maker's concern for poetics is observable, it is clear that the list has been designed for performance of a kind, if only by the solitary reader for his own pleasure. The second factor is the remarkable co-operative effort of a range of memory systems (episodic or semantic, visual, spatial, and auditory), all of which contribute to the performance. And, last, there is the sustained suspense which is part of any performance of this kind. This suspense is felt both by the singer, working under pressure, in performance, and the listeners, who will the list to continue uninterrupted to its end. Their engagement will keep them silent and absorbed for the sake of, and for the pleasure of, listening. Homer's lists are amongst the many special moments of his epic performance. They do not, as Beye suggests, reduce 'the ornate emotional, pictorial and dramatic material to its essentials', nor do they simply reflect an 'indexing, collecting mentality': rather, they can bring excitement and pleasure to oral performance even as they enrich the narrative in their own, often individual, ways.[54]

We should, therefore, pay attention to Homer's lists and catalogues as components of rather than as interludes in performance. They are not always an essential ingredient of the story itself; but they are used at different times to regulate, to structure, and to colour the telling. And they

---

[54] Beye, 'Homeric Battle Narrative', 369. Beye's sentiments echo those of Page, *History*, 136. For a response to Page, see Hope Simpson and Lazenby, *The Catalogue of Ships*, 158.

are undeniably part of the performance. The major lists and catalogues, by virtue of the number of entries which they include, are showpieces. They are designed to give clear evidence of the singer's diverse skills as poet and as performer. His audience will appreciate his ingenuity, his powers of memory, and his assiduity in working up a performance piece which demands, in some cases, careful rehearsal of traditional material, in others poetic craft, and, in every case, considerable practice, as he works with all the resources of his mind. The demonstration of these skills is particularly appealing to listeners who, as occasional list-makers themselves, know how difficult it is to overcome the limitations of memory. What sets the accomplished singer apart, however, is his delivery: given his command of technique, his performance will be that of a virtuoso. List-singing or catalogue-singing on a grand scale is therefore a remarkable feat, as Homer himself testifies: a feat of exceptional memory and of performative skill. It is his listeners' involvement in the singer's performance no less than their delight in his achievement which holds their attention and draws their applause.

3
Homer's Descriptive Segments: Their Composition and their Role in the Narrative

On at least twenty occasions in the course of the *Iliad* Homer slows the flow of narrative and allows himself to dwell on an object in the possession of one of his characters. He asks us to envisage a goblet, a bowl, a robe, or a lyre and, for a few moments, to hold that image before our eyes. For the most part these objects are familiar, even mundane; they are the furniture of everyday living. But these items are also extraordinary, because we encounter them in the *Iliad* in a context of war and suffering and because they are all endowed with remarkable qualities which set them apart from others of their kind.[1] This is an epic poem; these items are prized possessions. The poet tells us, for example, of Pandaros' bow (*Il.* 4. 105–11), the robes in Priam's store-chamber (*Il.* 6. 289–95), Meriones' helmet of boars' tusks (*Il.* 10. 261–71), Nestor's cup (*Il.* 11. 632–7), Andromache's head-dress (*Il.* 22. 468–72), the corselet taken from Asteropaios (*Il.* 23. 560–2), and the mixing bowl offered as a prize for the footrace at the funeral games for Patroklos (*Il.* 23. 740–7).

The poet's practice in the *Odyssey* is similar; but, it is not exactly the same. There are over a dozen passages, somewhat fewer than we note in the *Iliad*, which describe items designed for practical purposes, such as a key, a

---

[1] For comment on Homer's incorporation of the domestic into the high moments of epic, see e.g. E. Auerbach, 'Odysseus' Scar', in *Mimesis: The Representation of Reality in Western Literature*, trans. W. Trask (Princeton, NJ: Princeton University Press, paperback edn., 1968), 3–23, at 22, who observes that Homer is not afraid 'to let the realism of daily life enter into the sublime and tragic'.

mixing bowl, or a brooch. Like the material objects of the *Iliad*, these items, through the quality of their workmanship and through their associations with particular events and particular people, have already acquired a special significance; their value and their history set them apart as heirlooms.

What is the poet's purpose in lingering over such items? Certainly, he uses descriptions which contain a certain amount of detail to impress on his listeners the vividness of visual memory. His detailed account of a prized possession becomes a guarantee of the authenticity of the tale, for concrete details make stories seem more accurate; they imply attentiveness on the part of the observer, who is now the storyteller, and offer a certain reassurance that the central points of his or her story are also remembered correctly.[2] To some extent also the poet is celebrating the objects in question, as items which are beautiful and therefore significant in their own right. And he uses his descriptions to reflect in turn on the heroic lifestyle: on the acquisitive nature of the hero and on the heroic custom of gift-exchange in the mediation of friendships and alliances. But he has another motive. This we conclude from the distribution of such passages. Almost without exception these descriptions occur in association with events which we are to see as significant in the narrative line. When, at a critical point, the poet turns his eyes from one of his characters and his or her concerns, rests his gaze on something intimately connected with that character at the time, and describes it for us, he is effectively prolonging the dramatic moment. This technique is familiar to us in another medium, that of film.[3] And the purpose is much

---

[2] For discussion of how a storyteller achieves authenticity through inclusion of detail, see D. Tannen, *Talking Voices: Repetition, Dialogue, and Imagery in Conversational Discourse* (Cambridge and New York: Cambridge University Press, 1989), 138–40. For important discussion from a cognitive viewpoint, see D. Rubin, *Memory in Oral Traditions: The Cognitive Psychology of Epic, Ballads, and Counting-out Rhymes* (New York and Oxford: Oxford University Press, 1995), 56. In the *Odyssey*, the more self-reflexive of the epics, Homer builds this relationship, between description and authenticity, into the tale itself: e.g. the stranger's description of the golden brooch (*Od.* 19. 226–31) establishes his credibility in Penelope's eyes.

[3] On this point see M. Edwards, *Homer: Poet of the* Iliad (Baltimore and

the same. It is not that the poet is proclaiming the importance, or the centrality, of the object he describes; rather, he
is insisting on the significance of the scene in which that
object happens to play a minor role.[4] Because the poet's
descriptions of these small treasures render the items
themselves memorable, the occasions with which they are
associated remain in our memories also.[5] This is a reason for
the poet's focus on the boars' tusk helmet which is lent to
Odysseus for the daring night-raid on the Trojan camp; on
the individual items of Agamemnon's armour (corselet,
sword and shield) which he takes up in preparation for his
ἀριστεῖα, his ferocious attack on the Trojans; on Nestor's
great cup, from which he will be drinking when Patroklos
interrupts a quiet conversation with Machaon (the prelude
to a pivotal scene in the *Iliad*); on Andromache's head-dress
at the moment when she sees Hektor's body being dragged
by Achilleus across the plain; and on the golden brooch
which Penelope had pinned to Odysseus' mantle as he
prepared to leave Ithaka at the outbreak of the Trojan
War. When Penelope asks the stranger in her palace what

London: The Johns Hopkins University Press, 1987), 82–7, at 86; S. Richardson,
The Homeric Narrator (Nashville, Tenn.: Vanderbilt University Press, 1990), at
61–2. Auerbach, on the other hand, claims that Homer has simply created the
impression of retardation: see Auerbach, *Mimesis*, esp. at 4–7. Auerbach argues (at
7) that the Homeric style knows only a 'uniformly illuminated, uniformly objective'
present, hence the poet's need to represent phenomena in a 'fully externalized
form' (6). There is no doubt that Homer delights in recreating the physical
presence of material objects. I shall argue that these recreated objects have a role
to play both in the tale and in its telling; and that retardation, or the prolonging of
the dramatic moment, is part of that latter function. See also A. B. Lord, *The
Singer of Tales* (Cambridge, Mass.: Harvard University Press, 1960; New York:
Atheneum edn., 1965), 86–7, on the practice of Yugoslav epic singers.

[4] See G. Lukács, 'To Narrate or Describe?', trans. Hanna Loewy, from *Probleme
des Realismus* (Berlin: Aufbau-Verlag, 1955), reprinted in G. Steiner and R. Fagles
(eds.), *Homer: A Collection of Critical Essays* (Englewood-Cliffs, NJ: Prentice-
Hall, 1962), 86–9. Following G. E. Lessing, *Laocoön* (first pub. 1766), trans. E. A.
McCormick (Baltimore: The Johns Hopkins University Press, paperback edn.,
1984), ch. 16, Lukács observes that Homer does not aim to produce in words a
detailed account of what he wants us to see, for this would be superfluous to the
story. What is remarkable about all those objects which Homer describes in the
course of the *Iliad* is that they have been caught up in human affairs at a critical
moment in the narrative. This, Lukács claims, is the source of their poetic quality.

[5] On imagery as a 'powerful aid to memory', see Rubin, *Memory*, 46–8, at 48.
And see Introduction, above, on the memorability of imagery and its function as a
peg for other information.

Odysseus was wearing when he met him twenty years before, the stranger's accurate description of that brooch, from memory, reassures Penelope. She will make the stranger her confidant. These descriptive passages, therefore, are by no means digressions, in the narrow sense of the word, from the storyline; they are tied to their context, no matter how far from the present moment Homer may appear to take us.[6]

My study of Homer's descriptive mode begins with an analysis of the form of the small but elaborated descriptive passages which are scattered through both the *Iliad* and the *Odyssey*. Commentators have noted one or another feature within individual passages of formal description; but such passages have not yet been subject to this kind of scrutiny.[7] Such passages, delightful and distinctive as they are in some respects, are in others routine. This we shall see if we observe their form. In seeking reasons for their homogeneity, we shall look again at the resources of memory: the contribution of visual memory and of what has been termed implicit knowledge. Special consideration will be given to that element through which the poet prolongs his description and individualizes the item in question: a brief narrative, or perhaps simply a fragment

[6] See N. Austin, 'The Function of Digressions in the *Iliad*', *GRBS* 7 (1966), 295–312, esp. 299–300, 303, and 307, where he observes that '[e]xpansions are not ornaments but an essential part of the drama'. And note the comments of F. Zeitlin, 'Figuring Fidelity in Homer's *Odyssey*', in B. Cohen (ed.), *The Distaff Side: Representing the Female in Homer's* Odyssey (New York and Oxford: Oxford University Press, 1995), 117–52, at 117–18, on the significance of visual objects in the *Odyssey* as 'focusing elements' (117).

[7] For commentary on individual items, see e.g. G. S. Kirk, *The* Iliad: *A Commentary*, i (Cambridge: Cambridge University Press, 1985), on the sceptre at *Il.* 2. 101–8, the aegis at *Il.* 2. 447–9, and the bow at *Il.* 4. 105–11, esp. on 110. T. M. Andersson almost anticipates such a study in his brief reference to what he calls 'genetic description': see *Early Epic Scenery: Homer, Virgil, and the Medieval Legacy* (Ithaca and London: Cornell University Press, 1976), 35. On the other hand, A. S. Becker's recent book, *The Shield of Achilles and the Poetics of Ekphrasis* (Lanham, Md.: Rowman and Littlefield, 1995), overlaps my discussion in a minor way. He studies description as a rhetorical exercise, looking at 'the particular ways in which the language of ekphrasis directs our attention' (3). To this end Becker (41–4) sets up an order of 'levels of representation' in Homeric descriptions—*res ipsae*, *opus ipsum*, *artifex* and *ars*, and *animadversor*—through which he studies (51–77) a number of smaller descriptive passages from the *Iliad*, before he begins his study of the shield (87–148). Whereas Becker considers description as a rhetorical exercise, I shall study Homer's descriptive passages as memory-based discourse.

of a narrative.[8] In the course of this discussion another, related, issue is raised: the use which the storyteller makes of descriptive passages and his audience's reactions to them. In this context we shall examine the appropriateness of the term 'objective', which has often been used to describe Homer's narrative style. We consider a new analysis, and different terminology, which characterizes more truly the Homeric style and describes more accurately the means by which Homer awakens emotional response in his audience. Finally, we take up Lukács' point that set-piece description, or ekphrasis, is uncharacteristic of the Homeric epic; and we review reasons why the poet might rarely undertake that type of composition.[9] The aim of this chapter is to increase our understanding of the descriptive mode in the *Iliad* and the *Odyssey* and to observe some of the means by which an improvising oral poet works to make his story more effective.

NARRATION AND DESCRIPTION AS MODES OF DISCOURSE

The narrative mode, which we identify with storytelling of all kinds, including heroic tales, is characterized by those necessary interrelations of action and reaction, and cause (whether reason or purpose) and effect, which I have described in my Introduction.[10] The interconnective logic of the causal chain which underpins narrative makes it relatively easy to recall the thread of a story. A descriptive segment, however, is unlike narrative in that it has no fundamental substructure of this logical kind. Indeed, in our Western literary tradition, the descriptive genre is relatively unconstrained: it could be characterized by its lack of guiding principles or what we might call rules.

---

[8] This chapter is principally concerned with those passages of description which are prolonged by a narrative element. These may be distinguished from those shorter passages which include elements of description but no narrative (e.g. *Il.* 11. 628–9).

[9] Lukács, 'To Narrate or Describe?', at 87–8.

[10] The causal chain is the backbone of the narrative: for discussion, see Introduction, above.

Unlike Homer's descriptions, the majority of which are dedicated to personal possessions, literary descriptions in the tradition with which we are familiar are not so confined in their subject-matter. Quite simply they record notable attributes of any item, any setting, or any place, in no prescribed order and with various degrees of elaboration. Some descriptions may be brief evocations; others may be prolonged. In terms of structure or vocabulary, therefore, one literary description may have little in common with another.[11] And yet, although this generalization may be true of descriptive discourse in literary works, it does not apply to the kinds of descriptions we offer our listeners in oral discourse. These tend to the stereotypical. In offering a description we regularly work within the following agenda: size–capacity–shape; material; colour; workmanship–maker; value. Those elements which the speaker deems relevant will be covered briefly, and in any order. They will be supplemented by two further contributions: the speaker will note a remarkable feature (why would an item be worth describing otherwise?) and, finally, he or she may give some account of the item's origins, a 'history' which explains its significance in terms of human behaviour or of human relationships.[12] Indeed, it is typical in conversation, as Charlotte Linde has observed in her study of the ways in

[11] For discussion and examples, from a literary perspective, see D. Lodge, *The Art of Fiction* (London: Secker & Warburg, 1992), 56–60; for analysis of description in a written tradition from a cognitive point of view, see G. Miller, 'Images and Models, Similes and Metaphors', in A. Ortony (ed.), *Metaphor and Thought*, 2nd edn. (Cambridge: Cambridge University Press, 1993), 357–400, at 358–63. A recent work of fiction which offers us a rich harvest of literary description is A. S. Byatt's *Possession: A Romance* (London: Vintage, 1991). Byatt uses the Victorian era as the setting for one of her two parallel stories and evokes Victorian literary style in generous descriptive passages. Note her descriptions of items of significance: from domestic furnishings (e.g. at 148) to pins and brooches on sale in a second-hand store (258–61). Byatt describes, at 260, the jet brooch owned by her heroine, Maud: a significant object, in that it forges a link between the two stories.
[12] The item, for example, may have been purchased, or given as a gift, or found: any of these scenarios is material for a story. We may find the 'conversational' description pattern in literary description also, notably in cases in which an author consciously strives to recreate everyday speech patterns. See e.g. Byatt, *Possession*, 276: two speakers in conversation each describe a ring in accordance with the description agenda outlined above: *material, workmanship, feature, history.*

which we organize such discourse, for descriptions of
objects in space to give way to the temporal sequences of
narrative.[13]

HOMER'S DESCRIPTIVE MODE

Nor does this generalization apply to Homer. Consider again
the passages of description which we encounter in the epics.
Homer's descriptions of objects are predictable in three
respects. First the objects described, in that they belong to
the heroic world, are inherently superior in respect of their
material and their manufacture. Second, his descriptions,
like ours in conversation, are rarely of a point for point
'photographic' nature. He assumes, as we do, that his
listeners will refer to their visual memory to supply fundamental information about items of this kind.[14] There is no
need for the poet to describe commonly known items, mental
images of which his audience can retrieve promptly from
long-term memory. As he describes a handsome cup or a
bowl, for example, we bring to mind a generic cup or bowl
from our own store of images. We then embellish this or
modify it in accordance with the details which Homer
supplies.[15] Third, the descriptions themselves, although
relatively brief, are not assembled at random. They are in
fact constructed in accordance with a loose format which will
be recognizable to us all, at least to the extent that we see
these descriptive passages as characteristic of epic style. Let
us examine the way in which Homer assembles such passages, in order to identify this format.[16]

[13] For examples and discussion, see C. Linde, 'The Organization of Discourse',
in T. Shopen and J. M. Williams (eds.), *Style and Variables in English* (Cambridge,
Mass.: Winthrop, 1981), 84–114, at 104–10.

[14] An exception is his description of the boar's tusk helmet of *Il.* 10. 261–71.
Homer's uncharacteristically careful account of the construction of this type of
helmet (261–5) suggests that he may have been describing something which he felt
might be unfamiliar to his listeners. For discussion of the role of visual memory in
the recall of song, and on the dual coding hypothesis, see Introduction, above.

[15] For valuable discussion of what goes on in a person's mind as he or she hears
or reads a descriptive passage, see Miller, 'Images and Models', at 358–63.

[16] See Tables 2 and 3 for summaries of Homer's descriptions of objects in the
epics.

TABLE 2: An Analysis of Passages in Homer's *Iliad* in which Objects are Described[a]

location	object	summary description	material	workmanship	size, value	feature	history
2. 101–8	sceptre	—	—	101	—	—	102–8
2. 447–9	aegis	447	—	—	449	448–9	—
4. 105–11	bow	—	105–9	110–11	109	111	106–8
5. 722–9	chariot (and wheels)	724	723–4, 727	725	723	724–6, 729	—
6. 289–95	robe	289, 294	—	289–90	294	294–5	290–3
7. 219–23	shield	(219)	220, 222–3	220–1	219	223	220–3
9. 186–8	lyre	186–7	—	187	—	187	188
10. 261–71	helmet	—	262–5	265	—	263–5	266–71
11. 19–28	corselet	—	(16)	implied	—	24–8	20–3
11. 29–31	sword	—	(16)	—	—	29–30	—
11. 32–7	shield	33	(16), 33–5	32	—	36–7	—
11. 632–7	cup	632	633–5	implied	636–7	633–5	632
12. 294–7	shield	294	295	295–6	—	296–7	295–6
16. 220–5	chest	222	—	222	—	225	222–4
16. 225–7	goblet	—	—	225	—	225–7	225–7
18. 478–82	shield	478	(474–7)	478	478	479–80	369–477
22. 468–72	headdress	468	—	—	—	470	470–2
23. 560–2	corselet	—	561	implied	—	561–2	560
23. 740–9	bowl	—	741	741	741–2	742–3	743–9
24. 234–7	cup	234	—	—	235–6	235–7	234–5
24. 453–6	bolt	—	454	—	454–6	454–6	—

[a] I have for the most part omitted those brief descriptions, such as that of Athene's gown, at 8. 384–6, which do not include the elements *feature* and *history*.

TABLE 3: An Analysis of Passages in Homer's *Odyssey* in which Objects are Described[a]

location	object	summary description	material	workmanship	size, value	feature	history
1. 96–8	Athene's sandals	96	97	—	—	97–8	—
1. 99–101	Athene's spear	99	—	—	100	99	—
4. 125–32	Helen's workbasket	130	125, 132	131	—	132	125–30
4. 614–19 (cf. 15. 114–19)	mixing bowl	614	615–16	615, 617	614	616	617–19
9. 196–211	Maron's wine	196–7	—	—	205	205–7	197–205
9. 240–3	entrance stone	240	243	—	240–1, 241–2, 243	—	—
15. 105–8, 123–8	wedding gown	105	105	105, 126	107	108	125–8
18. 292–4	gown	292	—	293	292, 293–4	293–4	—
18. 295–6	necklace	295	296	295	—	296	—
19. 55–8	Penelope's chair	—	56	56–7	56–8	57–8	56–8
19. 226–31, 256–7	brooch	256	226	227	—	228–31	256–7
19. 232–4	tunic	232	233–4	implied	—	234	—
21. 6–7	key	7	7	6	6	7	—
21. 11–41	great bow	—	—	—	—	38–41	13–38

[a] I have for the most part omitted those brief descriptions which do not include the elements *feature* and *history*.

A description of any object from this epic world is often introduced by a phrase which announces it to be a thing of beauty, or, in the case of equipment for war, an efficient tool. We therefore bring to our mind's eye an item which is in prime condition. So Achilleus' lyre (*Il.* 9. 186–7) is sweet-sounding (λιγείη) and beautiful (καλή); his travelling box (*Il.* 16. 222) is lovely (καλῆς); and his shield (*Il.* 18. 478) is sturdy (στιβαρόν); Nestor's cup (*Il.* 11. 632) is very beautiful (περικαλλές); Andromache's head-dress is σιγαλόεντα, shining, or splendid (*Il.* 22. 468); Helen's workbasket (*Od.* 4. 125–30, 133–5) is one of a number of beautiful gifts (κάλλιμα, 130); and the brooch which Penelope had pinned to Odysseus' cloak is described (*Od.* 19. 256) as shining (φαεινήν).[17] I shall use the term *summary description* to represent this first element. It is an element which is often rendered in a perfunctory fashion, as we deduce from the poet's reference to a limited vocabulary: καλός, περικαλλής, κάλλιμος, φαεινός, and σιγαλόεις. Next, the *material* (usually a metal) or the *workmanship* of the item is noted: Pandaros' bow is made from the polished horns of a wild goat (τόξον ἔυξοον ἰξάλου αἰγὸς ἀγρίου, *Il.* 4. 105–6); Asteropaios' corselet is of bronze (χάλκεον, *Il.* 23. 561); the bolt on the door of Achilleus' hut (*Il.* 24. 454) is of pine (εἰλάτινος); the gowns in Priam's storechamber are of rich and varied work (παμποίκιλα ἔργα, *Il.* 6. 289); Achilleus' lyre (*Il.* 9. 187) is finely crafted (δαιδαλέη); his chest, like his lyre, is δαιδαλέης (*Il.* 16. 222); the cup within it is τετυγμένον (*Il.* 16. 225); the krater offered by Achilleus as a prize is of silver *and* well-crafted (τετυγμένον, *Il.* 23. 741). From the *Odyssey* I note amongst other examples Helen's workbasket, which is of silver (ἀργύρεον, *Od.* 4. 125); Penelope's chair of silver and ivory (δινωτὴν ἐλέφαντι καὶ ἀργύρῳ, *Od.* 19. 56); and Odysseus' cloak of purple wool (χλαῖναν πορφυρέην οὔλην, *Od.* 19. 225).

The foregoing qualities, *summary description*, *workmanship*, and *material*, are often announced in a triplet of

---

[17] I read σιγαλόεις and φαεινός as general terms of beauty. Notice that Homer has reserved the general term φαεινήν for Penelope's brief description of the brooch (*Od.* 19. 256–7). Odysseus, however, does not use the general term, as his task had been to give precise account of its appearance (*Od.* 19. 226–31).

adjectives, in which the combination of καλός (beautiful) and
δαιδάλεος (finely crafted) is frequently used: at *Il.* 9. 186–7,
for example, note the adjectives describing the lyre, φόρμιγγι
λιγείῃ, καλῇ δαιδαλέῃ. Note also the adjectives which describe
the shield at *Il.* 11. 32–3 (ἀμφιβρότην πολυδαίδαλον ἀσπίδα
θοῦριν) and at *Il.* 12. 294–5 (πάντοσ᾽ ἐΐσην, καλὴν χαλκείην
ἐξήλατον). Adjectives occur in groups of three also in the
Odyssey. The key to the chamber in which were stored all
Odysseus' possessions, including the great bow, is beautiful,
bronze, and artfully curved (εὐκαμπέα . . . καλὴν χαλκείην,
Od. 21. 6–7). The robe which Antinoos would offer as a gift
to Penelope (*Od.* 18. 292–3) is large, beautiful, and elaborate
(μέγαν περικαλλέα πέπλον, ποικίλον). And Odysseus' cloak is of
purple wool, with a double fold (πορφυρέην οὔλην . . . διπλῆν,
Od. 19. 225–6).

Third, the object being described is distinguished as
being exceptional by one remarkable *feature* of its construction (again, metal is often an indicator of value): in the eyes
of the poet, the aegis (*Il.* 2. 448) has golden tassels;
Achilleus' lyre has a bridge of silver (ἐπὶ δ᾽ ἀργύρεον ζυγὸν
ἦεν, *Il.* 9. 187); Nestor's cup is remarkable, being set with
golden nails (χρυσείοις ἥλοισι πεπαρμένον, *Il.* 11. 633) and
with two doves of gold on either side (*Il.* 11. 634–5);
Pandarus' bow has a golden string hook (χρυσέην . . .
κορώνην, *Il.* 4. 111).[18] The mixing bowl which Menelaos is
to present to Telemachos is silver, its rim worked in gold
(χρυσῷ δ᾽ ἐπὶ χείλεα κεκράανται, *Od.* 4. 616); the handle to the
handsome bronze key which gives access to Odysseus'
possessions is of ivory (κώπη δ᾽ ἐλέφαντος ἐπῆεν, *Od.* 21. 7).
And the front part of the pin which Odysseus had worn in
his cloak was distinguished by an elaborately worked scene
depicting a hound and a fawn (*Od.* 19. 227–31). In almost
every case it is through reference to such a feature that
Homer particularizes the item. Otherwise, an object may be
distinguished by an indicator of a different kind: for example, the robe for Athene is far below all the others in the
store-chest (*Il.* 6. 295); the robe which Helen will give to

---

[18] Note that at *Il.* 22. 470 the adjective marking value, χρυσέη, is transposed from
the head-dress to Aphrodite; and at *Il.* 16. 222 the adjective (here ἀργυρ-) is
transposed from Achilleus' box to Thetis.

Telemachos is likewise accessible only with difficulty (*Od.* 15. 108).[19] Fourth, some reference might be made to *remarkable size, weight, capacity*, or *value*. Note such references at *Il.* 2. 448–9 (the aegis which Athene holds has a hundred tassels, each worth a hundred oxen):

τῆς ἑκατὸν θύσανοι παγχρύσεοι ἠερέθονται,
πάντες ἐϋπλεκέες, ἑκατόμβοιος δὲ ἕκαστος·

From its edges float a hundred all-golden tassels
each one carefully woven, and each worth a hundred oxen.

At *Il.* 6. 294, the dress to be offered to Athene is the largest, μέγιστος; Nestor's cup, at *Il.* 11. 636–7, is so heavy that any man but Nestor would strain to lift it:

ἄλλος μὲν μογέων ἀποκινήσασκε τραπέζης
πλεῖον ἐόν, Νέστωρ δ' ὁ γέρων ἀμογητὶ ἄειρεν.

Another man with great effort could lift it full from the table, but Nestor, aged as he was, lifted it without strain.

Pandaros' bow, at *Il.* 4. 109, is fashioned from horns sixteen palms in length (ἐκκαιδεκάδωρα); the mixing bowl, however, donated by Achilleus at the games for Patroklos is remarkable for its modest size. And yet, although it has a capacity of only six measures, in its beauty it far surpasses all others on earth by far (*Il.* 23. 741–3):

ἓξ δ' ἄρα μέτρα
χάνδανεν, αὐτὰρ κάλλει ἐνίκα πᾶσαν ἐπ' αἶαν
πολλόν

The bronze key which will give Penelope access to Odysseus' treasures is so heavy that to lift it she needs a capable hand (εἵλετο . . . χειρὶ παχείῃ, *Od.* 21. 6).[20] The mixing bowl

---

[19] On this see G. S. Kirk, *The* Iliad: *A Commentary*, ii (Cambridge: Cambridge University Press, 1990), 199.

[20] There has been much discussion about the apparent inappropriateness of the epithet παχείη, used to describe what we might expect to be the more delicate hand of a noble lady. For the extensive bibliography see J. Russo, M. Fernandez-Galiano, and A. Heubeck, *A Commentary on Homer's* Odyssey, iii (Oxford: Clarendon Press, 1992), 148–9. I propose, *contra* Parry, that the epithet is not an example of a formula used without thought for its context: see M. Parry, 'L'Epithète traditionnelle dans Homère', in A. Parry (ed.), *The Making of Homeric Verse: The Collected Papers of Milman Parry* (Oxford: Clarendon Press, 1971), 151.

which Menelaos is to give Telemachos is said to be of the highest value (τιμήεστατόν ἐστι, *Od*. 4. 614).

Many descriptions are abandoned at this point; but in several others the poet goes further. He offers a *history* of the item, sometimes briefly, sometimes at length. This element is usually introduced by or presented in a relative clause.[21] I shall take up the discussion of the *history* at a later point in this chapter.

THE DESCRIPTION FORMAT AND MEMORY

Although I have set these elements down as though they occur in a fixed order, a close study of each passage will reveal that Homer does not always follow this sequence. But despite the fact that the order of elements is not fixed, and that the poet may omit one element or another, Homer's descriptions of personal possessions touch on some or all of the following topics: *summary description*, *material*, *workmanship*, *feature*, *size–weight–value*, *history*.[22] I shall refer to this cluster of elements as a description format. The format itself is a schematic representation of a certain abstract pattern of organization specific to the descriptive genre.

I suggest that this particular noun-epithet combination is Homer's rendering of that element of the description format which is under discussion above, *remarkable size* and *weight*. It is not Penelope's hand that he has in mind, but the bulk and the weight of the key. The description format, which guides Homer's description of items, has cued the notion of *weight*, which in turn has led him to this formula (cf. *Il*. 21. 403–5, Athene picks up a huge stone). For a helpful note on Homer's use of χειρὶ παχείῃ to indicate the weight of what one holds in one's hand, see T. Eide, 'A Note on the Homeric *ΧΕΙΡΙ ΠΑΧΕΙΗΙ*', *Symbolae Osloenses*, 55 (1980), 23–6.

[21] For such histories attached to descriptions of items, see *Il*. 4. 106–8; 6. 290–2; 9. 188; 10. 266–71; 11. 20–3; 11. 632; 16. 222–4; 22. 470–2; 23. 560; 23. 743–7; *Od*. 4. 125–30, 617–19 (= 15. 117–19); 9. 197–211; 19. 56–8; 19. 256–7; 21. 13–41. Note that a relative clause is not used at *Il*. 23. 743–7 or at *Od*. 19. 256–7. Note also the displacement of the 'history' of Odysseus' pin (*Od*. 19. 256–7), from the 'stranger's' description (in which omission of such an element is not surprising) to the unhappy words of confirmation spoken by Penelope. Homer uses the history of the pin to create a poignant moment in the relations between Penelope and the 'stranger'.

[22] This is a considerable refinement of Walter Arend's observation: see *Die Typischen Scenen bei Homer* (Berlin: Weidmannische Buchhandlung, 1933), 33, where he notes the predictable nature of descriptions, which regularly include information in response to the unspoken questions *von wem?* and *wie?*.

This abstract pattern is stored in memory as implicit knowledge. The function of formats of this kind is not to cue explicit or declarative information, as do the situational and instrumental scripts described in Chapter 1, but to provide cues on how to proceed in discourse of various kinds.[23] This kind of knowledge is the outcome of a routine cognitive process, by which information about certain events or tasks is acquired unconsciously and stored in such a way that it represents the sum of past experience (in this case, of description) without specific reference to any single past event.[24] The resulting pattern is retained in memory as a 'table' or 'format'.[25] A format can be readily accessed, like so many of the more explicit sequences—scripts or schemas—which we store in active memory. The poet, as he begins his description of an item, will draw on this abstract knowledge base which will guide him, as it were automatically, through this segment of song.[26]

Since the format which we observe in Homer appears to correspond to the description agenda which we ourselves follow in everyday conversation (and which I have outlined above), we may conclude that the poet did not learn this

[23] For overview, see Introduction, above; and note especially Rubin, *Memory*, 190–1. See also E. Dube, 'Literacy, Cultural Familiarity, and "Intelligence" as Determinants of Story Recall', in U. Neisser (ed.), *Memory Observed: Memory in Natural Contexts* (San Francisco: W. H. Freeman, 1982), 274–92. Implicit memory will assist the poet also in the composition of a variety of speech-acts (for discussion, see Ch. 1, above) and in the procedures of telling a well-formed story (see Chs. 5 and 6, below).

[24] For a relevant experimental study, see A. Reber, 'Implicit Learning and Tacit Knowledge', *Journal of Experimental Psychology: General*, 118 (1989), 219–35, who notes, at 222, the 'unconscious' and 'nonreflective' nature of implicit learning; for a series of detailed studies of a number of aspects of implicit memory, see S. Lewandowsky, J. Dunn, and K. Kirsner (eds.), *Implicit Memory: Theoretical Issues* (Hillsdale, NJ: Lawrence Erlbaum, 1989); for valuable discussion and a study of the role of implicit memory in the learning and composition of ballads which is highly relevant to the Homeric scholar, see D. Rubin, W. Wallace, and B. Houston, 'The Beginnings of Expertise for Ballads', *Cognitive Science*, 17 (1993), 435–62, esp. at 436–8 and 452–7.

[25] For the analogy of the 'table', see D. Broadbent, P. Fitzgerald, M. Broadbent, 'Implicit and Explicit Knowledge in the Control of Complex Systems', *British Journal of Psychology*, 77 (1986), 33–50; at 48–9.

[26] Given that this is an unconscious process, the poet would have been surprised to learn that his descriptions of items could be reduced to a common abstract structure; just as we may be surprised when we make the same discovery.

format by listening to a master-singer and imitating his practice. Rather, as he sang, his descriptive segments may well have been cued by that same description format which served him in everyday discourse, and which he had acquired unconsciously, early in life, through listening to the discourse of others and through his own active trial-and-error attempts at descriptive talk.

It is important to note that a description format does not generate particulars of description or their precise formulation. It simply offers the poet a sequence of options, each of which he may follow up or disregard: it generates pointers to formulae rather than the formulae themselves. The description format allows the oral poet (as, indeed, it allows us all) to economize on effort. The effort saved is quite simply the effort of deciding what, precisely, to describe. Nevertheless, the singing of descriptive passages still requires a degree of effort and invention: the selection of the appropriate vocabulary of description (although, to judge from Homer's usage in the thirty or so passages under discussion, he limits himself to a pool of expressions of general application) as well as the selection, and the telling, of an appropriate *history* (which may be either invented or prescribed by tradition). It is by this latter means that the poet establishes the significance of an item.

NARRATIVE IN DESCRIPTION

Rarely in either the *Iliad* or in the *Odyssey* does Homer sustain passages of pure description. His descriptions in the epics may cover only two or three lines of text; they are rarely more than seven or eight lines in length.[27] There are two reasons for this economy: the needs of the audience and the needs of the poet. Let us begin with the audience—particularly a listening audience. Their interest in the declarative sentences of description is limited.[28] Listeners

---

[27] Lessing, *Laocoön*, ch. 16. Two notable exceptions to the general rule, the shield of Achilleus and the palace of Alkinoos, will be discussed below.

[28] This is one reason why descriptions in oral storytelling are brief: a good storyteller is always responsive to his listeners and their preferences. Note the

typically find narrative a more engaging medium: they are interested in its onward movement, and they are interested in the character, the relationships, and the motivation of the actors.[29] Besides, as has been argued in cognitive science, narrative is an expression of the sequential nature of all human experience; our memories may well be organized on this very principle. If this is so, then it is not surprising that we find it easy to engage with and to follow narrative. Indeed, most of us can testify to the greater power of narrative over pure description and to our preferences for the former.[30] After all, it is the narrative sections (most often cast as *history*) of Homer's descriptions which remain most vividly in our memories. We can remember the origins of Andromache's headdress, of the gowns in Priam's store-chamber, of Agamemnon's corselet, and of the golden pin in Odysseus' cloak long after we have forgotten the details of their appearance which Homer has provided.

But the reasons for Homer's preference for the narrative mode are not attributable only to the needs and preferences of his audience. As a performing poet he finds it easier to hold in memory and to sing a passage of narrative than a

contrast in this respect with literary descriptions. Nevertheless, there are dangers in prolonged set-piece description even in writing. On this, see Lodge, *The Art of Fiction*, 60: 'a succession of well-formed declarative sentences, combined with the suspension of narrative interest, will send the reader to sleep'. This view was challenged by some participants at 'Epos and Logos', Durban, 1996, who referred to their own favourable responses to set-piece description. But I would argue that this conference, which takes as one of its themes the composition of texts, draws together a skewed sample of the population; and that the responses of these conference participants are not typical of the responses of all listening or reading audiences.

[29] This is the central point of Lukács' discussion: see Lukács, 'To Narrate or Describe?', 87. On the pleasures of narrative, see E. A. Havelock, *The Muse Learns to Write: Reflections on Orality and Literacy from Antiquity to the Present* (New Haven and London: Yale University Press, 1986), 75–6; and for a neat summation of narrative's power of attraction, see A. S. Byatt, *Still Life* (Harmondsworth: Penguin, 1986), 58, on narratives as 'intoxicants' or 'tranquillizers'.

[30] I cannot claim the following as a reliable test, but I use it as anecdotal evidence to illustrate my point. I returned to Byatt, *Possession*, in the course of writing this chapter, because I had recalled that the author had used a keepsake, a jet brooch, as an element in her story (see n. 11, above); and I assumed that Byatt would have included a description of that item. Before consulting the book this second time, I was able to recall without difficulty the history of the brooch and the part it plays in the narrative; but I did not remember any detail (beyond *material*) of its appearance. Yet the brooch is described in all its particulars.

sustained descriptive piece. Narrative, as I have noted above, is easier to call to mind and to perform because of its logical chain of cause and effect.[31] The poet, therefore, only rarely forsakes the narrative mode to undertake sustained set-piece description. Indeed, he often uses narrative—whether a story or a story fragment—to expand or supplement the limited descriptive material which he offers us:[32] for example, consider the functions of the *history* of the boars' tusk helmet (*Il.* 10. 266–71); of Agamemenon's corselet (*Il.* 11. 20–3); and of Priam's cup (*Il.* 24. 234–5):

> ἐκ δὲ δέπας περικαλλές, ὅ οἱ Θρῆκες πόρον ἄνδρες
> ἐξεσίην ἐλθόντι, μέγα κτέρας·

and [he] brought out a goblet of surpassing loveliness that the men of Thrace had given him when he went to them with a message

The poet uses his histories in the same way in the *Odyssey*. Note that the description of the wine which Odysseus offers to the Cyclops is considerably enriched by its history (*Od.* 9. 197–211); as is the description of the gift which Menelaos is to give to Telemachos (*Od.* 4. 617–19):

> ἔργον δ' Ἡφαίστοιο· πόρεν δὲ ἑ Φαίδιμος ἥρως,
> Σιδονίων βασιλεύς, ὅθ' ἑὸς δόμος ἀμφεκάλυψε
> κεῖσέ με νοστήσαντα·

This is the work of Hephaistos. The hero Phaidimos, the Sidonians' king, gave it to me, when his house took me in and sheltered me there on my way home.

Homer's preference for narrative over description is conspicuous in a number of other passages in the *Iliad*. Although the passages here are in effect description, the poet has chosen to render them almost entirely through narrative. These 'descriptions' are not concerned with objects but with

---

[31] Havelock, *The Muse Learns to Write*, 76, summarizes this preference neatly: 'A language of action rather than reflection appears to be a prerequisite for oral memorization'.

[32] As Becker, *The Shield of Achilles*, notes at 54: 'the bard . . . translates objects in space into actions in time': cf. the comment of Linde, above, on description in everyday oral discourse. On the poet's preference for narrative, see Lessing, *Laocoön*, ch. 16.

individuals and their dress and sometimes with larger entities, such as dwellings. When Hera approaches Zeus with the intention of diverting him from the battle around Troy, for example, we know exactly how she is dressed. But we know this not because Homer has described her appearance. Rather, he has recounted each step of her preparations for this enterprise, including all the negotiations necessary (*Il.* 14. 159–223). In place of description we have narrative.[33] Just as when the poet sings a catalogue-song, which includes fragments of stories, so it is with descriptive passages: it appears to be difficult for the poet to resist the pull of narrative.[34]

THE DESCRIPTION OF PLACE IN THE *ODYSSEY*: THE ROLE OF SPATIAL MEMORY

The *Odyssey* offers more varied evidence of the singer's descriptive practice than does the *Iliad*. As in the *Iliad* we note that some descriptions are presented as narrative: Eumaios' hut, at *Od.* 14. 5–22; or Odysseus' bed fashioned out of an olive tree trunk, at 23. 189–201; and the hero's changed appearance, at 6. 229–35. On the other hand, the *Odyssey* is remarkable for its non-narrative descriptions of landscape and of dwellings: the landfall near Crete (3. 293–6); a comparison of Sparta and Ithaka (4. 602–8); Kalypso's cavern in the grove (5. 58–73); the rocky coastline of Scheria (5. 401–5); a description of Ithaka (9. 21–7); the cave of Polyphemos (9. 219–23); and, above all, the description of Alkinoos' palace, 7. 84–132, which has no narrative or even quasi-narrative content.[35] Given the inclusion of such

---

[33] See also Homer's description (through narrative) of Achilleus' hut (*Il.* 24. 448–53).

[34] On the poet's use of narrative in catalogue-singing, see Ch. 2, above. The extended simile, which offers description through comparison, is another instance of this habit. The simile may begin in descriptive terms but it, too, will slip into the narrative mode. For further discussion, see Ch. 4, below. And see Lord, *Singer*, 86–92, on the wealth of description in Yugoslav epic, which likewise emerges from and slides into narrative.

[35] This latter description, which offers the listener a tour through the palace, takes us across the threshold, into the great hall, past the fifty serving women at

passages, which do not follow the identifiable pattern of the description format (which generates descriptions of prized possessions in both epics), the *Odyssey* does indeed appear closer to literary discourse in a written tradition than does the *Iliad*. But, although the poet has allowed himself no opportunity to demonstrate these particular skills of sustained description in the *Iliad*, the setting for which is barely registered and almost unvaried throughout the course of the narrative, we cannot argue that the poet of the *Iliad* was incapable of such passages, had he wished to include them. Rather, his almost unfailing reluctance to describe setting at any length in his *Iliad* was a choice he made in his desire to keep his listeners' attention on the action itself—and, more importantly, on the actors. The *Odyssey*, on the other hand, is a different kind of epic. Much of its interest is to be found in the adventures of its hero, a man who rejoices in the challenges of the unknown, and who meets those challenges with resourcefulness and energy: this is the man whom the poet describes at various points as πολυκερδής (very crafty), πολύμητις (full of guile), πολυμήχανος (inventive), πολύτροπος (ingenious), and πολύτλας (much enduring). Variety of setting is integral to an epic which makes such a man its hero. It is essential to their appreciation of the Odysseus-story that the audience be able to envisage each of the demanding, and in many cases life-threatening, environments in which the hero finds himself. The poet, with performance in mind, would have prepared in advance these longer descriptive passages, in which he describes the nature and form of landscape or dwelling. In structuring his descriptions of dwellings, he would have taken advantage of spatial memory. He would have called to mind a generic image of an appropriate house and proceeded to 'tour' the house in his mind, working with a spatial map and matching image to word. Spatial memory would have made it possible for him to order his ideas and to rehearse his sustained account of Alkinoos' palace, for example.[36] Descriptions of landscape,

their tasks, out into the orchard, the vineyard, and the vegetable garden, and finally to the springs which supply the house and the town.

[36] On spatial memory and the use of a spatial map to aid recall, see Introduction and Ch. 2, above. For an account of the role of spatial memory in everyday

however, would have been produced in accordance with a
mental model visualized by the poet. He describes the key
features of what he sees; for it is the visual image in this case
which prompts language. It is our task, as audience, to
recreate in *our* mind's eye what *he* sees and describes. Our
efforts may be only partly successful: the 'memory image' or
model which we produce may be quite vague. It almost
certainly will be different from that of the poet.[37] There is no
underlying cognitive pattern, or format, in descriptions of
scenery and landfall, of the kind that we find in the case of
small objects.

THE *HISTORY* ELEMENT AND ITS ROLE

We certainly delight in the small stories which Homer offers
us as part of his descriptions—as stories. But Homer has
included them not for that reason alone. He uses the *history*
element—the story of how an item came into the possession
of its current owner—quite deliberately as a motif of dual
reference: it refers in the first instance to the object itself,
but it also takes us beyond the physical reality of the object
to tell us something of its sentimental value for its owner or
of its broader significance in the owner's life.[38] Each of the
items he describes is in one way or another a souvenir: a gift
offered to cement a friendship, a keepsake which evokes
joyous memories, or a trophy of war. The memories which
each object evokes serve to tell us more about its owner, or
about the situation in which he or she is placed. Let us
briefly consider a number of examples from the *Iliad* before
we move to the *Odyssey*.

description, see Linde, 'The Organization of Discourse', at 104–13 ('The apart-
ment description'). As for Homer, we see evidence of the poet's reference to a
spatial map in his account of the palace of Alkinoos: the organization of the
description of the palace is based on a mental map of a typical great house of C8 (on
this see A. Heubeck, S. West, and J. B. Hainsworth, *A Commentary on Homer's
Odyssey*, i (Oxford: Clarendon Press, 1988), on *Od*. 6. 304).

[37] For comment, see Miller, 'Images and Models', at 358–63.

[38] For an excellent discussion, see J. Griffin, *Homer on Life and Death* (Oxford:
Clarendon Press, 1980), ch. 1.

Early in the *Iliad* the poet gives us an account of Agamemnon's sceptre (*Il*. 2. 101–8). In this passage description is perfunctory (2. 101: *workmanship*), but a narrative traces the impressive history of the sceptre in the world of men and its significance as a token of authority and power (2. 102–8). This history, for all that it is sparely told, nevertheless gives us a standard against which we should measure the man who now holds it. The man in question is Agamemnon, who, from the beginning of this narrative, has shown himself to be ineffectual as ruler.[39] This narrative segment, therefore, allows us to gauge how far Agamemnon falls short of that standard. At another point of the *Iliad*, when the embassy from the Achaians approaches Achilleus, his friends find him delighting in the sound of his lyre (9. 185–9). It is a remarkable scene: a warrior engaged in the pursuit of leisure. And it is a striking image of Achilleus, whom we remember from his previous appearance in the narrative as the combative hero, ready to stand up to his king. So the lyre suggests something about Achilleus' state of mind now that he is in self-imposed exile from the active life. He is searching for a means to fill in time. And, for all that, the lyre, paradoxically, is a reminder of that life for which he yearns. It is, as Homer tells us in this *history*, a souvenir of Achilleus' earlier campaign against Eëtion's stronghold; it reminds us of the active life he has led as a hero and the successes he has enjoyed in the past. It is not fortuitous, therefore, that the songs he sings are κλέα ἀνδρῶν, songs of men's fame. For my third example from the *Iliad*, I consider the moment when Andromache sees her husband's body being dragged behind Achilleus' chariot, and she collapses and tears away her head-dress. This head-dress represents memories of Andromache's marriage day, a happy day which had appeared to hold nothing but promise. It is this head-dress to which the poet draws our attention. He sees the poignancy of Andromache's gesture; and he points it out to us, using the image of the head-dress and an account of the memories it represents to make real to us this young woman's grief and her sense of loss (22. 468–72):

[39] Cf. Griffin, *Homer on Life and Death*, 9–10.

τῆλε δ' ἀπὸ κρατὸς βάλε δέσματα σιγαλόεντα,
ἄμπυκα κεκρύφαλόν τε ἰδὲ πλεκτὴν ἀναδέσμην
κρήδεμνόν θ', ὅ ῥά οἱ δῶκε χρυσέη 'Αφροδίτη
ἤματι τῷ ὅτε μιν κορυθαίολος ἠγάγεθ' Ἕκτωρ
ἐκ δόμου 'Ηετίωνος, ἐπεὶ πόρε μυρία ἔδνα.

and far off
threw from her head the shining gear that ordered her head-dress,
the diadem and the cap, and the holding-band woven together,
and the circlet, which Aphrodite the golden had once given her
on that day when Hektor of the shining helmet led her forth
from the house of Eëtion, and gave numberless gifts to win her.

We should note in this context that in the *Iliad* Homer uses the *history* element to remind us of events which pre-date either the Trojan War or the quarrel in its ninth year and which continue to resonate in the tale: the lyre recalls Achilleus' destruction of Eëtion's city (cf. *Il.* 6. 414–28); Andromache's head-dress reminds us, of course, of her marriage to Hektor (cf. *Il.* 6. 392–8); the robes in Priam's storechamber remind us of Paris' abduction of Helen (cf. *Il.* 3. 46–51, 442–6); the cup which Priam includes with his ransom offering to Achilleus (*Il.* 24. 234–7) allows us to appreciate the respect in which Priam has been held as king of Troy. To reiterate, these small items are by no means opportunities for digression; rather, through Homer's descriptions (and especially through the *history* which he includes), they become instruments of cohesion. Lynn-George's phrase 'a distant past haunts the present' neatly captures the gentle pathos which these small histories evoke.[40]

As in the *Iliad*, when the poet celebrates prized possessions in the *Odyssey*, he includes a *history* element. But these histories are less tightly focused. The history of Helen's work-basket (*Od.* 4. 125–32) takes us back to an unspecified time when, according to Homer, she and Menelaos were in Egypt. There they were welcomed by Polybos and his wife in Thebes; the work-basket was a gift from Polybos' wife to Helen. Likewise, the mixing-bowl which Menelaos will give Telemachos (4. 614–19) is a gift which he himself had received

---

[40] I borrow the phrase from M. Lynn-George's valuable critique of Auerbach: see *Epos: Word, Narrative, and the* Iliad (Basingstoke and London: Macmillan, 1988), 1–49, at 8.

on his way back to Sparta from Troy. He now gives it to Telemachos to mark his visit to his home, and to seal a bond of friendship between social equals. Thus we see Telemachos accepted as an adult in an adult world. Odysseus' great bow (21. 11–41) was a gift of Iphitos, who exchanged it with Odysseus, then on the brink of manhood, as a mark of friendship for a sword and a spear. As we have observed above, the history of prized possessions in the *Iliad* is used to unify the tale and to enrich the backdrop against which we understand the story of the great quarrel and its consequences. The poet's practice in the *Odyssey* appears to me to be different. The *history* element in the *Odyssey* for the most part draws attention to the practice of gift-giving and to its significance in the relationship between giver and receiver. The stories told, together with the context in which they are told, indicate that the poet is reflecting on the nature and practice of gift-giving as a powerful social ritual between social equals; he is recording observations of this ritual, which binds people in friendship in the present and preserves the remembrance of that moment of giving for the future, as a μνῆμα ξείνοιο φίλοιο (a memory of a dear friend, *Od.* 21. 40).[41] As Homer understands the practice, gifts such as those exchanged by his heroes have the power to carry memories from one generation to the next, and beyond. The gift which best illustrates my point is a gift for which history is being made at the moment of giving. It is the gown which Helen presents to Telemachos; its story is foreshadowed in Helen's words (*Od.* 15. 125–28):

> δῶρόν τοι καὶ ἐγώ, τέκνον φίλε, τοῦτο δίδωμι,
> μνῆμ' Ἑλένης χειρῶν, πολυηράτου ἐς γάμου ὥρην,
> σῇ ἀλόχῳ φορέειν· τῆος δὲ φίλη παρὰ μητρὶ
> κεῖσθαι ἐνὶ μεγάρῳ.

I too give you this gift, dear child: something to remember
from Helen's hands, for your wife to wear at the lovely occasion
of your marriage. Until that time let it lie away in your palace,
in your dear mother's keeping[42]

---

[41] One of the few exceptions to this practice in the *Odyssey* is the (more Iliadic) history of the chair in which Penelope sat when she interviewed the beggar (*Od.* 19. 56–8). The poet tells us that the chair was crafted by Ikmalios. It is a souvenir of the days when there was order in the palace: when the master was in the house.
[42] The prizes which Achilleus offers in the course of the Funeral Games in

TELLING A GOOD STORY:
THE SUBTLE MESSAGE OF INTERNAL
EVALUATION

As we have observed, the object which Homer has selected for description becomes a focus for a certain amount of what Labov has called evaluative information. This information, however, relates not to the object itself but to the individual with whom it is associated and the dramatic moment in which it plays a part.[43] Homer presents this information in such a way that we, the audience, are encouraged to draw our own conclusions about the individual or about his or her state of mind. Homer does not tell us directly what to think about these matters; rather, he points us towards certain conclusions, and he leaves us to reach them, on our own. I have drawn attention to instances of this practice above: consider, for example, the information which the poet shares with us when his gaze catches Andromache casting aside her head-dress; or when he observes Achilleus playing his lyre; or when Menelaos offers Telemachos a guest-gift. This storytelling strategy and its merits have been discussed by Tannen, who notes the greater force of so-called internal evaluation. She observes that when commentary on the narrative action is integrated into the story through the speech and actions of the actors, the audience is obliged to evaluate this information for themselves in order to find its significance. Tannen contrasts internal evaluation with external evaluation: in this latter mode the storyteller steps outside the narrative to communicate evaluative information directly.[44] It is not difficult to locate external evaluation in

honour of Patroklos are to be seen in the same light: they are to carry the memory of Patroklos into the future: see *Il.* 23. 740–9, esp. at 746–8.

[43] 'Evaluation' or 'evaluative material' is a term used in studies of narrative to identify the information which is necessary to listeners if they are to understand the motivation of the actors and if they are to know how to react to a particular dramatic moment, and to the tale as a whole. On this, see W. Labov, *Language in the Inner City: Studies in the Black English Vernacular* (Philadelphia: University of Pennsylvania Press, 1972), ch. 9, esp. 378–93.

[44] For a discussion of these contrasting modes, see first Labov, *Language in the Inner City*, 371–3, for a discussion of 'external' and 'embedded' evaluation. It is, however, Tannen who has made the observations and drawn the conclusions which

the comments of a narrator who says 'And this is the best bit', or 'I was really scared', for the storyteller has stepped outside the narrative to make his desired point. It is less easy to identify internal evaluation, which may be rendered by a variety of means: expressive phonology, repetition, lexical choice, emphatic particles, direct quotation, reports of speakers' mental processes, concreteness (through use of specific details), emphasis on people and their relationships, and on actions and agents rather than states and objects.[45] Tannen claims that internal evaluation—other things being equal—makes for more successful storytelling because it uses strategies that build on a 'sense of identification, or involvement, with characters and with tellers of stories'.[46] The natural consequence of internal presentation of evaluative material is that listeners are encouraged to make judgements for themselves. It is true that the evaluations which they make are guided by the storyteller. But what is important is that the listeners are not passive; they are participating in the storytelling—judging the actors, sharing their emotions, and perceiving the consequences of events in the distant past. They engage with the story because the storyteller has structured his or her telling with that end in view. The experience of listening will have been richer for them, and more satisfying, because of their active involvement.

Homer, in fact, uses both strategies described above: internal and external. We find evaluative information communicated internally in his descriptions of objects and their histories. We find it in direct speech, especially in cases where direct speech is set alongside indirect speech. An example is that critical moment in the narrative of the *Iliad* when Nestor attempts to persuade Patroklos to speak with Achilleus about taking up arms again. The old man reminds Patroklos, in indirect speech, of Peleus' words to his son, Achilleus (*Il.* 11. 783–4), as he set out for Troy:

I am reporting here: see D. Tannen, 'Oral and Literate Strategies in Spoken and Written Narratives', *Language*, 58 (1982), 1–21, at 4; 'The Oral/Literate Continuum in Discourse', in D. Tannen (ed.), *Spoken and Written Language: Exploring Orality and Literacy*, Advances in Discourse Processes, 9 (Norwood, NJ: Ablex, 1982), 1–16, at 8–9.

[45] Tannen, 'Oral and Literate Strategies', 6–8; 'The Oral/Literate Continuum', 8.
[46] Tannen, 'The Oral/Literate Continuum', 8.

Πηλεὺς μὲν ᾧ παιδὶ γέρων ἐπέτελλ᾽ Ἀχιλῆϊ
αἰὲν ἀριστεύειν καὶ ὑπείροχον ἔμμεναι ἄλλων·

And Peleus the aged was telling his own son, Achilleus,
to be always best in battle and pre-eminent beyond all others

But, when Menoitios addresses Patroklos on that same occasion, he recreates the actual words spoken (*Il.* 11. 786–9):

τέκνον ἐμόν, γενεῇ μὲν ὑπέρτερός ἐστιν Ἀχιλλεύς,
πρεσβύτερος δὲ σύ ἐσσι· βίῃ δὲ ὅ γε πολλὸν ἀμείνων.
ἀλλ᾽ εὖ οἱ φάσθαι πυκινὸν ἔπος ἠδ᾽ ὑποθέσθαι
καί οἱ σημαίνειν· ὁ δὲ πείσεται εἰς ἀγαθόν περ.

'My child, by right of blood Achilleus is higher than you are,
but you are the elder. Yet in strength he is far the greater.
You must speak solid words to him, and give him good counsel,
and point his way. If he listens to you it will be for his own good.'

The repetition of Menoitios' actual words has a profound effect on their immediate audience within the narrative, as Homer tells us (τῷ δ᾽ ἄρα θυμὸν ἐνὶ στήθεσσιν ὄρινε, *Il.* 11. 804) and as Patroklos' subsequent behaviour indicates. Homer has highlighted for us their importance to the action by choosing direct speech as the mode of expression.

We find other internal evaluative cues in the narrative itself (for example, the remarkably sympathetic account of the Cyclops as a caring and careful keeper of his flocks, which is conveyed through the narrative of *Od.* 9. 219–23); or in speech and narrative (the contrast of Aias the son of Oïleus and Antilochos at *Il.* 23. 780–92); or in the poet's 'biographies' of dying heroes in the *Iliad*, whose deaths have been made pathetic through the poet's brief, even bald, account of their lives.[47] In these passages, as in the *history* element of his descriptions, the poet sets past and present side by side, allowing our knowledge of the past to enrich our understanding of the present. Consider one such example, from the passage which records the death of the two sons of Merops at the hands of Diomedes (*Il.* 11. 328–34):

---

[47] For an exhaustive presentation of these 'obituaries', see Griffin, *Homer on Life and Death*, ch. 4.

Ἔνθ᾽ ἑλέτην δίφρον τε καὶ ἀνέρε δήμου ἀρίστω,
υἷε δύω Μέροπος Περκωσίου, ὃς περὶ πάντων
ᾔδεε μαντοσύνας, οὐδὲ οὓς παῖδας ἔασκε
στείχειν ἐς πόλεμον φθισήνορα· τὼ δὲ οἵ οὔ τι
πειθέσθην· κῆρες γὰρ ἄγον μέλανος θανάτοιο.
τοὺς μὲν Τυδεΐδης δουρικλειτὸς Διομήδης
θυμοῦ καὶ ψυχῆς κεκαδὼν κλυτὰ τεύχε᾽ ἀπηύρα·

There they took a chariot and two men, lords in their countryside,
sons both of Merops of Perkote, who beyond all men
knew the art of prophecy, and tried to prevent his two sons
from going into the battle where men die. Yet these would not
listen, for the spirits of dark death were driving them onward.
Tydeus' son, Diomedes of the renowned spear, stripped them
of life and spirit, and took away their glorious armour

The death of these two young men could have been avoided. Although this might be quite simply yet another sorry moment in the story of the Trojan War, Homer has personalized it. In telling us of the circumstances under which these particular young men came to Troy, he encourages us to think forward to the grief of their father, Merops, who, having failed to persuade his sons to stay with him, has now lost them to the battlefield. These few lines of fragmentary narrative, although apparently objective in presentation, nevertheless carry an evaluative message. In this case the poet has chosen the figure of the helpless father to serve as a standard by which we might measure the pathos of the moment (a father who could not keep his sons from the fighting now mourns them), just as in other 'obituaries' he has chosen as his motif an all too brief marriage and a young wife (for example, at *Il.* 11. 221–31, 241–5; 13. 427–35).

The poet makes use of a variety of means for evaluating his narrative internally. But we should bear in mind that it is remarkably difficult to construct a coherent tale without some form of external evaluation. In Homer evaluation in the external mode is expressed largely through his epithets (even the formulaic δῖος or φαίδιμος) and adverbs and equivalent phrases (ὑπόδρα ἰδών, at *Il.* 24. 559; νηλέϊ θυμῷ, at *Od.* 9. 272), but also through such means as the poet's occasional commentary, as narrator, on the action: for example, his comment on Patroklos' fate at *Il.* 11. 604, κακοῦ δ᾽

ἄρα οἱ πέλεν ἀρχή (and this was the beginning of his evil); or his comment at *Od.* 6. 66–7, after reporting Nausikaa's request to her father for transport to the river in order to go washing:

αἴδετο γὰρ θαλερὸν γάμον ἐξονομῆναι
πατρὶ φίλῳ·

       but she was ashamed to speak of her joyful marriage to her dear father

We know that Nausikaa had marriage in her mind; and we observe that she did not mention this when she spoke to her father. Homer at this point explains why.

HOMER AND OBJECTIVITY

With this discussion of internal and external evaluation we can resolve the debate about 'the often proclaimed objectivity' of Homer.[48] As Griffin remarks at the close of his discussion of Homer's narrative manner, the distinction between 'subjective' and 'objective' is less clear than has been suggested. He goes on to observe: 'Passages can be seen to produce the same emotional effect, whether expressed objectively in narrative by the poet, or subjectively in speech by one of his characters.'[49] Griffin is correct in his analysis. It is pointless and confusing to attempt to describe Homer's poetry in terms of objectivity and subjectivity; for even where Homer's style may give the appearance of objectivity, it rarely is objective, in the strict sense of the word. Consider, for example, the passages which Griffin notes as instances of Homer's 'dispassionate' manner: *Il.* 13. 578–80 (the death of Deipyrus) and *Il.* 15. 537–9 (Meges strikes the plume from the top of Dolop's helmet).[50] In each case Homer's account of events is restrained. But the events

[48] Ibid., 139. On the objectivity of Homer, see, for example, Auerbach, *Mimesis*, at 7, where he speaks of Homer's 'uniformly objective present'. See also Griffin's own comment (103), and the note thereto, on Homer's narrative manner, which he describes as 'generally speaking, objective'.

[49] Griffin, *Homer on Life and Death*, 139.

[50] Ibid., 134–5.

which he recounts (Deipyrus' helmet rolls in the dust under the feet of one of the Achaians; the freshly dyed plume of horsehair falls in the dust) themselves convey the pathos of the moment. The aspect of Homer's storytelling strategy which Griffin strives to identify and describe in the poet's 'pregnant utterances and scenes full of emotional weight, not explicitly spelt out but still present' is captured most accurately in Tannen's concept of internal evaluation.[51] It is this latter indirect (but by no means objective) strategy which underpins Homer's storytelling style in both epics. It is a strategy which he has adopted in order to engage his listeners in his tale and to bring them to the point where they feel for themselves its 'emotional weight'.[52]

THE SHIELD OF ACHILLEUS

There is in the *Iliad* a conspicuous exception to the principle that descriptions in an oral context are economical of effort: Homer's extended description of the shield crafted by Hephaistos for Achilleus (*Il.* 18. 478–608).[53] Although the description of the surface of the shield is ambitious, note that the description of the shield itself is in accordance with the Homeric format: the shield is sturdy (*summary description*, 478); it is huge (*size*, 478); it is carefully worked (*workmanship*, 479); it has a triple rim that glitters *and* a silver strap (*feature*, 480). The element *material* is subsumed in the preceding lines (474–7). The *history* of the shield has been expressed through the narrative (369–477): it has been made for Achilleus by Hephaistos at the request of Thetis. There follows, however, a remarkable account of the images

[51] Griffin, *Homer on Life and Death*, 139.

[52] For a valuable survey of some of Homer's modes of interaction with, and his closeness to, his audience, see M. Edwards, *The* Iliad*: A Commentary*, v (Cambridge: Cambridge University Press, 1991), 2–7.

[53] For a detailed account of this passage as a description of a work of art, see A. S. Becker, 'The Shield of Achilles and the Poetics of Homeric Description', *AJP* 111 (1990), 139–53; and *The Shield of Achilles*, 87–150, where see, esp., Becker's comments on the vivification of the image (139–41). See also O. Taplin, 'The Shield of Achilles within the *Iliad*', *G&R* 27 (1980), 1–21, on the role of the shield in making us think about war in relation to peace; and Edwards, *The* Iliad*: A Commentary*, v, 200–32, for valuable commentary on the passage.

worked onto the surface of the shield: the ekphrasis proper. Note that just as the description of the shield itself is introduced as pseudo-narrative (ποίει, 478), Homer uses ποιέω and synonyms to introduce each new scene on the shield, as though each were just being finished by the smith-god: thus he regulates the flow of description.[54] Homer gives us no indication how the scenes of community life which he envisages are distributed across its glittering surface. Our only certainty is the Ocean-river which runs around its rim (607–8). What is significant in the context of this chapter is that the format of the scenes is at times descriptive (for example, at 561–72, 590–605) but at other times—indeed, more often—it is narrative (for example, at 497–508, 509–40).[55] We see again that Homer, in the midst of description, reverts to narrative, as we would expect of a poet working in an oral tradition.

We might ask ourselves why Homer included in his song a passage of such length. I propose three functions. Certainly, the passage serves as a strategy of suspense: it delays the onward flow of narrative at a crucial moment, the moment when Achilleus is about to return to the fighting.[56] We see shorter descriptive passages used elsewhere to the same effect: note Homer's readiness to pause for description in *Iliad* 16, as Achilleus prepares to pour a libation before the departure of Patroklos into battle (the poet describes the chest in which he keeps the goblet at 16. 220–4; and the goblet itself at 16. 225–7); in *Iliad* 24, just before Priam enters Achilleus' hut to seek the ransom of his son (the poet describes the hut at 24. 448–53 (through narrative); and the bolt on its door at 453–6); in *Odyssey* 9, as a prelude to the great encounter with the Cyclops (he describes the entrance stone to the cave at 9. 240–3); and in *Odyssey* 21, before the contest of the bow (he describes the key to the storeroom at 21. 6–7; and Odysseus' bow at 21. 11–41). Second, as at *Il.* 11. 15–46, the description of Agamemnon's preparations for

---

[54] See *Il.* 18. 478, 482, 483, 490, 541, 550, 561, 573, 587, 590, 607.

[55] For Lessing's comments, see *Laocoön*, 95. Two other modes are represented: note the list at 483–9; and the simile at 600–1.

[56] Despite Auerbach's claim that the element of suspense is very slight in Homer (*Mimesis*, 4), we do feel suspense. It will not be the anxiety of the ignorant but the dread of the informed.

battle, Homer uses armour, or garb of any kind, to shed light on the man: that is, the information he offers here has an evaluative function. Since the smith-god himself is making the armour, we are assured of the invincibility of Achilleus amongst mortals. When the hero, in his magnificent war-gear, returns to the field, the battle around Troy will be conducted on different terms. And there is a third point to consider, and that is that the poet has worked up such a passage as a demonstration of his diverse skills: his power of imagination, his talent for evocative description, his memory for non-narrative discourse, and his performance-style.[57] Like a list-song or a catalogue-song, a composition, such as the description of the shield of Achilleus or the palace of Alkinoos, can be a showpiece: the poet has prepared in advance a special composition, which he may use if the occasion is right and the audience responsive. Like lists and catalogues, which offer a change of pace from narrative, a sustained descriptive piece offers listeners diversion from the narrative mode; and it provides an occasion for the poet's self-promotion.

Homer does not use his descriptions of cups, bowls, corselets and lyres simply to celebrate these items, as a kind of connoisseurship; and he is not proclaiming their centrality to the scenes in which they occur. He uses these descriptions in a number of ways which enrich our understanding: he defines his heroes by their delight in such fine possessions; through them he draws our attention to the gift-exchange rituals which bind the heroic world; and his steady accumulation of such passages suggests to us the splendid lifestyle of heroes in epic, if not in real life. But he uses them also as part of a broader storytelling strategy: to mark and prolong the dramatic moment, to assist us in reading the action of the poem, and to keep us involved in his tale.

---

[57] The question arises: how might the poet have remembered such a passage? I suggest that he worked up a number of scenes, each one representing an event (with its own logical sequence of action) in communal life. The scenes themselves are so general in nature that they have probably been based on episodic scripts which the poet stored in memory. A key word, such as 'war', 'peace', or 'harvest', would have been enough to stimulate his memory for each sequence. If spatial memory assisted the poet in recalling these scenes, it has left no conspicuous clue in the text.

My comments from a cognitive point of view on Homer's descriptive practice have been intended as an extension of other scholars' observations. Homer, when he sings in this descriptive mode, refers to an abstract procedural format which he has stored in memory as implicit knowledge. It is this format which supplies cues which lead the poet to a relatively narrow range of ideas, for which he can then seek the words and phrases he needs. In this respect, as in others, the poet's strategy resembles our own in oral discourse; in his reference to a description format he comes closer than we may have thought to everyday practice. Nevertheless, even when Homer is ostensibly describing an item, he may use narrative, as we do, to supplement descriptive terms. He is always ready to revert to the temporal sequences of narrative because he works more comfortably in this mode, in recognition of his own inclination and his audience's preferences, and because, in more ways than one, it makes for a livelier and a more engaging performance.

4

Similes in Homer: Image, Mind's Eye, and Memory

In this chapter I examine from a cognitive perspective a typical if not a defining feature of the epics: the simile.[1] My purpose is to draw into this discussion, which in the past has been for the most part descriptive or taxonomic, some evidence of a different kind.[2] My principal preoccupations will be the interactive relationship between imagery, which is at the heart of the simile, and memory—the way in which memory prompts an image, the way in which imagery and memory guide the expression of the simile, and the way in

[1] For the claim, see R. Martin, 'Similes and Performance', in E. Bakker and A. Kahane (eds.), *Written Voices, Spoken Signs: Performance, Tradition, and the Epic Text* (Cambridge, Mass.: Harvard University Press, 1997), 138–66, at 139, who demonstrates the close relationship between the language of lyric poetry and that of the Homeric similes and suggests that this relationship may explain why the extended simile is unique to Homeric epic alone among the epic traditions. Martin's study, along with that of L. Muellner, 'The Simile of the Cranes and Pygmies: A Study of Homeric Metaphor', *HSCP* 93 (1990), 59–101, marks a new interest in similes in Homer.

[2] For studies of a taxonomic kind, see W. Scott, *The Oral Nature of the Homeric Simile* (Leiden: E. J. Brill, 1974); C. Moulton, *Similes in the Homeric Poems* (Göttingen: Vandenhoeck and Ruprecht, 1977). For excellent, though relatively brief, overviews of similes, see M. Edwards, *Homer: Poet of the Iliad* (Baltimore and London: The Johns Hopkins University Press, 1987), ch. 12; *The Iliad: A Commentary*, v (Cambridge: Cambridge University Press, 1991), 24–41; and for a study of similes in terms of their poetics, see S. Nimis, *Narrative Semiotics in the Epic Tradition: The Simile* (Bloomington, Ind.: Indiana University Press, 1987), ch. 1. Earlier studies again are those of H. Fränkel, *Die homerischen Gleichnisse* (Göttingen: Vandenhoeck and Ruprecht, 1921; repr. 1977); M. Coffey, 'The Function of the Homeric Simile', *AJP* 78 (1957), 113–32; D. J. N. Lee, *The Similes of the Iliad and the Odyssey Compared* (Melbourne: Melbourne University Press, 1964); G. P. Shipp, *Studies in the Language of Homer* (Cambridge: Cambridge University Press, 1972), ch. 6; and C. M. Bowra, *Heroic Poetry* (London: Macmillan, 1952), who devotes some pages (266–80) to this device and its functions in a number of epic traditions. Fränkel's study of similes, as a comprehensive account of their content and function, is a landmark in itself. He raises many points which may now be confirmed at a more empirical level.

which imagery promotes recall—and the working out of this relationship in the Homeric simile. In short, we shall observe how a storyteller who is performing before a listening audience works with the resources of memory to generate this kind of comparative material, which draws on both imagery and language.

SIMILES AND 'PICTUREABILITY'

A simile, as we know, is a formal, verbal comparison, in which one idea or entity is compared with another idea or entity which has similar features. To effect this comparison, the 'target domain' (the idea under discussion) is explicitly 'mapped' by the domain of the simile (or the 'source domain').[3] This source domain, sometimes also called the vehicle, is usually concrete: that is, in Allan Paivio's words, it is 'pictureable'.[4] It should not surprise us that people prefer concreteness and pictureability in similes;[5] this preference for material which can be readily stored in and accessed from

---

[3] For the terminology, see G. Lakoff and M. Turner, *More than Cool Reason: A Field Guide to Poetic Metaphor* (Chicago: Chicago University Press, 1989), ch. 2, esp. at 63–4. For an alternative terminology, see R. Tourangeau and L. Rips, 'Interpreting and Evaluating Metaphors', *Journal of Memory and Language*, 30 (1991), 452–72, at 452–3: Lakoff and Turner's 'source domain' is referred to as the 'tenor' in Tourangeau and Rips's paper; and their 'target domain' is referred to as the 'vehicle'. On 'mapping' a set of correspondences, see Lakoff and Turner, at 4; Tourangeau and Rips, at 453.

[4] A key text is A. Paivio, 'The Mind's Eye in Arts and Science', *Poetics*, 12 (1983), 1–18, who states, at 6, that his study considers memory and imagery together because 'imagery itself is a memory phenomenon'. Paivio's paper is a useful introduction to this field of cognitive research. For a comprehensive survey of recent work on imagery and memory in the field of cognitive psychology and its application to oral song, see D. Rubin, *Memory in Oral Traditions: The Cognitive Psychology of Epic, Ballads, and Counting-out Rhymes* (New York and Oxford: Oxford University Press, 1995), ch. 3. For relevant discussion of image and language, the dual coding theory, and the function of imagery in aiding understanding and recall, see Introduction, above.

[5] For discussion, see A. Katz, 'On Choosing the Vehicles of Metaphors: Referential Concreteness, Semantic Distances, and Individual Differences', *Journal of Memory and Language*, 28 (1989), 486–99, at 487–8; for his results see 495. Katz's discussion considers metaphors rather than similes. But the two entities have so much in common that there would be little or no difference in the findings if the experiment were reconstructed to examine similes. On the common ground shared by similes and metaphors as non-literal comparisons, see A. Ortony, 'Beyond Literal Similarity', *Psychological Review*, 86 (1979), 161–80.

memory as image is consistent with the findings I have reported in earlier chapters.

We expect that a simile (the source domain) will have properties in common with the target domain. But the two domains cannot overlap completely. Investigations have shown that similes, like metaphor, work at two levels. Certain specific aspects of target domain and vehicle *must* be similar; others are of necessity dissimilar. The selected vehicle will be one which draws attention to the similarities between the two domains while remaining sufficiently distant so as to emphasize the differences.[6] Why does a speaker select as a vehicle an image which is conspicuously dissimilar from the target domain? A distinctive or, to take this further, a bizarre comparison will catch the attention of the listener, and hold it; and because it demands and receives a greater amount of processing time it will be more memorable.[7] As for the informativeness of such an unconventional comparison, Andrew Goatly looks to information theory, which states that the more predictable an item is the less information it carries.[8] Unconventional comparisons, therefore, are rich in information because of their novelty and their unpredictability. On the other hand, a striking comparison must be carefully monitored by a storyteller, since it may become a distraction from, rather than an enhancement of, the meaning of the passage in which it appears. We should remember, too, that a readily pictureable vehicle which generates some kind of emotion, such as our fear of wild creatures—lions or wolves—or which evokes the pathos of a helpless creature near death, will favour a transfer of that emotion from the vehicle to the target domain and thus enhance its memorability.[9]

---

[6] See Katz, 'On Choosing the Vehicles of Metaphors', at 487–8 and 495: 'The selected vehicles are sufficiently distant to emphasize differences but sufficiently close to maintain similarities' (495).

[7] See M. McDaniel and G. Einstein, 'Bizarre Imagery as an Effective Memory Aid: The Importance of Distinctiveness', *Journal of Experimental Psychology: Learning, Memory, and Cognition*, 12 (1986), 54–65, at 55. Note, however, McDaniel and Einstein's conclusions, at 63–4: although bizarre imagery is more easily accessed in comparison with more mundane images, it does not assist in any remarkable way in promoting the recall of material associated with it.

[8] See A. Goatly, *The Language of Metaphors* (London and New York: Routledge, 1997), at 164–5.

[9] See ibid., 158: 'if images are based on specific experiences which were once

How do we process a simile? When we hear or read those formal verbal signals which announce a comparison (words and phrases, for English speakers, like 'like', 'just as . . . so', 'as . . . so'), we prepare ourselves for the mapping exercise alluded to above. As we process the ensuing comparison, we draw on our repertoire of semantically linked images and bring to our mind's eye the appropriate picture. If, for example, we have to deal with the simile '[s/he is] as wholesome as new bread and butter', a comparison which has long delighted me, we will bring to mind and note both its salient (but dissimilar) and its less obvious (but shared and, therefore, highly relevant) features.[10] The salient features are the bread—I imagine it as a thick slice from a wholemeal loaf—and its cool, fresh, and natural spread. These obvious features are important because they fix an image in our mind's eye and thereby ensure the potency of the comparison. The visual image may well be supplemented by our memory for touch, smell, and taste: when all senses are engaged in this way the memorability of the simile is enhanced. What is crucial to the comparison is that we are being invited to understand an individual's character in terms of the wholesomeness of fresh, simple, but sustaining food. This understanding derives from our everyday, non-technical knowledge about diet and nutrition. So, when we compare an individual to a slice of bread and butter, we are declaring him or her to be sincere, unaffected, and good.

It is interesting to note that in reading the bread and butter simile we are obliged to overlook one essential element: the use of butter in the quantity I envisage is now recognized as being unadvisable for one's health. Because this attribute does not accord with the features of the target domain, for which simplicity and wholesomeness are the critical factors, we do not include that element in our reading of the simile. As we have noted

actually perceived, they are likely to be associated with the emotions they produced at the time of perception'. See also Tannen's useful discussion of imagery and its contribution to storytelling in terms of both understanding and involvement, in D. Tannen, *Talking Voices: Repetition, Dialogue, and Imagery in Conversational Discourse* (Cambridge and New York: Cambridge University Press, 1989), ch. 5.

[10] A. S. Byatt, for example, uses the simile in 'The Glass Coffin', in *The Djinn in the Nightingale's Eye* (London: Vintage, 1995), 3–24, at 16.

above, it is a common feature of similes that there is
incomplete correspondence between source and target
domain; and that in processing the simile some aspects of
the vehicle, even otherwise essential aspects, must be
disregarded. That is, our reading of the simile is inevitably
guided by our appreciation of the context in which it
occurs: just as the simile assists us in reading the action
of the narrative, so the action of the narrative provides us
with cues for reading the simile.[11]

The ability to *read* a simile depends, as Paivio has
proposed, on dual faculties: the ability to project the suggested image in our mind's eye and simultaneously to access
the relevant information to which that image, serving as a
mental peg or reference point, directs us.[12] The relevant
information—the knowledge, for example, of the dietary
value of fresh bread—may be described as cultural knowledge. It has been acquired through actual and indirect
experience, all of which is recorded in episodic memory
(the memory for event sequences) as schemata or scripts.[13]
These scripts will be activated along with the relevant
images. Together, therefore, image and cultural knowledge
assist us in comprehending discourse, and in remembering it.

By contrast, when we *generate* a brief simile in conversation
or in informal storytelling we follow a similar course. If we
were asked to explain either our decision to use a simile or our
choice of material, we would in most cases reply that, at some
point of our narrative, the action of the tale evoked a memory
which appeared as a vivid image in our mind's eye;[14] because
this image caught for us the essence of the action, we judged

---

[11] See Katz, 'On Choosing the Vehicles of Metaphors', at 495; see also Ortony,
'Beyond Literal Similarity', who argues that the features which are salient for the
vehicle are crucial for interpreting the metaphor.

[12] On images as 'conceptual pegs', see Paivio, 'The Mind's Eye', 13–14.

[13] On episodic memory and the storage of episodic material as schemata or
scripts, see Ch. 1, above.

[14] In Gentner's words: 'Mental experience is full of moments in which a current
situation reminds us of some prior experience stored in memory' ('The Mechanisms of Analogical Learning', in S. Vosniadou and A. Ortony (eds.), *Similarity and
Analogical Reasoning* (Cambridge: Cambridge University Press, 1989), 199–241, at
199). And see also R. Schank and R. Abelson, 'Knowledge and Memory: The Real
Story', in R. Wyer (ed.) *Knowledge and Memory: The Real Story* (Hillsdale, NJ:
Lawrence Erlbaum, 1995), 1–85, *passim*.

that the pictorial quality of the image would be important in some way also to our listeners and to the story. In accordance with Paivio's dual coding hypothesis, words which would describe this remembered image would be prompted by the image as it came to mind.[15] This prompting function, which is fundamental to dual coding, is clearly of benefit to all storytellers as they cast about for the words they need; it must have been of great benefit to Homer, especially in his sustained performances before large audiences.

THE FUNCTIONS OF SIMILES

Imagery not only promotes recall; it also promotes understanding. Actual pictures, or diagrams, work as 'advance organizers' for readers or listeners as they process discourse such as narrative or explanatory text; they provide listeners or readers with a schema, a conceptual outline, which enables them to focus their attention and to organize their ideas appropriately, in order to build a mental model for understanding what is being presented to them in words.[16] It is important for us in the context of this discussion to observe that mental models, pictures in the mind's eye, can serve the very same functions, of promoting comprehension and recall, as do actual pictures and diagrams.[17]

Similes serve the storyteller and his audience in these and a variety of other ways. In collating a list of possible functions I have drawn principally on Goatly's valuable discussion of the functions of metaphor, which I have

[15] See Paivio, 'The Mind's Eye', at 8.

[16] On the important link between imagery and comprehension, see A. Glenberg and W. Langston, 'Comprehension of Illustrated Text: Pictures Help to Build Mental Models', *Journal of Memory and Language*, 31 (1992), 129–51, who study the cognitive processes which underlie the 'facilitative effects of pictures on text comprehension' (129). On 'advance organizers', see R. E. Mayer, 'Can You Repeat That? Qualitative Effects of Repetition and Advance Organizers on Learning from Science Prose', *Journal of Educational Psychology*, 75 (1983), 40–9.

[17] See J. D. Bransford, *Human Cognition: Learning, Understanding and Remembering* (Belmont, Calif.: Wadsworth, 1979), 123; M. Marschak and R. Reed Hunt, 'A Reexamination of the Role of Imagery in Learning and Memory', *Journal of Experimental Psychology: Learning, Memory, and Cognition*, 15 (1989), 710–20, at 710.

modified in the light of the cognitive material presented in my Introduction.[18]

The first function is that of *explanation* and *modelling*, in which a simile may be used to explain a concept which is relatively abstract or unfamiliar through familiar images; in this function the simile serves as an 'advance organizer'. A second function is *reconceptualization*, which goes beyond the earlier function of explanation; we use literary similes, especially, to bring about a completely fresh understanding of experience. A simile may well open the way to observing relationships which are implicit in the narrative; thus it will assist in creating a richer reading than would ordinarily be available from the narrative itself. A third function is that of *filling lexical gaps*; we resort to similes when there is no word or form of words available to us to describe an action or an event—or, if there is, we cannot recall it at the moment we need it. A fourth function is that of *expressing emotional attitude*; this, according to Goatly, is one of the major functions of metaphor, especially as it occurs in literature.[19] Such impact derives from the tension within a metaphor or a simile between the notable similarities and dissimilarities between it and the target domain and the emotional associations of each. *Decoration* and *hyperbole* are taken together as a fifth function, whereby concepts are simply elaborated in another guise, the guise of a simile, for the purpose of drawing attention to themselves. A sixth function of the simile emerges from the mutual understanding between speaker and listener: the *cultivation of intimacy*. Intimacy may develop between a speaker and his or her audience, for example, when the speaker chooses vehicles for comparison which refer directly to the experience of his listeners or readers. Next, just as metaphor can be used, consciously or unconsciously, to structure the development of a text, so may a simile; an explanatory function and a *textual structuring* function may operate together. The next-to-final category brings together

---

[18] Goatly, *The Language of Metaphors*, at 148–67. I omit those functions which seem to me to be exclusively the focus of metaphor: ideology; disguise; humour and games; and calls to action. Cf. Fränkel's discussion of the Homeric simile, *Die homerischen Gleichnisse*, 98–9; and that of Martin, 'Similes and Performance', 139–47.

[19] Goatly, *The Language of Metaphors*, at 158.

three items: *enhancing memorability, foregrounding,* and *informativeness.* These functions are together related to the vitality and the imagistic quality of the comparison. As we have observed already, similes which evoke vivid or even exaggerated images seize the audience's attention and enhance understanding and memory. Finally, a simile, unlike a metaphor, is a form of repetition, although repetition in this case is effected in new terms. As repetition, the simile works towards increased understanding and emphasis, as we have noted already; but it serves a further pragmatic purpose: that of *prolonging the audience's pleasure* in the narrative moment.

By way of summary, I follow Goatly in proposing that the functions of similes fall into three broad categories: some are ideational, for they express new ideas about the topic; some are interpersonal, in that they build new relations between speaker and listener; and some, since they are concerned with the organization and presentation of the message, are textual. Many similes in their context will at any one time serve a number of purposes, from all three of these categories.

SIMILES AND THEIR CONTEXT

Are similes a literary phenomenon? Or are they part of everyday discourse? The answer to this question is implicit in much of the discussion above. But I draw attention to Tannen's observations on the relationship between everyday talk and literary discourse. She points out that all those forms which we have long considered to be literary forms, such as repetition, the use of imagery and detail, and tropes which operate on meaning, such as metaphor and irony, are, in fact, forms which are 'spontaneous, pervasive, and often relatively automatic' in everyday talk; they have been 'borrowed' from spoken discourse and polished—or 'intensified'—for use in more formal literary discourse, to achieve much the same rhetorical effect.[20] Similes, we must conclude, are likewise

---

[20] D. Tannen, 'Repetition in Conversation: Towards a Poetics of Talk', *Language*, 63 (1987), 574–605, at 574–5. And cf. Fränkel, *Die homerischen Gleichnisse*, at 110, who speculates that epic poetry took up images which were already used for purposes of comparison and shaped them into the similes which we now read.

part of everyone's repertoire, and always have been. In spoken discourse we use a limited range of images (drawn from everyday life, from the animal world, and from our cultural heritage) for pictureable terms of comparison. Our similes may be brief and stereotypical; but it is clear that the ability to access them and to use them to advantage is not restricted to the great poet who writes, or to the great poet, like Homer, who sings, even though Homer's similes are in some ways different from our own. We all understand, for the most part, subconsciously, how to construct and how to read a simile.

THE SIMILE IN HOMER: THE IMAGE AND ITS MESSAGE

In the Homeric simile, as in similes which we devise and use today, the source domain is usually an image which is readily pictureable: a lion, for example, or a bird, a falling tree, or a bright-coloured poppy. And the comparison is presented in a fashion similar to our own pattern of expression. Just as certain words and phrases in English signal similes, so there are predictable words and phrases in the Homeric epics (for example, the pattern ὡς . . . ὥς) for the same purpose.[21] Leaving aside the language of the similes, there is one striking respect in which the Homeric simile is unlike those which have been discussed above. The similes with which we are familiar in everyday English are relatively brief, as though the speaker is unwilling to claim too much of his or her listener's attention for what could be viewed as a mere decorative flourish.[22] In Homer the brief simile—the single image produced from the resources of memory—is the exception. There are relatively few of this kind.[23] By contrast, the so-called extended simile (which is, more accurately, a 'less condensed' simile, for reasons which I discuss below) is

---

[21] For a complete list of such introductory expressions see Lee, *Similes*, 17–21.

[22] For example, 'He ran like the wind'; 'We worked like Trojans'; 'She swims like a fish'.

[23] See e.g. *Il.* 2. 764, 800; 4. 462; 5. 299; 6. 295; 8. 215; 11. 129, 485; 13. 500, 754; 14. 499; 19. 17, 381; 20. 244; 21. 29, 237; 22. 460; *Od.* 7. 106; 8. 280; 9. 289; 10. 124; 12. 433.

the norm. Similes of this kind may extend over at least three lines of text (to use the terminology of a literate culture), describing an image in detail and/or narrating a sequence of events. Similes of even five and six lines of text are familiar to readers of Homer.[24] Let us consider two examples of the brief simile before we turn to the so-called extended simile.

When Achilleus leaps up to supervise the preparation of Hektor's body for its return to Troy, he is compared by Homer to a lion: λέων ὣς (*Il*. 24. 572).[25] Through this simile the storyteller invites us to locate points of correspondence between his hero and a creature of the wild. We note both the salient (but dissimilar) and the less obvious (but shared and relevant) features of the comparison. The salient features of the lion—his four paws, his reddish mane, his sharp teeth—are important in that they hold its image in our mind's eye.[26] What is more important is that we also bring to bear on the issue what we know of the instinctive behaviour of lions and the fear which men and animals feel in their presence.[27] So when we compare Achilleus to a lion we are observing that the hero shares the lion's readiness for action, his uncompromising single-mindedness, and his power to terrify.[28] These particular lion-like qualities

---

[24] See e.g. *Il*. 2. 459–63; 4. 141–5, 482–7; 5. 136–42, 522–6, 554–8; 6. 506–11; 10. 183–6; 11. 113–9, 172–6, 474–81, 548–55, 558–62; 12. 41–8, 146–50, 299–306; 13. 137–42, 471–5; 15. 263–8, 271–6, 624–8, 630–6, 679–84; 16. 156–63, 259–65, 384–92, 745–50, 765–9; 17. 53–8, 61–7, 674–8, 725–9, 747–51; 18. 207–13, 318–22; 20. 164–73; 21. 257–62, 573–8; 22. 26–31; 23. 760–3. For a sampling of the extended similes in the *Odyssey*, see *Od*. 6. 130–4; 8. 523–30; 16. 216–18; 17. 126–30; 19. 109–14; 23. 233–8. For discussion of a possible reason for the comparatively small number of extended similes in the *Odyssey*, see below.

[25] For a discussion of this analogy expressed as a metaphor rather than a simile, see Lakoff and Turner, *More Than Cool Reason*, at 195–7.

[26] Would Greeks have known lions? For brief discussion, see G. S. Kirk, *The* Iliad*: A Commentary*, i (Cambridge: Cambridge University Press, 1985), 269; Edwards, *The* Iliad*: A Commentary*, v, 36, at n. 43. Kirk notes that lions were known in Asia Minor and Northern Greece. An awareness of the name, the general appearance, and the nature of lions was possibly part of the cultural knowledge of the audience of traditional epic, even if, as Kirk notes, this information was distorted by hearsay and imagination. The image itself and this further information would be separately but simultaneously accessed in memory.

[27] For the most part, we make assumptions about the behaviour of lions (or, for that matter, about any members of the animal kingdom) in terms of our understanding of our own human characteristics and behaviour.

[28] My discussion here draws on that of Lakoff and Turner, *More Than Cool Reason*, at 195–6.

define Achilleus at this point of the tale. They explain what it is that could cause Priam, or even us, the audience, to fear him. As a consequence, we feel a moment of anxiety on Priam's behalf as the simile is expressed. Indeed, I cannot agree with Edwards, who claims that this short simile is used to add emphasis but 'has no more special effect than a standard epithet'.[29] Neither of the simple analogies described here appears to me to be a cliché. Each has its own force, which derives from both its pictureable quality and the bundle of information which we access as we bring this image to mind.[30]

When the Kyklops kills two of Odysseus' companions (*Od.* 9. 289), he seizes them and slaps them ($\H{\omega}\varsigma$ $\tau\epsilon$ $\sigma\kappa\acute{\upsilon}\lambda\alpha\kappa\alpha\varsigma$) against the ground.[31] The Kyklops' slaughter of Odysseus' men, Homer suggests, resembles the unsentimental killing in the rural world of unwanted new-born pups. We feel a moment of shock, because the two acts do not to us seem compatible. We ourselves may not be used to dealing with dogs in this way, but we understand the rationale for what is being described. When Homer makes us realize that the Kyklops treats humans with as little sympathy as we might treat pups, we recoil. The force of these similes does not lie so much in language *per se*, but, in the first instance, in the image which is conjured up in our minds. We promptly evaluate that image in terms of our cultural knowledge, and we respond to it both in those terms and emotionally.[32] The storyteller's language simply serves as a prompt and a guide, to stimulate us to perform the exercise of visualization and to ensure that the picture which we build up is appropri-

---

[29] Edwards, *Homer*, at 102.

[30] This apparently simple lion-simile conceals a wealth of association. When the poet uses the simile here, in the closing phases of the *Iliad*, he refers us back to all the more developed lion-similes of the epic, which describe a warrior's violent behaviour in battle (see, for example, *Il.* 5. 161–2; 11. 113–19; 15. 630–6). At this late point of the narrative the bundle of lion-related information to which we have access when we call to mind its image will have been modified by those earlier descriptions. I thank Janet Watson for this observation.

[31] The image is made more powerful by the auditory effect of onomatopoeia: $\kappa\acute{o}\pi\tau$' (290). Martin, 'Similes and Performance', at 149, comments on the frequency with which Homeric similes report the sound of an action.

[32] Although these bare similes contain few directly expressed evaluative terms, they nevertheless convey their message through a simple, striking image: cf. the powerful $\phi\grave{\eta}$ $\kappa\acute{\omega}\delta\epsilon\iota\alpha\nu$ (like the head of a poppy) of *Il.* 14. 499.

ate.[33] It is the cognitive and affective outcomes of this process, whereby we refer to our memories to assist us in constructing the scene, that remain in our minds even as the narrative moves on.

When we as an audience are processing the simple analogies which I have cited above, we are set a task by the storyteller: to evaluate the point of the simile for ourselves. What is it about Achilleus which reminds the poet of a lion? In what way does the killing of Odysseus' men resemble the killing of an unwanted pup? And why is this latter scene, in Polyphemus' cave, so shocking? Homer leaves this task to us, thereby engaging us in both the analogy and the narrative into which it is integrated. This strategy of 'internal evaluation', whereby the storyteller requires his or her listeners to draw their own conclusions on the basis of the material provided, has been discussed in Chapter 3, where I contrasted internal and external evaluation as two distinct storytelling strategies.[34] The consequence of internal evaluation is that the audience, other things being equal, is engaged by the narrative, whether cognitively or emotionally; external evaluation keeps listeners and readers at a distance from the tale: they are required to follow the storyline, but they are not invited to play any part in its interpretation. Homer's brief similes, therefore, as minor exercises in internal evaluation, draw us into the story. His extended similes function in a slightly different fashion. The poet wants to draw us into the story and invites us to evaluate it for ourselves; but his concern to direct us to other conclusions as well leads him to a more detailed presentation.

HOMER'S SO-CALLED EXTENDED SIMILES

As I have already noted, the poet often presents similes in more leisurely form. In this respect, his style of presentation is quite different from our own. We prefer, in everyday talk at least and for reasons which I have set out above, to keep our

[33] For discussion, see Lakoff and Turner, *More Than Cool Reason*, at 90–1.
[34] For discussion and references, see Ch. 3, above.

similes brief; Coffey suggests that this may have been true also of everyday speech in the world of Homer.[35] Indeed, it has been argued that it is Homer's preference for the so-called extended simile which distinguishes the *Iliad* and the *Odyssey* not only from everyday speech but also from other epic traditions.[36] And yet Muellner observes that extended similes are themselves condensations; and that, as such, they are akin to Homer's brief similes.[37] He argues that in a traditional medium, like Homeric epic, it is possible for a singer to omit from the surface of discourse elements which are held in memory by everyone. The extended simile and the brief simile are compressed versions of the same image or image sequence. I agree with his proposition, but I wish to rework his explanation, so that it can be accommodated to what we know about human cognitive behaviour. I propose, in line with my discussion above, that the narrative content of all similes is activated by the poet's memory for imagery; as the poet accesses visual data, he has access also to relevant scripts from episodic memory, where his experience of event-sequences is recorded. Although the singer's expression of a script may be detailed, it is unlikely that it will ever be as comprehensive as the script which he holds in memory. The narrative content of a simile, therefore, will be a condensation of that highly specific scripted information. Thus we have brief similes, which are highly condensed, and extended similes, which are less condensed. I shall, however, continue to refer to Homer's longer similes by the familiar term: the extended simile.

The real difference between the two modes of presentation—the simple simile and the extended simile—lies in the greater explicitness of the latter. Whereas in the simple analogy the relationship between source domain and target domain is not made explicit, and the audience becomes involved in the storytelling through the task of evaluation,

[35] Coffey, 'The Function of the Homeric Simile', at 114–15.

[36] See n. 1, above; and Bowra, *Heroic Poetry*, 275–80. For a contrary view, see P. Damon, *Modes of Analogy in Ancient and Medieval Verse* (Berkeley and Los Angeles: University of California Press, 1961), ch. 1, 'Homer's Similes and the Uses of Irrelevance'. For a listing of the longer similes, see above.

[37] For Muellner's valuable comments on so-called 'extended' similes, see 'The Simile of the Cranes and Pygmies', at 66.

in the extended simile the relationship between the two domains is generally elucidated through a brief narrative or narrative fragment which incorporates a number of pertinent details: thus the simile maps itself more completely over what is now an event-sequence and through it the poet encourages the listener to envisage the scene and to complete the comparison, as he, the poet, wishes it to be seen.[38] Lakoff and Turner point out a reason for this accumulation of detail: it limits possible image-mappings and thus facilitates and directs our interpretation of the action along the lines intended by the poet.[39] That is, by reinforcing his simile with further detail, the poet retains considerable, although not complete, control of our reading of both the simile and, therefore, the action. There is, however, almost inevitably some irrelevant material; just as in our own similes there is material which does not correspond to the target domain, so there is material of this kind in Homer's comparisons.[40]

It could be suggested that the explicitness of similes such as these may make them less interesting to us, since less effort is required of us if we are to interpret them.[41] But I do not accept that the extended simile is less interesting. Indeed, it retains its power to engage through the very detail which the poet includes. I draw attention to Tannen's comments on the role of imagery in narrative. She observes that details are important to us as listeners;[42] their particularity and their familiarity create a kind of intimacy—the intimacy of recognition. And she notes that a scene made vivid by the use of detail may spark an emotional response; this, in its turn, promotes greater involvement and deeper understanding in the listener.[43]

---

[38] For discussion of the extensive mapping of simile over narrative event, see Fränkel, *Die homerischen Gleichnisse*, ch. 1.

[39] Lakoff and Turner, *More than Cool Reason*, at 91.

[40] Perfect correspondence in every detail is pointless in similes: see my discussion, above.

[41] Cf. G. Miller, 'Images and Models, Similes and Metaphors', in A. Ortony (ed.), *Metaphor and Thought*, 2nd edn. (Cambridge: Cambridge University Press, 1993), 357–400, at 375.   [42] Tannen, *Talking Voices*, ch. 5.

[43] Ibid., 135: 'Images, like dialogue, evoke scenes, and understanding is derived from scenes because they are composed of people in relation to each other, doing things that are culturally and personally recognizable and meaningful.' On involvement through emotional response, see above.

Furthermore, as Edwards comments, the obvious point of comparison in the extended simile may itself overlie a 'deeper and more significant, unstated meaning' which listeners or readers are expected to locate for themselves.[44] Let us consider two examples which will illustrate how the extended simile exercises its force within the narrative.

When the poet at *Il.* 13. 389–91 describes the fall of Asios in battle at the hands of Idomeneus (cf. *Il.* 16. 482–6, the fall of Sarpedon), he likens Asios' collapse, after a fatal strike from his opponent's sword, to the falling of a great tree—an oak, a poplar, or a pine—which has been felled by carpenters who wish to use its timbers for ship building.[45]

> ἤριπε δ' ὡς ὅτε τις δρῦς ἤριπεν ἢ ἀχερωΐς,
> ἠὲ πίτυς βλωθρή, τήν τ' οὔρεσι τέκτονες ἄνδρες
> ἐξέταμον πελέκεσσι νεήκεσι νήϊον εἶναι·

He fell, as when an oak goes down or a white poplar
or like a towering pine tree which in the mountains the carpenters
have hewn down with their whetted axes to make a ship timber.

The scene which the poet describes is achieved by invoking the tree-felling script familiar to his listeners from their experience of the everyday. He provides a number of details: the carpenters, their axes, the tree (and its location, in a mountain forest), and its fall. What brings the description to life, however, is one particular item: these men are said to be ship builders. But the ship builders are not crucial to the comparison. What is essential to the comparison is the size of the tree and the emotions which a spectator might feel on seeing and hearing its slow fall to the ground. We know that Homer wishes us to think along these lines here, because he has chosen trees known for their great height; and he gives us an explicit cue in his epithet βλωθρή (towering) (390). Why, then, has he expanded his simile, to include the carpenters and their intentions? We may identify a number of reasons. The first is that the poet wishes to set the image of men alongside the image of the great tree which dwarfs them. Such is the size of Asios. Having introduced men into the scene,

---

[44] See Edwards, *Homer*, at 104.

[45] For similar tree-similes, see Simoeisios' fall in *Il.* 4. 482–7 and Imbrios' at *Il.* 13. 178–80. For discussion of the Simoeisios-simile, see Moulton, *Similes*, 56–8.

Homer introduces a motive for their presence; he is too much a storyteller to leave this as a loose end. And, as we have noted, details such as these are necessary to us if we ourselves are to interpret and respond to the scene which we visualize. What better in this case than to attribute to the carpenters the intention of using this great tree as ship-timber? This point too testifies to Asios' stature. A third reason lies beneath these others. This has to do with the emotions we might feel as spectators, whether we watch this scene or visualize it. The introduction of men and their purposeful and productive occupations points up, by contrast, the pathos of the target scene: the wasteful killing, on the battlefield, of one of the bold Trojan allies. There is nothing productive about this.[46] At this point the target domain and the source domain are violently at odds, to such an extent that we cannot overlook the disparity. The simile, therefore, vivid because of its detailed imagery, gains further affective force through a bold, unexpected, and unstated contrast of opposites.[47] The image, along with—and because of—the evaluative material associated with it, stays in our minds.

A second simile, now from the *Odyssey* (16. 216–18), is unusual, since it paints men as a hostile force. At the moment of recognition and reunion, Telemachos and Odysseus weep (213–15). The sound of their voices is like (indeed, it is greater than) the shrill cry of vultures whose fledglings have been stolen away by countryfolk (216–18).

> κλαῖον δὲ λιγέως, ἀδινώτερον ἤ τ' οἰωνοί,
> φῆναι ἢ αἰγυπιοὶ γαμψώνυχες, οἷσί τε τέκνα
> ἀγρόται ἐξείλοντο πάρος πετεηνὰ γενέσθαι·

[A]nd they cried shrill in a pulsing voice, even more than the
                                                    outcry
of birds, ospreys or vultures with hooked claws, whose children
were stolen away by the men of the fields, before their wings grew
strong

---

[46] Whether Greeks felt ambivalent or not about setting out to sea in ships, the building of ships was essential to their livelihood. This is the sense in which I use the term 'productive'.

[47] For a similar comment on the simile of *Il.* 12. 278–86, see R. Lattimore, *The Iliad of Homer* (Chicago: University of Chicago Press, 1951), 43. On the memorability of bizarre or distinctive imagery, see above.

What is the point of comparison in this case? Now that
Odysseus and Telemachos have been reunited, they can at
last weep. It is not joy which brings their tears, but the
pent-up sorrow of years of separation. The grief of father
and son is deeply felt: each weeps at last the tears which he
might have shed during their time apart.[48] To be sure that
we understand their tears Homer calls up the image of
great birds mourning the loss of their young. The information that the fledglings were taken from the nest by
countryfolk allows us to complete a story. Thus we
become involved in the sorry tale, and our emotions are
engaged. Indeed, the simile works twice over. In the first
instance, the grief of father and son is described in terms of
the shrill cries of the birds; in the second, Odysseus' own
grief, as a parent who feared he may never be reunited
with his son, is caught in the image of the parent bird
deprived of its chicks by the depredations of men. This
image, which has been given added force by virtue of the
emotions associated with it, replays the dramatic moment,
with its affective links, for our greater understanding—and
our pleasure.

THE CONTENT OF AN EXTENDED SIMILE

It is worth noting that each of the extended similes which I
have discussed above touches in some general way on
everyday life. They are by no means exceptional in the
epics; a large proportion of Homer's extended similes
represent aspects of daily life in the wider world remote
from the battlefield of the *Iliad* and the troubled realms of
the *Odyssey*, whether the poet makes reference to activities
that might be conducted in a rural context, an everyday
understanding of the weather, or the behaviour of animals in

---

[48] For commentary on this simile, categorized as a 'reverse simile', see H. Foley,
' "Reverse Similes" and Sex-Roles in the *Odyssey*', *Arethusa*, 11 (1978), 7–26, at 7.
Foley notes that, although Odysseus has just regained his son, Homer marks this
moment, paradoxically, with an image of bereavement. For reservations about, and
defence of, the simile, see A. Heubeck and A. Hoekstra, *A Commentary on the
Odyssey*, ii (Oxford: Clarendon Press, 1989), 275.

the wild.[49] This, indeed, is as we would expect. The simile, if it is to be effective, must connect with the experience of the audience; and it must offer a contrast to its target domain. Homer, therefore, is deliberately using a limited body of material, to which all his listeners can in some way relate. The point of choosing this material is not simply to describe a world of peaceful and productive activity. He uses these familiar scenes as explanatory models, to engage us in an assessment of what is unfamiliar to us, the world of war, and to help us appreciate what is happening on the battle-field or in that other realm of competitive male activity, games.[50] We might consider, for example, the image of the widow who weighs out her wool so carefully, illuminating that moment in battle when both sides are so evenly balanced that neither gives way to the other (*Il.* 12. 433–5); or the contest of the Lesser Aias and Odysseus, who compete for the winner's prize of victory in the foot-race in honour of Patroklos, running as close to each other as the κανών (the shuttle, which passes through the warp threads) runs close to the weaver's breast, yet does not quite touch it (*Il.* 23. 760–3).[51]

And yet, when he uses a simile, Homer is breaking down the illusion that we are direct observers of the action. At these moments he recalls his listeners from the storyworld to

---

[49] For general comments on Homer's similes which compare warfare with crafts and craftsmanship, see Scott, *The Oral Nature of the Homeric Simile*, 107–13. For a useful categorization of similes, which demonstrates that Homer, as we do, drew on a limited range of material for his comparisons, see J. Redfield, *Nature and Culture in the* Iliad: *The Tragedy of Hector* (Chicago and London: Chicago University Press, 1975; Phoenix edn., 1978), at 188–9, who groups the similes of the *Iliad* under four headings: weather and natural phenomena, human activities of a productive nature (see his n. 60 for examples), hunting and herding, and wild animals amongst themselves. All of these could be reconciled with the life experiences (at first- or second-hand) of an audience of this epic tradition (cf. M. Nilsson, *Homer and Mycenae* (London: Methuen, 1933), at 275–7; and Muellner, 'The Simile of the Cranes and Pygmies', at 73, who explains the apparent authenticity of the similes as 'a transformation of traditional lore . . . into a coherent, generative, poetic system . . .'). On the linguistic lateness of the extended Homeric similes, see the comments of Shipp, *Studies in the Language of Homer*, ch. 6. For a contrary view, see Muellner, 'The Simile of the Cranes and Pygmies', at 97–8.

[50] See Redfield, *Nature and Culture*, at 186–7.

[51] For a discussion of the simile, in terms of weaving technology, see W. Leaf and M. Bayfield, *The* Iliad *of Homer* (London: Macmillan, 1895), 569.

the realm of performance; and, as he interrupts his narrative with comparison or description, he reminds us of the role he plays as mediator and guide.[52] Such a break, midway through a stretch of battle narrative, may well be refreshing to the audience; it may give them the opportunity to focus elsewhere for a moment before the storyteller draws them back, also by way of the simile, to the narrative. Thus the simile which compares the rebound of an arrow from Menelaos' corselet to the rebound of beans and chickpeas in the blast of the winnowing fan (*Il*. 13. 588–90) provides a pause in the narrative and an opportunity to bring to the mind's eye images of rural life; but the storyline of the narrative proper cannot be forgotten, because the events in the world of the simile reflect events in the storyworld.

SIMILES WHICH OVERSHOOT THE MARK

The majority of Homer's similes are extended by narrative in the form of a story or story fragment; and we have studied a number of examples above. There I was concerned to demonstrate Homer's use of detail in connection with his strategy of internal evaluation. I turn now to observe the way in which he marries the narrative of the simile with the progress of the storyline. Let us consider a straightforward example: the comparison of Agamemnon to a lion.

When Agamemnon is in the midst of his ἀριστεία (his ferocious attack on the Trojans), described in *Iliad* 11, he is likened, at 113, to a lion. The image is developed at 113–19, when he is likened to a lion which has just broken into the lair of a deer and has snatched her young (νήπια τέκνα) and torn them apart (113–15).[53] The doe is terrified, unable to help.

---

[52] See S. Richardson, *The Homeric Narrator* (Nashville, Tenn.: Vanderbilt University Press, 1990), 64–6, at 66, 198. For further commentary on this phenomenon, see Ch. 5, below. Although the poet interrupts his story, he does not interrupt his performance. And yet, in invoking the everyday world, he allows his audience a moment's respite: the images of the simile come readily to mind.

[53] For commentary on this simile and the series of lion-similes which are generated in this episode, see B. Hainsworth, *The* Iliad: *A Commentary*, iii (Cambridge: Cambridge University Press, 1993), 237–8.

She gathers the last of her strength and runs to escape the beast. The details which convey her sheer terror are conveyed as images in the τρόμος αἰνός (the quivering which seizes her, 117) and her sweating as she flees (ἰδρώουσα, 119). This story, however, is fragmentary, in that we have no resolution: we don't know whether the doe actually makes her escape. But, in terms of the action of the simile, what happens to the doe is irrelevant. For the narrative of the simile should do no more than parallel the story of Agamemnon and the Trojans to this point; it should go no further. What is critical to the simile are those elements which describe the current plight of the Trojans, who see two companions brought down by Agamemnon and in fear, like the doe, run to escape him.

When the poet extends his simile through narrative, what he offers is, as it were, a commentary on the scene which runs in the cinema of his mind's eye.[54] The words and phrases he requires for his song will be stimulated by the images themselves as the small scene he is viewing unfolds: this is a function of dual coding. The poet's task at this point is therefore relatively easy: narrative, by virtue of its relationships of cause and effect, comes readily to us all.[55] The storyteller, furthermore, may choose whether he will compress his narrative, alluding only to the principal elements of the story from which the simile is drawn, or whether he will expand it with detail by giving full expression to relevant scripts. The expansion of a simile is not a chore. It is an option which the poet readily selects, for imagery, memory and linguistic processes (notably, his formulas) combine to assist him as he sings.

There are, however, traps for the poet who extends his simile into narrative. Given that narration is natural and relatively easy for the poet, it may happen on occasion that he takes the narrative of his simile beyond the point which he has reached in the narrative proper, with the result that the simile ceases to be relevant, confusing the audience and overshadowing the action of the main narrative.[56] I should

---

[54] For a description of storytelling in similar terms, see Introduction, above.

[55] On the activity of narrating and its relation to episodic memory storage, see Ch. 1, above.

[56] For a similar comment, see Fränkel, *Die homerischen Gleichnisse*, at 105–6.

concede the possibility, of course, that the narrative of the extended simile may on occasions have been intended to foreshadow what is to happen in the story itself; and that some similes are at certain points so condensed or so allusive that we today do not understand their meaning.[57] I shall, however, consider a number of examples of what I regard as narrative over extension, not as a reproof to Homer but because those instances which do not conform to our expectations provide us with opportunities to learn more about the cognitive processes which underlie the production of the simile, and of narrative.

Let us consider the simile (*Il.* 4. 141–5) through which the poet describes the dark blood which flowed from Menelaos' wound when Pandaros' arrow pierced his corselet (134–40). Here the poet claims that his intention is to compare the visual impact of Menelaos' blood on the pale skin of his thighs and legs to a vivid purple dye with which a woman from Asia Minor paints an ivory piece (141–2). If that is so, then the remaining narrative elements of the simile (142–5) are, strictly speaking, pointless:[58]

> παρήϊον ἔμμεναι ἵππων·
> κεῖται δ' ἐν θαλάμῳ, πολέες τέ μιν ἠρήσαντο
> ἱππῆες φορέειν· βασιλῆϊ δὲ κεῖται ἄγαλμα,
> ἀμφότερον κόσμος θ' ἵππῳ ἐλατῆρί τε κῦδος·

> to make it a cheek piece for horses;
> it lies away in an inner room, and many a rider
> longs to have it, but it is laid up to be a king's treasure,
> two things, to be the beauty of the horse, the pride of the horseman

The narrative of the simile, from 142–5, goes beyond what is necessary in terms of the main narrative line. This fragment

[57] See, on my first point, G. Duckworth, *Foreshadowing and Suspense in the Epics of Homer, Apollonius and Vergil* (Princeton, 1933; reprint edn., New York: Haskell House, 1966), 14–15. For an example of possible foreshadowing, see *Il.* 22. 26–31; but note Duckworth's comments (15) on the dangers of reading announcements of the future into comparisons. And, on my second, see Muellner, 'The Simile of the Cranes and Pygmies', esp. at 98. I am not persuaded by Muellner's argument, that our failure to follow Homer's difficult similes is entirely due to our own lack of experience in the tradition. It may be so in some cases; but I cannot accept that that factor explains away all our difficulties in the interpretation of some similes.

[58] Strictly speaking, they are pointless; yet, as I have shown above, it is the inclusion of human participants and their productive activities which cultivates intimacy, introduces pathos to the scene, and makes it memorable.

is true to the *Iliad* in its leisurely style and in the cultural milieu which it invokes: its reference to great kings, to their delight in fine craftsmanship, and to their pleasure in the accumulation of the rare and the beautiful. Nevertheless, it is with some surprise that we find ourselves returned to a point of correspondence which had been reached earlier in the simile: to the brothers' reaction of horror, at 148–52, when they see Menelaos' blood and the wound itself.

Kirk suggests that the extension of the simile (143–5) implies the unique value of Menelaos to the Achaians.[59] Such a reading would be hard to justify, since it is the relationship between the brothers which is brought to the fore in the following lines (148–82). Rather, the poet has been seduced by his image of the craftswoman and her fine work (141–2) and has allowed the story of the fate of the ivory piece to distract him. The development of the comparison, which keeps our attention on the cheekpiece, weakens the original force of the comparison and, in offering superfluous material, is confusing. Nevertheless, this problematic moment in the narrative, which reveals an unexpected incompatibility between narrative and simile, has thrown some light on the mental processes which generate this genre.

An extraordinarily powerful simile is that of *Il.* 16. 156–63. Here the poet compares the fighting spirit of the Myrmidons, now at last armed for battle, with the lust for blood of wolves (156–7):

> οἱ δὲ λύκοι ὣς
> ὠμοφάγοι, τοῖσίν τε περὶ φρεσὶν ἄσπετος ἀλκή

> And they, as wolves,
> who tear flesh raw, in whose hearts the battle is tireless

In fact, the simile quickly moves beyond the point at which it coincides with the main narrative. We soon see the wolves gorging themselves on a stag brought down in the mountains: they feed, they drink, they regurgitate clotted blood (ἐρευγόμενοι φόνον αἵματος, 162), and their bellies are full (περιστένεται δέ τε γαστήρ, 163).

---

[59] See Kirk, *The* Iliad: *A Commentary*, i, 345–6.

Despite Nimis's, and Janko's, defence of the extension of the simile as an instantiation of the meal which we might otherwise expect at this point of the preparations for battle, I suggest that the poet has quite simply allowed the simile to go beyond the limits defined by the narrative proper at this point.[60] The feasting of the wolves does not describe the present situation; rather, it looks ahead to the performance of the Myrmidons in battle, alongside Patroklos. It anticipates, for example, their attempt to strip the armour from and dishonour the body of Sarpedon (544–7) and might be compared with the battlefield performance of Agamemnon, like a lion among cattle, at *Il.* 11. 172–6. I propose, therefore, that the poet has allowed the scene in his mind's eye (the scene of the simile) to run ahead of the narrative proper. And, forgetting that he must co-ordinate the two, he has continued to sing his simile-song.[61]

The image of wolves glutted with blood is readily pictureable, to the extent that the animals and their bloodied jowls divert our attention from the Myrmidons. The possibility of distracting his audience from the narrative proper, however, may for the poet be a risk worth taking. But his weakness at this point, on my reading, has been his failure to correlate his descriptions of the actual performance of Achilleus' men with the promises which he has made. The Myrmidons' achievements in the subsequent

---

[60] Nimis, *Narrative Semiotics in the Epic Tradition*, 23–42, esp. at 41, attempts to justify the inclusion of the wolves' meal, claiming that a meal is an established element of preparations for battle (cf. *Il.* 19. 145–237). The expected but unrealized meal is transformed therefore into a negative meal: the meal of the wolves. See also R. Janko, *The Iliad: A Commentary*, iv (Cambridge: Cambridge University Press, 1992), 338–9. I point out, however, that a meal, if that is what the wolves' meal is intended to represent, is completely out of the question at this point of the narrative. Fully armed men cannot eat and drink; they do so before donning their cumbersome war-gear. And note that a meal is not included in the narrative of the preparations for the great day of battle in *Il.* 11.

[61] On the relative ease with which he can compose narrative, see above. For other examples of similes which lose their relevance as they are developed, see *Il.* 17. 674–8 (the relationship of Menelaos to Antilochos is not an eagle–hare relationship); *Il.* 22. 308–10 (nor is Hektor and Achilleus' relationship that of an eagle to a lamb—or a hare). And see Muellner's discussion ('The Simile of the Cranes and Pygmies', at 65) of the irrelevant element at *Il.* 2. 462. On such slips of attention, see A. Baddeley, *Human Memory: Theory and Practice* (Hove and London: Lawrence Erlbaum, 1990), ch. 6, esp. at 127.

battle do not seem (with the exception of *Il.* 16. 544–7) to justify the powerful comparison.

As a third example I choose a simile which compares Sarpedon in battle to a lion eager for food, resolved to risk the herdsmen's spears in his hunger for the meat of their lambs (*Il.* 12. 299–306):

> βῆ ῥ᾽ ἴμεν ὥς τε λέων ὀρεσίτροφος, ὅς τ᾽ ἐπιδευὴς
> δηρὸν ἔῃ κρειῶν, κέλεται δέ ἑ θυμὸς ἀγήνωρ
> μήλων πειρήσοντα καὶ ἐς πυκινὸν δόμον ἐλθεῖν·
> εἴ περ γάρ χ᾽ εὕρῃσι παρ᾽ αὐτόφι βώτορας ἄνδρας
> σὺν κυσὶ καὶ δούρεσσι φυλάσσοντας περὶ μῆλα,
> οὔ ῥά τ᾽ ἀπείρητος μέμονε σταθμοῖο δίεσθαι,
> ἀλλ᾽ ὅ γ᾽ ἀρ᾽ ἢ ἥρπαξε μετάλμενος, ἠὲ καὶ αὐτὸς
> ἔβλητ᾽ ἐν πρώτοισι θοῆς ἀπὸ χειρὸς ἄκοντι·

[H]e went onward like some hill-kept lion, who for a long time
has gone lacking meat, and the proud heart is urgent upon him
to get inside of a close steading and go for the sheepflocks.
And even though he finds herdsmen in that place, who are
                                                        watching
about their sheepflocks, armed with spears, and with dogs, even so
he has no thought of being driven from the steading without
                                              some attack made,
and either makes his spring and seizes a sheep, or else
himself is hit in the first attack by a spear from a swift hand
                                                          thrown.

Described by Kirk as the finest lion-simile in the *Iliad*, this extended simile not only covers the story of the lion and his search for food but dwells also on the urgency of his need (κέλεται δέ ἑ θυμὸς ἀγήνωρ, 300).[62] Here, too, the poet appears to be tempted to move beyond the limits which the narrative proper sets him. But on this occasion he turns temptation to advantage. At 305–6 he shows his audience the possible outcomes: either the lion will spring out and take his prey or he will be struck by a spear thrown by one of the herdsmen. That is, the poet has used his simile to model the ways in which this small story might develop. As an 'advance organizer', to use Mayer's term, the narrative of the simile sharpens our interest in the hero's fate.[63]

---

[62] See Hainsworth, *The* Iliad: *A Commentary*, iii, 351.
[63] See Mayer, 'Can You Repeat That?'. For further commentary on 'advance

All three similes which I have discussed are drawn from the *Iliad*. We are aware that similes are more frequent in this epic than in the *Odyssey*. The reason for this is that the backdrop to the action of the *Odyssey*—and the cast of actors—is of itself much more varied. Variety of setting reduces the pressure on the poet to build variety into his song in other ways.[64] The similes in the *Iliad*, therefore, are designed to serve all the separate functions set out above (such as reconceptualization, intimacy, and emotive force) and more: they are designed to assist in distinguishing individuals and their actions in a narrative which lacks the imagistic richness of the *Odyssey*.

VISUAL MEMORY AND THE SIMILE
IN AN ORAL TRADITION

The expression of a simile, which is verbal, is triggered by an image which has sprung to mind. This is consistent with Paivio's dual coding hypothesis. It is an observation which encourages me to revise Scott's claim that Homer's similes were the products of verbal memory and his implication that they had little connection with the mind's eye.[65] A more economical approach is to argue that Homer produced his similes in the same fashion that we all do. It is in response to an image which springs to mind that the poet finds the

organizers', see above. For examples, on the other hand, of the simile as a source of unambiguous foreshadowing, see first, *Il*. 12. 41–8, in which Hektor is compared to a lion who will not flee (and his courage kills him, 46) and, second, the simile which compares Achilleus to a star, the Dog Star, a κακὸν σῆμα (a sign of evil, *Il*. 22. 26–31, at 30). The element of foreboding is deliberate here; cf. *Il*. 5. 4–6, where it is absent. Edwards, *Homer*, at 105–6, suggests other instances: *Il*. 18. 318–22 (Achilleus, like the lion, will set out on a course of vengeance); *Il*. 23. 222–3 (the simile looks ahead to Achilleus' own death and the grief of his father); and *Od*. 6. 102–8 (Odysseus will compare Nausikaa to Artemis, at 151–2). It is possible that the memorable simile of the widow weighing the wool which she will sell in order to support herself and her children (*Il*. 12. 433–5) looks ahead to a moment when the balance tips in favour of one side or the other. For discussion of this aspect of this simile, see Hainsworth, *The Iliad: A Commentary*, iii, 362.

[64] For comment on this point, see Scott, *The Oral Nature of the Homeric Simile*, at 120–1. And cf. my discussion in Ch. 3, above, on the greater frequency of descriptive passages in the *Iliad*, by comparison with the *Odyssey*.

[65] See Scott, *The Oral Nature of the Homeric Simile*, at 162–4.

words to sing. The simile he is singing is not a memorized sequence of words; rather it is the verbal account of an image—or a series of images. It is these images, the visual code, which have given him access to the verbal code, to the words he sings.

One of the oral poet's essential assets is his visual memory. His memory for images is a powerful tool, first, because it is efficient (the majority of us find it easy to bring images to mind); second, because an image is very effective as a mnemonic aid; third, because it functions as a cue for the retrieval of other material; and, fourth, because the poet's visualization of the unfolding story and of the images which become his similes directs him to the words he needs—that is, to the formulaic phrases of his tradition. The speedy response of visual memory and his capacity for dual coding are indispensable to the oral poet, who depends on the efficiency of all the functions of memory to generate his song. The poet who works in writing, by contrast, has time to ponder. The ability to retrieve and to generate visual imagery, and associated scripted material, quickly and with a minimum of effort is far less important to him than it is to the oral storyteller.

We have noted Homer's preference for extending his similes with additional narrative material. This is the mark of a skilled oral poet at work, one who wishes to expand his song for the continuing pleasure of his audience, and who delights in narrative because he can produce it with ease, supported as he is by the episodic nature of his memory.[66] Here again we see the poet working with the resources of memory as he performs.[67] By accommodating his presentation to its structures he makes his task easier. What is interesting to me is that the strategies he has adopted to assist him in conveying his point to his audience through

[66] On the singer's use of similes in the expansion of song, see A. B. Lord, *The Singer of Tales* (Cambridge, Mass.: Harvard University Press, 1960; New York: Atheneum edn., 1965), at 79 (Avdo fills out Mumin's story).

[67] Cf. the comment by D. Rubin, 'Stories about Stories', in R. Wyer (ed.), *Knowledge and Memory: The Real Story* (Hillsdale, NJ: Lawrence Erlbaum, 1995), 153–64, at 157: 'Oral traditions have developed forms of organization and strategies . . . [which] make use of the many strengths and avoid the weaknesses of human memory.'

singing a simile—his reference to visual memory, his exploitation of scripts, his preference for narrative in the formulation of similes—have all left their mark on the song. What
may have originally been a series of enabling strategies for
the poet now plays its part in enhancing the pleasure of the
audience.

THE SIMILE IN PERFORMANCE

As Muellner has argued, similes are an integral part of the
tradition which Homer has inherited; and he has drawn on
this tradition for his own purposes.[68] But Muellner does not
suggest the form in which this inherited material may have
been transmitted; nor does he speculate on how the poet
prepared his similes for the moment of performance. Scott
uses evidence which he has gathered on repeated similes to
argue for both a repertoire of similes and a certain degree of
preparation in advance of performance.[69] The simile, he
notes, could have been prepared in advance and stored in
much the same way as a typical scene, one which describes
the arming of a warrior or the preparation of a meal, might be
stored. But Scott and Muellner view 'storage' in terms of
language.[70] By contrast, the secret of recall lies in the images
which underpin each simile. The fact that there are so few
extended similes which are repeated detail for detail and
word for word in the two epics suggests that verbal response
alone was not the key to the simile.[71] If we approach the issue
of preparation through Paivio's dual coding hypothesis, we

[68] See Muellner, 'The Simile of the Cranes and Pygmies', 65–6, 96–9.

[69] See Scott, *The Oral Nature of the Homeric Simile*, at 127–40. For the repeated
similes, see 129–30. These are as follows: *Il.* 5. 782–3 = *Il.* 7. 256–7; *Il.* 5. 860–
1 = *Il.* 14. 148–9; *Il.* 6.506–11 = *Il.* 15. 263–8; *Il.* 11. 548–55 = *Il.* 17. 657–64; *Il.*
13. 389–91 = *Il.* 16. 482–4; *Od.* 4. 335–9 = *Od.* 17. 126–30; *Od.* 6. 232–
4 = *Od.* 23. 159–61. It should be noted that there are comparatively few similes
of any length in the two epics which are repeated word for word.

[70] See Scott, *The Oral Nature of the Homeric Simile*, at 162: 'Similes were taken
from the poet's memory harking back to the inherited diction of the oral tradition
rather than created from the poet's eye glancing on a memorable landscape.'

[71] By way of example, contrast the cattle-yard similes at *Il.* 11. 548–56 and
17. 657–64, in which the image is similar, but the expression of each simile at the
outset, at least, is different.

might better understand the nature and the purpose of rehearsal. In rehearsal, Homer visualizes a scene. The images he sees lead him to the language he needs. He may 'perform' this sequence many times in private, until he is satisfied with the way the simile is developing, with its correlation with the story, and with his presentation. If he rehearses as described, the co-operation of visual imagery and language processes will be all the more efficient when he sings before his audience.

That an oral poet such as Homer practised for performance is without question, as we have observed in the case of the extended lists which he has included in his epics.[72] Storytellers today have more often than not practised their stories in advance: they have run over the event sequence, devised a style of narration appropriate to their tale, and called up the language in which to express it. We all find ourselves, at one time or another, rehearsing a story which we aim to tell before an audience of family or friends.[73] This desire to practise is driven by our need to tell a story effectively: a successful telling will be to our credit; a failed telling will cause us to lose face.[74] Professional storytellers in an ancient oral tradition would have been driven by the same impulse; they would rehearse their songs before performance.

Homer's similes are more than occasional grace-notes which characterize and define epic song. My account, in this chapter, of the complex function of the simile is an extension of Edwards's position. He sees the simile as a 'technique of expansion'; it is a 'means of creating a pause', which enables

---

[72] On the rehearsal of lists, see Ch. 2, above; and see also R. Schank and R. Abelson, 'Knowledge and Memory: The Real Story', at 74–7.

[73] For a delightful moment in fiction, when a storyteller who wishes to give the impression of spontaneity as he tries to recapture for his listener the intensity of an experience in his past is caught out, see D. Lodge, *Small World* (London: Secker & Warburg, 1984), 72: 'That's a very fancy metaphor, Philip,' said Morris. 'I can hardly believe you've never told this story before.' Philip has been practising this tale.

[74] For discussion of the consequences of a failed story, see W. Labov, 'The Transformation of Experience in Narrative Syntax', in *Language in the Inner City: Studies in the Black English Vernacular* (Philadelphia: University of Pennsylvania Press, 1972), 354–405, at 366.

the poet to hold still the action and to add new thoughts or contrasting emotions.[75] I, however, argue for a stronger position: that the simile is completely integrated into the epic, serving the singer, the audience, and the song itself.

In his conclusion to his work on similes Moulton laments that he has been unable to uncover a 'key' to the Homeric simile. He explains that the search for a key has been made impossible for him because of the enormous variety of similes in Homer. Although he recognizes a single common denominator—that the similes present concrete details—he remarks that this is 'virtually meaningless' for purposes of analysis.[76] I wish to differ. If there is any key to the similes it is precisely this, banal as it may seem, that they are all readily pictureable. It is this quality which unites them in their service to the storyteller, as mind's eye and memory work together to give expression to song. It unites them in their service to the audience, as memory and mind's eye interpret what is heard or read. And it unites them in their service to the song itself, in the many ways in which I have described above, whether similes serve to clarify what has been described within the narrative, to enlarge on it, to emphasize it, to evaluate it, or to enhance it; or whether they work to involve the audience's emotions in the action through their play on image and memory. For the goal of the simile is, in one way or another, to prolong the pleasure of a selected narrative moment and thereby to make that moment recognizable, vivid, and unambiguous—in short, memorable—for its listening audience.

[75] See Edwards, *Homer*, at 109. On the simile as a 'descriptive pause', see also Richardson, *The Homeric Narrator*, at 64.

[76] See Moulton, *Similes*, at 155; and cf. Coffey, 'The Function of the Homeric Simile', at 132.

5
Homer's Script for Storytelling: The Evidence of the Invocations

Homer calls upon his Muse, or the sisterhood of Muses, a number of times within the *Iliad* and once only—at the outset—in the *Odyssey*.[1] In the invocations which introduce each epic he asks the Muse to inspire his song; and in those which occur in the course of the *Iliad* he appeals for inspiration for a single segment or episode—the singing of the great Catalogue of Ships, or the song which describes a turn in battle. There has been considerable discussion over the years about the kind of assistance which the poet/narrator is seeking and, indeed, about the kind of relationship, between poet and Muse, which an oral singer such as Homer might have envisaged.[2] These aspects of the invocations have been carefully studied and profitably discussed elsewhere.[3] Nevertheless, my study will begin

---

[1] Such invocations are at *Il.* 1. 1–7; 2. 484–7, 761–2; 11. 218–20; 14. 508–10; 16. 112–13, and at *Od.* 1. 1–10.

[2] For discussion in narratological terms of the identity of poet and narrator in Homeric storytelling, see I. de Jong, *Narrators and Focalizers: The Presentation of the Story in the* Iliad (Amsterdam: B. R. Grüner, 1987), ch. 1. Calame, working with Benveniste's concept of 'enunciation', reaches a similar conclusion: see C. Calame, *The Craft of Poetic Speech in Ancient Greece*, trans. J. Orion (Ithaca and London: Cornell University Press, 1995), introduction.

[3] On the issues of knowledge, memory, poetic craft and performance, see P. Murray, 'Poetic Inspiration in Early Greece', *JHS* 101 (1981), 87–100 (esp. her conclusions at 99–100); C. Macleod, 'Homer on Poetry and the Poetry of Homer', in *Collected Essays* (Oxford: Clarendon Press, 1983), 1–15, esp. 4–6; W. Thalmann, *Conventions of Form and Thought in Early Greek Epic Poetry* (Baltimore: The Johns Hopkins University Press, 1984), 126–9; A. Thornton, *Homer's* Iliad: *Its Composition and the Motif of Supplication* (Göttingen: Vandenhoeck and Ruprecht, 1984), ch. 2; de Jong, *Narrators*, 41–54; M. Finkelberg, 'A Creative Oral Poet and the Muse', *AJP* 111 (1990), 293–303; *The Birth of Literary Fiction in Ancient Greece* (Oxford: Clarendon Press, 1998); C. Segal, *Singers, Heroes, and Gods in the* Odyssey (Ithaca and London: Cornell University Press, 1994), ch. 6; A. Ford, 'Epic as Genre', in I. Morris and B. Powell, *A New*

with a brief account of poetic inspiration, to establish what assistance the singer believes that he receives from the Muse; we then consider Homer's addresses to his Muse in the context of—and as part of—the performance itself. We shall observe how the poet's invocations, especially those of the *Iliad,* achieve their effect, and what they reveal to us about Homer's understanding of how stories are shaped. This survey of the invocations of the *Iliad* will be concluded with some consideration of a related phenomenon, the so-called 'faded' invocation, several occurrences of which we note in the *Iliad.* Finally, we address the proem to the *Odyssey.*

In the course of this chapter I draw on work on conversational strategies by the linguist Charles Goodwin; and there will be reference throughout to research into the shaping of stories, summarized in my Introduction. There we considered the properties of stories as analysed by Labov and Waletzky, and we observed how, from an early age, we learn how to shape the stories we tell, partly by observation and largely through practice in conversation, with the guidance of adults, who pass on their expectations of successful storytelling to the next generation. We store this intuitive knowledge about the presentation of a story in memory as a scripted format or a generalized schema, which generates a series of prompts whenever we hear or whenever we choose to tell a story. This is the kind of abstract knowledge which has been described as implicit knowledge; it may be set against the explicit knowledge of situational scripts. My discussion, below, of the distribution of the poet's invocations to his Muse will make particular reference to two elements of the storytelling format: namely, *complicating action* and *resolution.*

Companion to Homer (Leiden: E. J. Brill, 1997), 396–414; and see also W. Minton, 'Homer's Invocations of the Muses: Traditional Patterns', *TAPA* 91 (1960), 292–309; and 'Invocation and Catalogue in Hesiod and Homer', *TAPA* 93 (1962), 188–212.

THE MUSE, THE POET, AND THE SONG

Let me summarize my stand on the question of inspiration, through reference to what Homer says about his relationship with the Muse. The Muse stirs the bard to sing— Μοῦσ' ἄρ' ἀοιδὸν ἀνῆκεν ἀειδέμεναι κλέα ἀνδρῶν (the Muse stirred the bard to sing the famous actions of men, *Od.* 8. 73). She is his teacher—ἤ σέ γε Μοῦσ' ἐδίδαξε, Διὸς πάϊς, ἤ σέ γ' 'Απόλλων (surely the Muse, Zeus' daughter, or else Apollo has taught you, *Od.* 8. 488). *He* performs but *she* has provided the inspiration (hence the bard's appeal at *Il.* 1. 1: ἄειδε, sing; *Od.* 1. 1: ἔννεπε, tell me; *Od.* 1. 10: εἰπὲ καὶ ἡμῖν, tell us, too). She is, as the bard understands it, responsible for the song. My reading of how the relationship is viewed by the poet is in general accord with that of Calame, who notes that in the case of oral song, for which the poet's memory is crucial, 'the Muses contribute to establishing the Subject's competence', and the Subject (that is, the poet) is then 'involved in the achievement, represented by the actual performance of the poem before the public'.[4] Finkelberg's closer analysis, however, is also valuable in this context, since she is concerned with the division of labour within the relationship.[5] She argues that the storyteller was responsible for acquiring technical skills, such as playing the lyre, and a competence in a range of epic subjects and their basic plots. I would add to this list the acquisition of vocal skills and, as noted above, in Chapter 1, the formulaic language of epic song.[6] The Muse, for her part, gave the poet the ability to *transform*

---

[4] See Calame, *Craft*, 77–8. Admittedly, Calame is more concerned with the ways in which the 'enunciator' and the 'narrator' (I use his terminology) address characters within the text, and (on the basis of these observations) with drawing some conclusions about the context of the original performance; he is less concerned with the terms of the relationships implied by his enunciative approach.

[5] See Finkelberg, *Literary Fiction*, 57.

[6] It is difficult to know how to interpret the punishment inflicted on Thamyris, who boasted that he could out-sing the Muses (*Il.* 2. 591–600). The Muses took away his wonderful singing (ἀοιδὴν θεσπεσίην) and his memory (599–600). Did Homer regard these as skills which 'belonged' to the poet—or were they skills which the Muses might choose to confer?

a subject into epic; it was she who 'stirred' him, enabling him to work a given story-line into song.[7] This interpretation is likely to correspond to reality. Most of us hold the causal chains of a number of stories in our memories. Not all of us, however, have the talent for telling these stories in an appealing and an authoritative fashion: that is, with the liveliness, the vividness, and the fluency which recreate for listeners the experience of 'being there'.[8] This talent for storytelling—or, for the poet of these monumental poems, this genius—would, in Homer's eyes, have been the contribution of the Muse.[9] As he understood it, she granted the ability to synthesize: she inspired him to create a marvellous story for his listeners using the skills he had learned and the material he himself had stored in memory.[10] As he sings, therefore, the poet believes he is responding to the inspiration of the Muse; without it, there would be no song.

In order to understand better what is implied when Homer turns his attention from his audience as a whole to his Muse and addresses her, I begin by asking whether it is possible to find some correspondence between Homer's behaviour as it is displayed in these records of epic performance, the *Iliad* and the *Odyssey*, and our own in everyday conversation. I raise this question because I am persuaded that there is.

---

[7] See Finkelberg, *Literary Fiction*, 57. Finkelberg remarks (at 59) 'the difference between "knowing" a story and transforming it into a song is as great as that between the general plot of the *Iliad* and the *Iliad* as an epic poem'.

[8] For Homer, the Muse had seen and, therefore, 'knew' what had happened. For discussion, see Ford, 'Epic as Genre', 404–5.

[9] For us, Homer's Muse is a fictitious entity. But, for Homer, the Muse has 'objective reality'. See the discussion in G. Dimock, *The Unity of the* Odyssey (Amherst, Mass.: University of Massachusetts Press, 1989), 5–8, at 8. See also Thalmann, *Conventions*, at 126–7; Segal, *Singers*, 138–9. Segal, in his discussion of Phemios' claim at *Od.* 22. 347, that he is αὐτοδίδακτος (taught by himself), argues (138) that the poet 'views his art as coming *both* from his own power and from a god'. He likens the poet to one of Homer's own warriors, who is inspired with the fighting spirit at the height of battle. The bard, like the warrior, can thus perform at his highest level. If the Muse withdraws her inspiration, he loses his genius for song.

[10] As Calame, *Craft*, 77, observes, however, even if the Muses are fictitious, the poet's invocation of them is the essential precondition for poetic communication.

Invocations 165

'KNOWING' AND 'UNKNOWING' RECIPIENTS

When we as speakers tell a story to a group which includes both first-time listeners and people who have participated in or witnessed the events which are the subject of our tale, we adapt our presentation in recognition of these differences in knowledge states. It is remarkable that when storytellers are aware of a 'knowing recipient' among their listeners, they display uncertainty about small points, even though they may be confident of their grasp of the tale; and they will hesitate, check details, and ask for confirmation.[11] It is their conspicuous concern for the accuracy of detail which is crucial to my argument: as Tannen observes, the authenticity of any story will in large part be judged by the persuasiveness of its detail.[12] The storyteller, therefore, in consulting his knowing recipient is including her in his performance and confirming, for his unknowing listeners, the reliability of his tale.[13]

In Homer's telling of the *Iliad*-story we find behaviour of the same kind; the same etiquette is being observed. To be sure, nowhere does Homer tell us that his Muse is part of his audience as a knowing recipient or that she actually listens to his song. But it is difficult to envisage any other possibility,

[11] The terms 'knowing' and 'unknowing' recipient are used by Goodwin in his analysis of the ways in which speakers present their discourse, and themselves, when the main addressee does not know what she/he is about to be told (that is, she/he is an unknowing recipient) but another member of the audience, the knowing recipient, does. For discussion and examples, see C. Goodwin, 'Designing Talk for Different Types of Recipients', in *Conversational Organization: Interaction between Speakers and Hearers* (New York: Academic Press, 1981), 149–66. Such speaking turns are often marked by request for verification or for points of detail: 'He was driving really fast, wasn't he?' or 'How many would you say we saw? Half a dozen?' or 'Robert will have to help me out with this. There were probably fifteen different varieties'. That is, Goodwin observes that, in order to 'maintain the appropriateness of his utterance for a recipient with a particular state of knowledge', the speaker appears to change his own state of knowledge (166).
[12] See D. Tannen, *Talking Voices: Repetition, Dialogue, and Imagery in Conversational Discourse* (Cambridge and New York: Cambridge University Press, 1989), 144, for an example of a storyteller's desire to specify detail. This, she notes, 'lends a sense of authenticity, of vivid recall'. See also my discussion of the importance of detail in Ch. 3, above.
[13] On these points see Goodwin, *Conversational Organization*, 159.

given that the poet behaves as though this were so, to the
extent that he invites the Muse to be part of his performance.[14] Observe, for example, that in the course of his song
the poet at intervals turns to his Muse, or in the case cited
below, the Muse and her sisters: he acknowledges, or
implies, that the Muse is one who knows (*Il.* 2. 484–5):

> Ἔσπετε νῦν μοι, Μοῦσαι Ὀλύμπια δώματ᾽ ἔχουσαι–
> ὑμεῖς γὰρ θεαί ἐστε, πάρεστέ τε, ἴστέ τε πάντα

Tell me now, you Muses who have your homes on Olympos.
For you, who are goddesses, are there, and you know all things[15]

He asks her to help him with factual details (2. 487, 761–2;
11. 219–20; 14. 509–10; 16. 113)—the kind of detail
(notably, details of names) which lends authenticity—and
with the performance of sustained passages of song (2. 488–
92). Of course, the poet expresses his deference in far more
formal terms than those we use in casual conversation. He is,
after all, addressing a deity; the poet's terms of address, in
their solemnity, indicate that this is by no means everyday
talk.[16] And yet there is a certain intimacy reflected in his
words. Although an invocation is normally phrased as a
subspecies of prayer, the poet's address does not follow the
scripted format for prayers:[17] he does not propose sacrifices,
gifts, or other offerings in return for the inspiration of the
Muse; nor does he remind her of past benefits. His relationship with her, we deduce, is based on a closer understanding. Despite its formal vocabulary, the poet's appeal is
recognizably true of life: we can account for the circumstances which gave rise to it in terms of our own experience.

---

[14] A sceptic may ask: does the Muse actually listen? I don't believe that this is
relevant to my discussion. What is important is that the poet encourages us to
believe that she does. Pindar, unlike Homer, actually acknowledges the Muse's
attentive presence: see *Paean* 6. 54–61.

[15] See also *Il.* 1. 1–7; 11. 218; 14. 508. For further discussion of the Catalogue
which follows this invocation, see Ch. 2, above.

[16] Nor are the poet's words an empty ritual: the story of Thamyris (*Il.* 2. 591–
600) persuades us that the poet is in earnest when he calls upon the goddess.

[17] On the close relationship of invocation to prayer, see A. Ford, *Homer: The
Poetry of the Past* (Ithaca and London: Cornell University Press, 1992), 19–20. The
poet's neglect of the full ritual is noted also in J. Strauss Clay, *The Wrath of
Athena: Gods and Men in the* Odyssey (Princeton: Princeton University Press,
1983), 9–10. For an example of what we might regard as the full expression of the
prayer script, see *Il.* 10. 284–94: Diomedes to Athene.

That is, in his addresses to his Muse, the poet models his behaviour on his everyday experiences of telling stories in the presence of someone who knows.

THE ADDRESS TO THE MUSE AND ITS MEANING FOR THE UNKNOWING RECIPIENT

Although the poet's invocation is addressed to the Muse, the narrator's knowing recipient, it inevitably works upon the unknowing audience in a number of ways.[18] In the first place, the initial appeal serves a practical function: it announces the performance. It is the signal for the audience to stop talking amongst themselves and to listen to his tale.[19] Second, the invocation illuminates for the audience the formal aspects of the poet's relation with his Muse. These are set out above. Third, in intruding into his song in this way, the poet makes a number of claims on behalf of the story he is about to tell and on his own behalf. By implication he assures his audience that his story will be a story worth telling; the Muse's role in the performance is a guarantee of its authenticity and its quality. For this reason it deserves their attention.[20] And, finally, through

[18] See Goodwin, *Conversational Organization*, 152, who notes that 'an action to a knowing recipient can be embedded within an ongoing action to an unknowing recipient'. We shall note below, however, a point at which the poet clearly shifts his attention from his knowing to his unknowing audience.

[19] It is equivalent to the institutionalized lowering of lights today in the theatre, or to the raising of a curtain. On storytelling as performance (in the sense of a show), see E. Goffman, 'The Frame Analysis of Talk', *Frame Analysis: An Essay on the Organization of Experience* (Harmondsworth: Penguin, 1975), 508–9. Such framing practices, designed to demarcate the performance from everyday activity, are not universal. Stephen Wild observes that in the case of Australian Aboriginal dramatic performances (through which Aboriginal groups commonly present their myths), the dividing line between preparation for performance and performance itself is 'so blurred that it is impossible to establish unambiguously': see S. Wild, 'Australian Aboriginal Theatrical Movement', in B. Fleshman (ed.), *Theatrical Movement: A Bibliographical Anthology* (Metuchen, NJ: Scarecrow Press, 1986), 601–17, at 602.

[20] The poet's self-recommendation and his recommendation of his song are, as de Jong observes, 'indirect and unobtrusive'; but this is nevertheless the firm implication of the introductory appeal: see de Jong, *Narrators*, 52. See also Ford, 'Epic as Genre', 406. For examples of indirect evaluative cues which signal the

each proem he offers a bare outline of the story to come. This, indeed, is one of the functions of any such passage: to foreshadow the tale, or some aspect of it.[21]

As for the appeals which are made in the course of the narrative, when the poet turns to his Muse (as he does in the *Iliad*, five times in all), Homer's words, again, have some impact on and some relevance for his actual audience. In effect they recall his listeners, temporarily, from the story-world to the realm of performance. In implying that the Muse herself is present, the poet reminds his unknowing listeners, again, of the extraordinary nature of the performance in which they participate, and of the part he plays in the entertainment.[22] Furthermore, for those whose interest has been flagging, the appeal is a bid to re-engage their attention

potential interest of the tale, consider the significance of the name of the hero in *Il.* 1. 1, the quantitative expressions in 1. 2 and 3, μυρί' (thousandfold) and πολλὰς (in their multitudes), and the reference to the βουλή (the will) of Zeus (1. 5). Likewise, in the *Odyssey*, note the force of πολύς (much/many), used on four occasions (*Od.* 1. 1, 3, and 4) both as an adjective in its own right and in compounds. The poet claims that these are both stories about great men, whose deeds are on a grand scale: these are stories worth telling. The singer's opening words serve the same evaluative function as the printed programme in the theatre today (which, apart from displaying credentials and providing background information that assists us in evaluating the performance, offers us an outline of the tale). On the functions of such a document, see M. L. Pratt, *Towards a Speech-Act Theory of Literary Discourse* (Bloomington: Indiana University Press, 1977), 112–13.

[21] It is a feature of a well-formed story, in the Western tradition at least, that its content or point will be introduced by a résumé, or abstract, of some kind: see W. Labov, *Language in the Inner City: Studies in the Black English Vernacular* (Philadelphia: University of Pennsylvania Press, 1972), 363–4, for a discussion of this element of story structure; and see my comments in the Introduction, above, and Ch. 6, below. The invocation which introduces the *Odyssey* might appear to be a poor fit. I take up this problem below.

[22] We should note, however, that although he interrupts his story, he is not interrupting his performance: he does not allow the audience to return to the world of every day. I distinguish, that is, between the 'realm of performance' and the 'story-world'. For similar distinctions, but with different terminology, see K. G. Young, *Taleworlds and Storyrealms: The Phenomenology of Narrative* (Dordrecht: Martinus Nijhoff, 1987), 15–18; and see also S. Richardson, *The Homeric Narrator* (Nashville, Tenn.: Vanderbilt University Press, 1990). It is interesting to observe, too, that Homer represents in his song his change of focus, as he turns from one kind of listener to the other. Notice his shift of focus from the Muse back to his audience in *Iliad* 2, before he begins the Catalogue. With the end of his appeal in the second person (2. 487) he insists on his need for the support of the Muses in his great task. At this point he speaks about the Muses in the third person (488–92; see esp. 492: μνησαίαθ', [the Muses] remembered): he is addressing his unknowing audience again.

before a special moment in performance: the singer may be about to catalogue the troops which gather to resume battle (this, at 2. 494–759, will be a bravura performance); or he may be about to sing in another characteristic mode, a stretch of battle narrative (for example, the narrative of Agamemnon's victorious sweep through the Trojans at 11. 221–83; the list-like narrative of the Achaian surge at 14. 511–22; or the last contest, at 16. 114–22, before the firing of the ships).[23] In short, the effect of the invocation, *vis-à-vis* the unknowing recipients, is meta-narrational: it interrupts the story to comment on, or draw attention to, some aspect of the tale or its telling.

THE DISTRIBUTION OF HOMER'S APPEALS

But why are Homer's appeals to his Muse distributed as they are? The poet, as we have noted, calls upon her on six occasions in the *Iliad* and once only in the course of the *Odyssey*. Why might the poet turn so often to his Muse in one epic, when he does not do so in the other? Why does he turn to her only in the earlier and middle phases of his *Iliad*-story and not thereafter?[24]

Minton, indeed, poses these very questions. He observes that Homer's invocations in the *Iliad* draw the listener's attention to critical moments in the story; and he notes that

---

[23] On this point see Murray, 'Inspiration', 90–1. The invocation may precede those stretches of battle narrative which are list-like (as the heroes who join battle are in turn identified) or catalogue-like (since they include biographical information, as at *Il*. 11. 221–83). We may ask why an invocation should precede the brief listing of the best and bravest of the Achaians (and their horses) at *Il*. 2. 763–9. For this is an unremarkable list, as it stands. It is brief; and it ends abruptly with its perfunctory reference to Aias. On this see also G. S. Kirk, *The* Iliad: *A Commentary*, i (Cambridge: Cambridge University Press, 1985), 241. What is interesting, however, is that the list gives way to a fine set-piece describing the unfocused activities of Achilleus, his men, and their horses (771–9). This passage provides a striking contrast to the Catalogue of Ships which precedes it; and it may indeed have been with this in mind that the singer sang his invocation at 761–2. Kirk, however, would not agree: see his note on 779.

[24] For a discussion of the three phases of the *Iliad*-story, see O. Taplin, 'Exploratory Charts', *Homeric Soundings: The Shaping of the* Iliad (Oxford: Clarendon Press, 1992), ch. 1.

the invocation in many cases precedes a particular pattern of events characteristic of the *Iliad*, which he defines as crisis–struggle–defeat.[25] In his argument to support his case, Minton examines each appeal in its context with considerable sympathy for the text; his explanation for the distribution of such appeals, however, is not the 'far-reaching' explanation which he had promised.[26] Rather, as Minton sees it, an invocation has a limited, content-related, function. He uses the same argument to explain the lack of any but an introductory invocation in the *Odyssey*: as there are no sequences of crisis–struggle–defeat within the epic, no invocations occur in the body of the poem.[27] And, as for the proem-invocation of that epic, it is included only because it heralds a 'vestigial' pattern of crisis–struggle–defeat.

Like Thornton, I am not persuaded that Homer's invocations are related solely to narrative content.[28] If this were so, we might have expected to find further invocations after that of *Il*. 16. 112–13: why does the poet not invoke his Muse before his account of the fighting over the body of Patroklos, or as an introduction to the encounter between Hektor and Achilleus? What I am seeking, by contrast with Minton, is a rationale which recognizes the meta-narrational aspects of such appeals, and which accounts for the presence of invocations *before* a certain point in the performance and the absence of such appeals *after* that point. I am moving, that is, towards an account which is performance-based rather than content-based.

Let us reconsider these invocations, in terms now of their distribution across the narrative. Homer's addresses to his Muse precede special moments in performance, heralding sustained stretches of song marked by considerable detail, such as a list or a catalogue. Furthermore, we observe that the invocations of the *Iliad* occur as accompaniment to the rising tide of action: they occur only in that part of the narrative which precedes the turning-point of the poem.[29]

---

[25] See Minton, 'Homer's Invocations', 295–7.
[26] Ibid., 295.   [27] Ibid., 307–8.
[28] See Thornton, *Homer's* Iliad, 43–4 and n. 38.
[29] Cf. the discussion in Thornton, *Homer's* Iliad, 41–4. Here Thornton, like Minton, argues that invocations signal intensification and heightened excitement. She argues that invocations occur at crucial 'turns' in the action, when the singer

In the *Iliad* the last of Homer's invocations occurs at
16. 112–13; it precedes the narrative of the firing of the
ships. This is a long-awaited moment, foreshadowed by
Homer earlier in the narrative at several points. It is the
event which will generate a sequence already advertised: the
firing of the ships (foreshadowed at 9. 601–2, 650–3) will
lead to Patroklos' entry into battle (forecast at 15. 64–5); as a
result of this he will die (foreshadowed or forecast at 8. 475–
7; 11. 603–4; 15. 65–6); and his death will bring Achilleus
back to the fighting (see 2. 694; 8. 474; 15. 68). The firing of
the ships, therefore, changes the course of the narrative. It
sets it on the path towards resolution.[30] After this turning-
point Homer does not invoke his Muse again; he now
refrains from intruding into his song in this marked fashion.
What is the effect of his apparent withdrawal on the
audience—and on the song? Once the final stage of the
narrative is under way (that course of events which leads
towards its resolution), the poet does not distract his
listeners from the story-world again: he allows them to
become completely absorbed in what is happening there.
In short, he creates the impression that the story carries
itself, by its own momentum, to its close.

The poet, that is, turns to his Muse and acknowledges her
contribution to his performance during that long period
when he is setting up his story, when he is weaving together
its complications. This is the narrative element which Labov
and Waletzky describe as *complicating action*.[31] The poet, like
any storyteller, knows that he must proceed carefully here, if

'desires from the Muses the exciting touch of immediate present reality' (44). That
is (if we express this point in Goodwin's terms), the Muse, as a knowing recipient,
has a role to play in the telling, in supplying or confirming the detail that represents
authenticity. But Thornton considers the invocations to be amongst the song's
'more ornamental' features (59); she does not compare the Iliadic pattern of usage
with that of the *Odyssey*; she seeks no wider explanation for their presence in the
epics.

[30] This turning-point, in the *Iliad*, is at 16. 123–4. As Taplin, *Homeric
Soundings*, observes, it represents 'a major turning-point' (18). The poet himself
has marked out this moment as being structurally significant (see 9. 650–4; and see,
too, Taplin's commentary at 174–8 and in his Appendix, at 291).

[31] On the properties of storytelling, see W. Labov and J. Waletzky, 'Narrative
Analysis: Oral Versions of Personal Experience', in J. Helm (ed.), *Essays on the
Verbal and Visual Arts* (Seattle: University of Washington Press, 1967), 12–44, at
32–41; see also Labov, *Language*, ch. 9, and my Introduction, above.

he is to recall in plausible order the appropriate sequence of events, if he is to assemble the random details which will be significant to the plot, and if he is to present these sequences in an engaging fashion. Indeed, given that the *Iliad* is a monumental poem—a poem of measured pace in which progress toward the turning-point is postponed and post-poned again (through episodes such as Agamemnon's dream, the Diomedeia, the embassy to Achilleus, and through the several reversals initiated by divine intervention)—an audi-ence might conceivably become restless. For these reasons the poet, as responsible narrator and inspired singer, at selected moments acknowledges the support of his Muse and thereby reminds his listeners that this is a song which will reward their patience. These invocations, therefore, mark special moments in performance. But they do not mark them all. Homer is careful not to use this device to excess. What is significant about the distribution of these appeals to the Muse is that it appears to indicate that the poet himself distinguished between the so-called complicating action of his tale (where he might interrupt his story to appeal to his Muse, thereby encouraging his audience to stay with him) and its path of resolution (when he might be confident that the steady movement of the narrative towards its end-point would hold his audience's interest; to break into the story here would be to distract the audience from the intensity of the moment).[32] The very distribution of Homer's addresses to his Muse might, therefore, be used as evidence that the scripted story format which Homer used was very similar to our own; and that Homer, whether instinctively or, as is more probable, as a result of observation and reflection, had a sound grasp of the principles of good storytelling.

HOMER'S 'FADED' INVOCATIONS

Running parallel with Homer's appeals to his Muse in the *Iliad* are a number of second-person addresses of some

[32] As Lodge observes, when the narrator calls attention to the act of narrating, the emotional intensity of the experience being represented is at that moment reduced: see D. Lodge, *The Art of Fiction* (London: Secker and Warburg, 1992), 10.

relevance to this discussion—the so-called 'faded' invocations.[33] The poet's question at 5. 703–4:

> Ἔνθα τίνα πρῶτον, τίνα δ' ὕστατον ἐξενάριξαν
> Ἕκτωρ τε Πριάμοιο πάϊς καὶ χάλκεος Ἄρης

Who then was the first and who the last that they slaughtered,
Hektor, Priam's son, and Ares the brazen?

is similar in form to the questions which we ourselves utter in mid-narrative, when we voice a question which we might have posed to a knowing recipient, and promptly respond to that same question ('Now who was there? I can tell you, it was. . .' or, as in the lines cited from Homer, 'Who, then, was the first and who the last that they slaughtered? It was . . .'). The same type of question–answer sequence is realized in Homer's questions at 8. 273:

> Ἔνθα τίνα πρῶτον Τρώων ἕλε Τεῦκρος ἀμύμων;

Then which of the Trojans first did Teukros the blameless
strike down?

and 11. 299–300:

> Ἔνθα τίνα πρῶτον, τίνα δ' ὕστατον ἐξενάριξεν
> Ἕκτωρ Πριαμίδης

Who then was the first, and who the last that he slaughtered,
Hektor, Priam's son

I agree with Minton, Edwards, and de Jong that we should read these pseudo-exchanges as being directed to the Muse.[34] First, the question in its form and in its function (for it will elicit a list-like response), is very similar to the question which concludes the poet's invocation to his Muse at *Il.* 1. 8:

---

[33] 'Faded' invocations are to be found at *Il.* 5. 703–4; 8. 273; 11. 299–300: cf. Minton, 'Invocation and Catalogue', 208–9. On such passages see also Minton, 'Homer's Invocations', 304 (note that Minton here wrongly identifies the invocation of *Il.* 16. 692–3 as one of this type); M. Edwards, *The* Iliad: *A Commentary*, v (Cambridge: Cambridge University Press, 1991), 3. These invocations are indeed faded. Not only is the identity of the addressee passed over, but the appeal which otherwise defines an invocation is also absent.

[34] See Minton, 'Invocation and Catalogue', at 208–9; Edwards, *The* Iliad: *A Commentary*, v, 3; and de Jong, *Narrators*, 45–50. Not all scholars agree, however: see Kirk, *The* Iliad: *A Commentary*, ii (Cambridge: Cambridge University Press, 1990), on 8. 273–6: 'a question not necessarily addressed to the Muse(s)'. Kirk does not propose an alternative.

Τίς τ' ἄρ σφωε θεῶν ἔριδι ξυνέηκε μάχεσθαι;

What god was it then set them together in bitter collision?

Second, the poet relies on the Muse for all other information which he seeks. It would be remarkable if he were to refer to and draw on a second source without due acknowledgment. It is significant, too, that these faded invocations are distributed across the poem in exactly the same way as the full invocations discussed above. The poet uses them to punctuate the narrative (and to communicate with his audience in the indirect ways described above) as he develops the complications of the tale; he refrains from using even these almost incidental forms in the course of its resolution. No faded invocation interrupts the poem after its turning-point.[35] From this moment the story proceeds steadily to its conclusion, through its cycle of violence, pain, and reconciliation, without any intrusion of this kind on the poet's part.

THE PROEM TO THE *ODYSSEY*

If we turn to the *Odyssey* we find a structure somewhat different from that of the *Iliad*. The proem to the epic almost immediately precedes what is, in fact, the turning-point of Homer's Odysseus-story. The proem (*Od.* 1. 1–21) ends with a reference to Poseidon's hostility to Odysseus.[36] And, with a smooth transition, the tale itself begins. Poseidon's

---

[35] It is relevant to mention Homer's use of apostrophe at this point. For Homer continues to address his characters in the story-world *after* the turning-point of the narrative. But there is no inconsistency here, as the poet (when he apostrophizes one of his characters—be it Patroklos, Menelaos, or Eumaios) is not taking his listeners out of the story-world—he is joining them in it. For further discussion of apostrophe in Homer, see E. Block, 'The Narrator Speaks: Apostrophe in Homer and Vergil', *TAPA* 112 (1982), 7–22.

[36] This fact (19–21), along with the information that all the other heroes who had escaped Troy by now had reached home (11–12), that Odysseus was at this point being detained by Kalypso (13–15), and that despite Poseidon's hostility, all the other gods were sympathetic, is a neat summary of essential background information essential to our understanding of the current situation and of some of the themes of the epic as a whole. Labov and Waletzky refer to this kind of information as 'orientation': see Labov and Waletzky, 'Narrative Analysis', 32–41, and my Introduction, above.

temporary absence from the halls of Zeus is noted: this absence allows Zeus, at Athene's prompting, to decree that the hero should be brought home (1. 76–9):[37]

ἀλλ' ἄγεθ', ἡμεῖς οἵδε περιφραζώμεθα πάντες
νόστον, ὅπως ἔλθῃσι·

But come, let all of us who are here work out his homecoming and see to it that he returns.

This is the turning-point. All that happens in the *Odyssey* from this moment on represents the resolution of the tale. Even the long digression into the past which reconstructs the events in the story-world that precede Zeus' decision in Odysseus' favour (Odysseus' own tale of his wanderings as far as Kalypso's isle, *Od.* 9–12) is woven into the resolution of the narrative. If my conclusions about Homer's use of the invocations in the *Iliad* have any validity, and given the unusual structure of the *Odysseus*-story (in which the resolution of the tale, to use Labov and Waletzky's terminology, begins at 1. 81), we should not expect that Homer will address his Muse again. And he does not.

The poet's depiction in the *Odyssey* of his relationship with his Muse has been analysed by a number of scholars.[38] Commentary on the proem has drawn to our attention the somewhat unsatisfactory nature of the content of the invocation which is at its head (1. 1–10), in its incomplete survey of the story as a whole, its imprecision, its inaccuracy, and its undue emphasis on one event, the slaughter of the cattle of Helios.[39] But these apparent insufficiencies may be viewed in another light: as remarkable features. The poet's suppression of Odysseus' name, the ambiguous epithet (πολύτροπον, resourceful) by which he is described at 1. 1, the poet's focus on the slaughter of the cattle of Helios, and his partisan stance all suggest a new concept of heroic song.[40] Even

[37] On the transition, see K. Rüter, *Odysseeinterpretationen: Untersuchungen zum ersten Buch und zur Phaiakis* (Göttingen: Vandenhoeck and Ruprecht, 1969), 53.
[38] See Clay, *Wrath*, ch. 1; Dimock, *Unity*, 5–13; Segal, *Singers*, ch. 6; V. Pedrick, 'The Muse Corrects: The Opening of the *Odyssey*', YCS 29 (1992), 39–62.
[39] See, by way of summary, West's valuable note on *Od.* 1. 1–10 in A. Heubeck, S. West, J. B. Hainsworth, *A Commentary on Homer's* Odyssey, i (Oxford: Clarendon Press, 1988), 67–9.
[40] For discussion, see Pedrick, 'The Muse Corrects', 43–50.

though this story-line will run in accord with a traditional agenda, that of the *nostos*-tale (the story of the homeward journey of a hero), it will be a story of a new kind. This is not simply an adventure-story; it is to be a song which will attempt to define its hero and, in that process, to explore his mind.

Two particular features of the poet's invocation are relevant to the present discussion. Both relate to the poet's words, τῶν ἁμόθεν γε, θεά, θύγατηρ Διός, εἰπὲ καὶ ἡμῖν (from some point here, goddess, daughter of Zeus, speak, and begin our story, 1. 10), his instruction to the Muse to begin the song at about the point where Odysseus' men slaughter the cattle of Helios. Notice that the poet feels no need to tell this particular *nostos*-story from the logical starting-point— that is, from its beginning. He asserts that the story he is about to tell will start *in medias res*. And, given that he identifies this advanced moment in the narrative as his point of departure, he gives us further insight into his knowledge of the construction of stories. We can conclude that he understands something of the flexibility of story structure and, on the other hand, of the constraints such flexibility imposes.

The invocation suggests that our poet knows that a story need not follow the order of events. He knows that he has some discretion in his presentation: he can postpone certain key events in the interests of suspense; he can omit certain key information in order to arouse curiosity.[41] And he knows that it is possible to use special techniques (in this case Odysseus' first person 'flashback' narrative) to return the audience to earlier events in the storyline.[42] Finally, he is aware that, although a successful story may begin anywhere along that chain of events which I have called complicating action, it may not begin later, that is, after the turning-point. Indeed, Homer's Muse selects a starting-point which is different from that which the poet at first proposed. She urges him

---

[41] See W. Brewer and E. Lichtenstein, 'Stories are to Entertain: A Structural-Affect Theory of Stories', *Journal of Pragmatics*, 6 (1982), 473–86. For further discussion, see Epilogue, below.

[42] For a note on Homer's possible pride in his flashback technique, see Heubeck, West, and Hainsworth, *The Odyssey: A Commentary*, i, 72.

to begin the telling at the latest possible point along the chain of complicating action, with its last event. If we were to seek a reason for this choice, the fact that she urges this last possible point is the key. It is not a poetic motive which is the guiding factor here; rather it is a pragmatic motive.[43] The poet accepts her advice. This is the confident choice of a bold storyteller who well understands how to manipulate his story material to the best advantage.

It is noteworthy that it is the poet himself who has initiated the move to begin his telling in the middle of things. Here we see the poet as sometimes proactive in a relationship which is, as I have remarked above, otherwise deferential. And yet his proactivity is modified by the apparent casualness of τῶν ἁμόθεν γε (from some point here, *Od.* 1. 10). These words, however, are not deliberately offhand. Rather, they represent a further instance of the slight hesitation that a storyteller feels in the presence of the listener who knows. The poet is not so assertive that he will urge the Muse to start at a particular point. His contribution to this novel presentation has been the proposal that the tale start at a point other than the beginning. It is for the Muse to select the appropriate place.

My reading of the remainder of the proem of the *Odyssey* has been much influenced by Pedrick's recent study of this passage, in which she develops an idea proposed by Dimock, that the verses which follow the invocation (1. 11–21) represent a response by the Muse to the proposal which the poet has set out in his invocation.[44] As she says, '[T]he proem of the *Odyssey*, and in particular the request for a starting point in verse 10, are unusual and powerful enough to create the illusion that this narrator has a problem on his hands which needs the Muse's help'.[45] What we have, therefore, in lines 1–21 is the report of a consultation between poet and Muse, in which he (at 1–10) puts himself into a 'posture of needing correction'; and she responds with amendments to his

---

[43] On the contrast, see Segal, *Singers*, at 140. For discussion, see Clay, *Wrath*, at 39–53; Pedrick, 'The Muse Corrects', 52 (where Pedrick observes that the late start allows the poet to include the *Telemachy*).

[44] See Dimock, *Unity*, at 12–13: he reads *Od.* 1. 11–21 as the words of the Muse—not of the poet inspired by the Muse.

[45] See Pedrick, 'The Muse Corrects', 41.

proposal.[46] There is, however, no change of speaker through-out the proem: it is the poet/narrator who gives voice to the Muse's response. The effect of this negotiation, according to Pedrick, is to point up the power of the goddess. This is true. But I find it useful, too, to read this negotiation as a consultation modelled on real-life interaction. It parallels, in today's terms, the kind of negotiation that we witness in academic life between an advanced student (who tentatively proposes an expression of ideas which he or she has developed) and a supervisor (his or her knowing listener, who, being more experienced, responds, suggesting a more effective way of achieving the same end).[47] Indeed, as we have noted, the Muse modifies the poet's proposal in several ways: in the choice of starting-point, in the structure and focus of the projected story, and in the introduction of new and relevant information which provides a smooth transition for the poet into the song proper (at 22).[48] But, on the whole, she is in sympathy with the poet's project of defining and exploring his hero. This is confirmed by the irony with which she imitates the singer's reluctance, in his invocation, to mention Odysseus by name. Throughout her segment of the proem she refers to the hero obliquely, by means of the pronoun: through τόν (13), οἱ (17), and οἷσι (19). Only at verse 21, as she brings the proem to its end, does she name the hero. It is this deliberate restraint on her part which makes the vignette complete: an artfully contrived portrayal of the collaborative relationship between poet and Muse.[49]

THE MARGINALIZED MUSE

Does Homer's failure to address his Muse again in the *Odyssey* imply that he has ceased to communicate with her, or she with him? To be sure, because of the structure

---

[46] See Pedrick, 'The Muse Corrects', 42–3.

[47] Thus we have exchanges marked by hesitation, such as 'I am thinking of starting with this', which is, in effect, a request for confirmation or amendment from the knowing listener.

[48] As Pedrick notes, the Muse's proposals are 'radical but in a real sense complementary': see Pedrick, 'The Muse Corrects', 57.

[49] For comment in a similar vein, see ibid., 58–9.

of his story, the poet refrains from consulting the omniscient
Muse in the course of his tale: in effect, he marginalizes her.
As a consequence, the way is open for him to promote
himself as poet and to recommend his skills as creative
artist. He seizes the opportunity. The singer of the *Odyssey*
integrates his professional preoccupations, with poetry, with
the nature of narrative, and with the pragmatics of performance, into his song. At several points he describes the telling
of a story; he offers his listeners a demonstration of his own
understanding of the performative context within which he
works. He recreates with care the efforts of a storyteller to
tell an engaging tale and some of the possible responses,
non-verbal and verbal, of his listeners. That is, the poet's
self-consciousness becomes part of—indeed, it is one of the
themes of—his own performance.[50] And yet the Muse is not
entirely forgotten. Although she is not drawn into the
singer's performance, she is acknowledged in other ways,
on the lips of others: notably, in Odysseus' tribute to
Demodokos and his Muse (8. 479–81) and in Phemios'
reminder to Odysseus of the Muse's contribution to his
song, at 22. 347–8:

> θεὸς δέ μοι ἐν φρεσὶν οἴμας
παντοίας ἐνέφυσεν.

> but the god has inspired in me the song-ways
of every kind.

Homer's invocations are not, as Minton suggests, linked
with the content of his tales. Nor are they distributed at
random through his songs. My discussion has demonstrated
that there is across the two epics a discernible pattern of
usage, which is performance-related. The invocations arise
naturally as a consequence of the ancients' belief that the
Muse was the source of inspiration for epic song. The poet
appeals to his Muse as he puts his story together. He
appeals to her because she has seen and, therefore, knows,
and because it is the common communicative practice to

---

[50] For further discussion, with examples, see Macleod, 'Homer on Poetry';
W. Suerbaum, 'Die Ich-Erzählungen des Odysseus', *Poetica*, 2 (1968), 150–77;
Pedrick, 'The Muse Corrects', 42, at n. 13; Segal, *Singers*, 126–34. And see
Epilogue, below.

defer to a knowing recipient. The Homeric invocation, even as it confirms a relationship between singer and Muse, also plays a role in mediating relations between singer and audience. In its meta-narrational function it makes comments on poetic inspiration, on the cultural importance of what is to be transmitted in song, and on the skills of the performer. And it offers a muted commentary on the progress of the narrative as it moves from the development of its complications to the turning-point which precedes its resolution. It is the poet's reluctance to break into the narrative after this point which is significant, as it indicates that the singer himself was fully cognizant of the scripted format which underlies storytelling of all kinds; it testifies to his 'sense of story'.

6

The Story Format and the Generation of 'Rings'

This chapter returns to a topic raised in my Introduction and developed in Chapter 3: the topic of memory expertise. There I discussed how we acquire expertise in routine tasks, how we store information about those tasks in memory, and how we access it. As we have already observed, expertise of this kind is retained in procedural or implicit memory as a 'table' or a 'format':[1] the format will provide a series of cues to action. This is so even in the case of verbal tasks, such as trying to persuade someone to undertake a particular course of action; rebuking someone for something he or she has done (or failed to do); refusing an invitation; giving a description of a personal possession; or telling a story. The format will not prompt words or phrases; it prompts a sequence of actions.

In this chapter the presentation of stories in Homer will be under consideration once again: in particular, the format which underpins the telling of a story, some aspects of which we considered in Chapter 5. I shall use the results of research in the fields of linguistics and cognitive psychology to re-examine the story format which we all use both in casual conversation and on more formal occasions; and to propose a way by which we might understand a particular surface pattern in narrative texts from the ancient world which has caught the interest of classicists. This is the pattern which we have come to know as 'ring composition'.

---

[1] See above, Introduction, 'Is there a Script for Storytelling?'; and Ch. 3.

RING COMPOSITION: THE TERM AND
ITS APPLICATION

It is only in the last fifty years that scholars have become familiar with the concept of ring composition.[2] The term itself, ring composition, describes a certain arrangement of elements within a unit of discourse such as a story or a digression within a story.[3] When the same element, the same idea, or the same notion, appears at the beginning and at the end of a story, this repetition has been identified as a ring; when a number of elements within the unit are handled individually in a certain sequence (A, B, C . . .) and then rehandled in the reverse order (. . . C, B, A), the outcome is a number of rings. In either case, scholars have referred to the style which generates such ringlike patterns in a text as ring composition.

Most scholars today hold that ring composition is a premeditated pattern appearing on the surface of the text, and that this symmetrical ordering of material serves a mnemonic or an aesthetic function.[4] Many also believe that

---

[2] For an account of early observations of ring composition see D. Lohmann, *Die Komposition der Reden in der Ilias* (Berlin: de Gruyter, 1970), 5–7.

[3] For commentary on the device and examples, see W. van Otterlo, *De Ringcompositie als Opbouwprincipe in de Epische Gedichten van Homerus* (Amsterdam: Noord-Hollandsche Uitg. Mij., 1948); J. Notopoulos, 'Continuity and Interconnexion in Homeric Oral Composition', *TAPA* 82 (1951), 81–101; B. A. van Groningen, *La Composition littéraire archaïque grecque: Procédés et réalisations* (Amsterdam: Noord-Hollandsche Uitg. Mij., 1958), 51–6. See also F. Cairns, *Tibullus: A Hellenistic Poet at Rome* (Cambridge: Cambridge University Press, 1979), 193–202 (note Cairns's useful bibliography of ring composition at 194); W. Thalmann, *Conventions of Form and Thought in Early Greek Epic Poetry* (Baltimore and London: The Johns Hopkins University Press, 1984), ch. 1.

[4] According to Notopoulos, 'Continuity and Interconnexion', 97–8, it is a 'stylistic device', a 'consciously applied principle of composition'. Cairns, *Tibullus*, 195–6, claims that these formal thematic structures 'are, in origin, mnemonic features of oral poetry', which helped the poet in the arrangement of his material (in non-narrative sections and over longer sections of narrative) and helped the audience to follow him. See also B. Fenik, *Homer and the Niebelungenlied: Comparative Studies in Epic Style* (Cambridge, Mass.: Harvard University Press, 1986), 98, on ring composition as 'an arbitrary configuration'; and Lohmann, *Die Komposition der Reden*, 7–8, on ring composition as 'ein poetisches Kompositionsprinzip', and as ' "rhetorische" Kunstmittel'. J. Gaisser, 'A Structural Analysis of Digressions in the *Iliad* and the *Odyssey*', *HSCP* 73 (1969), 1–43, at 42, sees ring composition as both practical (in that it allows short passages to be inserted into the narrative and indicates the beginning and the end of a digression) and decorative.

ring composition is confined to the ancient world, that it is no longer practised; or, indeed, if it is practised still, we see it only in traditional songs and ballads.[5] Edwards' note on the device (in the context of Homeric epic) epitomizes these views: '[o]f the small scale structural devices which are used to order the presentation of material in Homer, ring composition is probably the least familiar to us and the hardest to appreciate without giving it our special attention'.[6]

But is the structure unfamiliar, or difficult to appreciate? Fowler makes the unsettling proposal that ring composition is 'perhaps one of the most obvious and psychologically natural ways of organizing material', in both oral and written composition.[7] Although he offers little discussion to corroborate his intuitions, his comment deserves further consideration for two reasons: first, because the view which he proposes is quite different from the common view of the device; and, second, because there is a body of evidence which will support his claim.

A STUDY OF STORYTELLING IN CONVERSATION

Let us examine ring composition—or what we classicists call ring composition—in the light of that study of the activity of storytelling, conducted by William Labov and

[5] Van Groningen, *La Composition littéraire*, 24: 'les procédés littéraires d'un autre peuple et d'un autre âge ne sont pas forcément les nôtres'. For a summary of the later history of ring composition, see Cairns, *Tibullus*, 196. David Rubin observes that ring composition is common in ballads, epic, and other oral traditions: D. Rubin, *Memory in Oral Traditions: The Cognitive Psychology of Epic, Ballads, and Counting-out Rhymes* (New York and Oxford: Oxford University Press, 1995), 274–8, at 274.

[6] M. Edwards, *The Iliad: A Commentary*, v (Cambridge: Cambridge University Press, 1991), 44. Edwards' comment is echoed by Rubin, *Memory*, at 275: he notes that ring structures are difficult to apply in a simple and mechanical fashion to ballads, because they require a sophisticated interpretation of the ballad. He goes on: 'Although this makes the ring structure difficult to use in a detailed quantitative fashion suitable for an experimental psychology journal, the evidence presented is clear enough to convince most sceptics that ring composition is a good description of many ballads.' I remain sceptical.

[7] See R. Fowler, *The Nature of Early Greek Lyric: Three Preliminary Studies* (Toronto: University of Toronto Press, 1987), 61–2. He adds, without further comment: 'one will hear examples [of ring composition] in any normal conversation'.

Joshua Waletzky, referred to in earlier chapters.[8] The outcome of this review should persuade us that the generation of rings is not a phenomenon confined to ancient literature; it is part of all oral storytelling, or at least of oral storytelling in our own culture, even today; and that the ringlike pattern which we associate with stories and episodes of stories is not the product of a ring-shaped template (which imposes formal constraints on the storyteller), nor is it a mnemonic device. Rather, this pattern which we observe in oral storytelling is an outcome of a storyteller's efforts to present his or her story in an acceptable and effective form.

Labov and Waletzky's research reveals that most oral anecdotes in our own tradition share a number of formal properties and reveal a common framework, namely, a structure or a format which we recreate automatically when we tell stories. It is likely that few of us are aware that our stories conform to a structural pattern; but we recognize these properties as soon as they are brought to our attention. Although I gave a brief overview of this framework in my Introduction, I shall describe it once again, using Labov and Waletzky's terminology for the most part, since I propose now to modify their identification of two properties critical to my discussion in this chapter. Then I shall analyse a number of stories from the ancient world to see whether they too might have been constructed in this way. Since we have in the Homeric epics examples of stories which were composed orally, and since Homeric ring patterns have been extensively studied, it is appropriate that a review of ring composition in the context of storytelling should begin with some stories from Homer.[9] Finally, I propose a tentative explanation for the development in a written context of the rhetorical figure which we call ring composition.

---

[8] See W. Labov and J. Waletzky, 'Narrative Analysis: Oral Versions of Personal Experience', in J. Helm (ed.), *Essays on the Verbal and Visual Arts* (Seattle: University of Washington Press, 1967), 12–44.

[9] Such patterns have been identified in other texts, such as those of Pindar or Thucydides. My intention at this point is to examine the practices of an early, oral storyteller and to compare them with the practices of oral storytellers today.

THE FORMAL PROPERTIES OF ORAL ANECDOTES

First, let us look at the formal properties of storytelling, as Labov and Waletzky describe them. When a storyteller sets out to tell a story, he or she is most likely to begin with a segment which Labov and Waletzky call an *abstract*. Storytellers may use their abstract in two ways. When someone says, 'Listen to this!' or 'Have I got something to tell you!', he is giving notice that he wants to tell a story, and that it may be some time before his listeners have a chance to speak again; that is, he is negotiating for the attention of his prospective audience. On the other hand, the storyteller may use his abstract as a guide to his listeners—as a summary or an evaluation of the story which he is going to tell.[10] The following are examples of abstracts of this second kind: 'Jim and Maria had to get a silent number'; 'I failed the test for my driver's licence'; 'I've had a terrible day'. The term 'abstract', in other words, covers two functions, each of which has a different focus. These two functions should be distinguished formally: we should recognize the frame of discourse as a significant element separate from the discourse itself. I use Polanyi's term, *entrance talk*, to describe the preliminary negotiation which goes on between the would-be story-teller and his potential audience.[11] The term *abstract*, therefore, can be reserved for that other, story-related function of the introductory segment: it will mark the

---

[10] For commentary on introductory clauses of this kind as a phenomenon peculiar to archaic poetry and a reflection of an archaic way of thinking, see van Groningen, *La Composition littéraire*, 62–9.

[11] For a detailed account of openings and closings as the means by which storytellers take their listeners from the real world of casual talk into a story-realm (in which a story is to be communicated) and, ultimately, return them to the real world, see K. G. Young, *Taleworlds and Storyrealms: The Phenomenology of Narrative* (Dordrecht: Martinus Nijhoff, 1987), 31–6. For discussion of how such transitions may occur, see G. Jefferson, 'Sequential Aspects of Storytelling in Conversation', in J. Schenkein (ed.), *Studies in the Organization of Conversational Interaction* (New York: Academic Press, 1978), 219–48. The terms *entrance talk* (or opening) and *exit talk* (on this closing element, see below) are suggested by L. Polanyi, 'Literary Complexity in Everyday Storytelling', in D. Tannen (ed.), *Spoken and Written Language* (Norwood, NJ: Ablex, 1982), 155–70.

clause or the clauses which indicate the scope or the point of the tale.

Entrance talk and abstract are regularly followed by one or more clauses which convey background information essential to the story. Without information of this kind the listener will not be able to make sense of the narrative which follows. Labov and Waletzky describe this segment as *orientation*. In the anecdotes which I am constructing, the following units might serve as orientation: 'Maria had been at home by herself'; 'I had been trying to park the car'; 'It was raining and I didn't have an umbrella'. It is not necessary, however, that all such material be presented *en bloc*; some information can be interwoven with the narrative: 'Maria went to answer the phone: she was at home by herself.'

The narrative proper comprises the clauses which report the events of the story. The clauses which precede the resolution of the tale (I discuss this element below) are described by Labov and Waletzky as the *complication* or *complicating action*, a term which I introduced in my discussion, in Chapter 5, of Homer's distribution of invocations through his epics. In the Western tradition a storyteller aims to communicate a particular temporal and causal sequence, but he may not always report the events and actions of the complicating action in the order in which they occurred.[12] When he chooses to leap ahead to later events, he will at some point in his narrative backtrack to fill in the omitted details which are necessary to the tale: Homer's *Odyssey* is an example of this kind of complex structure. The final event in this narrative sequence is its *resolution*, that is, the end-point of the chain of action which the storyteller is reporting: 'And so they asked for a silent number'; 'He told me that I'd failed the test'; 'And everything is wet: my clothes, my shoes, and my papers'.

---

[12] For temporal sequence as the basis of storytelling in a Western tradition, see Labov and Waletzky, 'Narrative Analysis', at 20–32. Temporal sequence is not, however, a universal characteristic of narrative structure: see L. Polanyi, 'So What's the Point?', *Semiotica*, 25 (1979), 207–41, at 208–9; A. L. Becker, 'Text-building, Epistemology, and Aesthetics in Javanese Shadow Theatre', in A. L. Becker and A. Yengoyan (eds.), *The Imagination of Reality: Essays in Southeast Asian Coherence Systems* (Norwood, NJ: Ablex, 1979), 211–43, at 216–20.

The story itself may end at this point, with the concluding event of the narrative. There is nothing more to tell.[13] But a storyteller may wish to confirm the point of the tale, or in some way to tie things off. In order to fulfil the first goal, storytellers often reiterate the resolution of the narrative; or they may comment on the action. And to fulfil the second, they will formally seal off the storytelling, perhaps opening a pathway back into the conversation which the story had suspended. Labov and Waletzky call these clauses the *coda*. Again, as in the case of the abstract, the coda may be subdivided into two categories. I use *coda* to describe that segment of the tale which pulls the story together: the resolution is reiterated or the action is evaluated. And it might take this form: 'So they have a silent number'; 'It was a frustrating experience'. I use Polanyi's term *exit talk* to describe the segment which bridges the gap between the events of the story and the present time or which notifies the audience that the performance is over: 'I just thought I'd let you know'; 'So I'm still catching the bus'; 'Now I'm going to find some dry clothes'.

A well-formed story, therefore, may proceed in the following fashion: entrance talk, abstract, orientation, complicating action, resolution, coda, exit talk.[14] Each of these elements may appear in any anecdote, but they are not all obligatory. When we tell stories to a few friends, for example, we may not feel it necessary to use entrance talk: we may be sufficiently confident of their supportive interest to launch directly into our abstract. Or, if we tell a story in response to a leading question or a leading remark, even an abstract may be unnecessary.[15] And, as has been noted

[13] Cf. van Groningen, *La Composition littéraire*, 70: 'on cesse quand on a traité le dernier morceau de la série, quand on n'a plus rien de nouveau à dire'.

[14] I have not discussed one further element which Labov and Waletzky identify: *evaluation*. This element, unlike those which I have described above, has no fixed place within the story (although evaluative comment often appears immediately before the resolution of the narrative). When evaluative information appears in the abstract, it may well appear also in the coda. On the evaluative element in any story, see Labov and Waletzky, 'Narrative Analysis', 33–9. See also my discussion, in Ch. 3, above, of Homer's evaluative strategies.

[15] On this point, see Jefferson, 'Sequential Aspects of Storytelling'; S. Ervin-Tripp and A. Küntay, 'The Occasioning and Structure of Conversational Stories', in T. Givón (ed.), *Conversation: Cognitive, Communicative and Social Perspectives* (Amsterdam and Philadelphia: J. Benjamins, 1997), 133–66, esp. at 161–2. And see below.

above, a story may well end with its resolution: it may lack both coda and exit talk. We may omit any of these elements, if we judge that our story in this form will be acceptable to our audience. We would have included them if we had felt that our audience needed them—and we may include them at another telling.[16] Indeed, if we were to tell a story in more formal circumstances to a wider audience, we would include most of the elements which have been described above. Our aim in incorporating those elements which surround the narrative proper is clearly pragmatic: we use the outer framing elements (entrance talk and exit talk) and the introductory and closing segments (abstract and coda) to ensure that our story gets a hearing and that our listeners will appreciate its point. These peripheral elements address the needs of the storyteller, who wishes his or her story to be a success, and of the audience, who must be given a certain amount of assistance if its members are to understand the narrative as the speaker intends. We decide which elements we should include on the basis of our assessment of the state of mind of our listeners and in the light of what we have learned about the structure of stories, through listening, imitation, guidance, and practice, over the years.

What is important in the context of this chapter is that this story format, when it is fully exploited within any one tale, opens the way to repetition or near repetition of words or of themes. It is possible that we might find a correspondence between entrance talk and exit talk (the elements which focus on the storyteller/audience relationship), or between the elements which introduce the narrative and bring it to an end: abstract and resolution, or abstract and coda.[17] When such correspondences between introductory and concluding

[16] A second telling of the same story may well be different in some formal respects (and in some of the details communicated), if the storyteller perceives that the new audience has different needs and expectations from those of his original audience. For discussion, see e.g. L. Polanyi, 'On Telling the Same Story Twice', *Text*, 1 (1981), 315–36, esp. 319–26.

[17] Such repetition may be useful when the storyteller is returning to the main narrative from a detour or a lengthy expansion (cf. Gaisser, 'A Structural Analysis', 42). But even if the resolution or coda does not repeat the theme of the abstract (which initiated the digression or the episode), the very presence of such an element acts as a sign that the detour or the episode is being terminated and informs the listener that he is being returned to the narrative proper.

elements occur in oral anecdotes, they are more likely to be the outcome of audience-directed strategy rather than a conscious embellishment of the narrative. It is equally possible, however, that we may find no correspondence between these introductory and closing elements. For example, when an abstract *evaluates* the events of the story and the resolution *reports* the outcome, there is no correspondence. Nevertheless, the story has an identifiable beginning and end: it is a well-formed story.

This analysis of everyday storytelling as we know it indicates that certain patterns, which remind us of the patterns of ring composition, may be produced in the normal course of storytelling. The story format can produce the equivalent of two rings within a single story—and more, if self-contained episodes or digressions are embedded within it.

STORIES IN HOMER: PATTERNS OF CORRESPONDENCE

Can we relate this everyday format to Homeric storytelling? Do these patterns of correspondence which we have observed in informal discourse throw some light on Homeric ring composition? With this possibility in mind, I turn to some of Homer's stories: to some episodes from the narrative of the *Iliad* and to some stories which Homer's characters themselves tell in the course of the narrative. I shall analyse these in terms of the story format which has been described above (a complete account of these episodes is provided in the accompanying Table); then I shall consider the implications of what we find.

At *Il.* 11. 91–100, Homer tells the story of the death of Oïleus. The poet begins this episode with an abstract. This is appropriate: he is moving from a general statement about the movement of battle to a specific sequence of events, the death of Bienor (which is noted but not described) and that of his companion. The key to the abstract is Ἀγαμέμνων . . . ἔλε . . . Ὀϊλῆα (Agamemnon killed Oïleus, 91–3). Within this abstract there is a certain amount of background material

TABLE 4: The Framework of Four Tales from Homer's *Iliad*
           (11. 91–100; 5. 541–60; 11. 670–762; 24. 602–13)

Il. 11. 91–100

91–3	abstract	Agamemnon killed (Bienor and) Oïleus
93	orientation	he was the companion of Bienor, the charioteer
94–8	complication	he faced Agamemnon, but Agamemnon stabbed him with his spear, which pierced his helmet
98	resolution	and killed him
99–100	coda	Agamemnon stripped him (and Bienor) and left their bodies exposed

Il. 5. 541–60

541–2	abstract	Aineias killed Krethon and Orsilochos
543–9	orientation	family background: four generations of the family line
550–8	complication	they reached Troy; they fought like lions
559	resolution	they were overcome by Aineias
560	coda	and they fell

Il. 11. 670–762

670–1	entrance talk	I wish I were young and strong as when
671–2	abstract	I killed Itymoneus in a quarrel
673–4	orientation	I was driving cattle which I had seized
674	complication	he defended them
675	resolution (a)	and was struck down by me; he fell
676	coda	and his people fled in fear
677–81	complication	we drove off many head of cattle and
682	resolution (b)	took them to Pylos
683–4	coda	I was young and did well; my father rejoiced
685–8	abstract	the spoil was divided
689–93:	orientation:	the Pylians had been worsted by the Epeians
689	abstract	the Pylians had been worsted
690	orientation	Herakles had come
690–3	complication	and killed the bravest of the Pylians
694–5	resolution	the Epeians despised us and committed outrageous acts against us
696–7	abstract	Neleus took many head of cattle as compensation
698–702:	orientation:	the reason for his anger:
698–9	abstract	a wrong was done Neleus in connection with his horses
700–1	orientation	they were on the way to a race
701–2	resolution	Augeias kept them
702	coda	and sent away the driver
703–5	resolution	Neleus, in anger, took a great deal of plunder and he gave the rest to the people
706–7	coda	so we administered the spoils and made sacrifice
707–17	complication	the Epeians came against us, with the Moliones; they laid siege to Thryoessa; Athene came to us and gathered an army
717–19	resolution	but Neleus would not let me go
720–1	abstract	but I distinguished myself in battle
722–3	orientation	by the river Alpheios
723–37	complication	the actions which preceded battle; the beginning of battle

738–46:	resolution (i):	Nestor was the first to kill a man:
738	abstract	I was first to kill a man and win his horses
738–41	orientation	Moulios' background
742	complication	he came on and I struck him
743–4	resolution	he fell in the dust and I took his horses
744–6	coda	the Epeians ran in terror
747–9	complication	I charged and took 50 chariots
750–2	resolution (ii)	I would have killed the Moliones, but for the Earthshaker
753–8	complication	we pursued the Epeians; Athene turned us back
759	resolution (iii)	I killed my last man
759–61	coda	and we returned to Pylos; all glorified Zeus amongst gods and Nestor amongst men
762	exit talk	this is the man I was

Il. 24. 602–13

602	abstract	Niobe remembered to eat
603–9:	orientation:	Niobe was grieving because her children were killed:
603	abstract	her twelve children were killed
604	orientation	six daughters and six fine sons
605–8	complication	Niobe compared herself to Leto and boasted of her offspring
609	resolution	Apollo and Artemis slew all her children
609–11	complication	her children, slain, lay unburied until
612	resolution	the Uranian gods buried them;
613	coda	but she remembered to eat

(93), which we identify as orientation: Homer tells us that Oïleus is the companion, indeed, the charioteer, of Bienor. At 94 the poet begins the narrative proper: Oïleus springs from his horses, and comes face to face with Agamemnon, who stabs him in the face with his spear. The path of the spearhead is traced, through helmet and bone (97–8). This minor tale is resolved at 98: δάμασσε δέ μιν μεμαῶτα (so he beat him down in his fury). The coda (99–100) evaluates the event in the terms of the battlefield: these bodies are coolly stripped by the victor and left to lie naked and exposed. In this brief tale there is correspondence between abstract and resolution: they form, as it were, a single ring. We should note, however, that it is not a question of repetition. The abstract looks ahead to the resolution.

Likewise, at *Il.* 5. 541–60, Homer tells how Aineias brings down the sons of Diokles. At the outset (541–2) he offers an abstract of the episode: Αἰνείας . . . ἕλεν . . . Κρήθωνά τε Ὀρσίλοχόν τε (Aineias killed Krethon and Orsilochos). The information which he provides at 543–9 is background material: here Homer describes briefly the family history of these twin sons.[18] Now comes the narrative. The young men came to Troy as part of the expedition of the Argives (551); they fought well and brought honour to Agamemnon (552–3); and they were killed by Aineias (553): τὼ δ' αὖθι τέλος θανάτοιο κάλυψεν (now fulfilment of death was a darkness upon them). Note that the death of the young heroes is retold (at 554–8) in the simile (itself a small story) which parallels their experience. The narrative of 550–8 is resolved at 559–60, when the young heroes, overpowered, fall (δαμέντε καππεσέτην). As in the previous example, abstract and resolution correspond. Again we might identify a single ring.

Some Homeric stories may yield more than one so-called ring, as the following ambitious tale told by Nestor will illustrate. When one of Homer's characters tells a story in his own voice, he may use entrance talk and exit talk to frame his story. The former will prepare his audience for what is to come; the latter will indicate that his tale is over. In Nestor's anecdote at *Il.* 11. 670–762, his entrance talk (670–1), εἴθ' ὣς ἡβώοιμι βίη δέ μοι ἔμπεδος εἴη ὡς ὁπότ'. . . (if only I were young now, and the strength still steady within me), announces the tale to come and is matched by his exit talk, which seals off the story and signals a return to normal conversational exchange: ὣς ἔον, . . . μετ' ἀνδράσιν (that was I, among men, 762). Within this outer frame we notice that Nestor tells a lengthy and rather rambling tale out of which emerge three larger episodes, each one exhibiting the properties which Labov and Waletzky

---

[18] For a fuller discussion of tales such as this, in which the material that we classify as orientation is expanded (and often, as at *Il.* 4. 474–7; *Il.* 13. 665–70; or *Il.* 16. 572–6, becomes a narrative, an 'obituary', in its own right) and the narrative proper is perfunctory, see J. Griffin, *Homer on Life and Death* (Oxford: Clarendon Press, 1980), ch. 4. It is the foregrounding of what would otherwise be classified as background material, to the extent that it is cast as narrative, as a small anecdote in itself, which unbalances the story—and engages the reader. This background material, as Griffin notes (104), gives 'status and significance' to an otherwise undistinguished subject. As a consequence we are surprised and affected by what the storyteller tells us. Not all scholars have understood this characteristic of Homer's obituaries: see e.g. C. R. Beye, 'Homeric Battle Narratives and Catalogues', *HSCP* 68 (1964), 345–73.

have identified. Each of these begins with an abstract. The first episode, the story of the original quarrel between the Pylians and the Epeians and the cattle raid led by the young Nestor, begins at 672 (ὅτ' ἐγὼ κτάνον Ἰτυμονῆα, when I killed Itymoneus) and continues into a new phase at 677 (συνελάσσαμεν (we drove off). The second begins at 685–8; its focus, expressed in its abstract, at 687–8, is the division of spoil by the chiefs (οἱ ... ἡγήτορες ἄνδρες δαίτρευον). This segment is, as it were, begun afresh at 696–7: ἐκ δ' ὁ γέρων ... εἵλετο (and the old man took for himself). This episode contains within it two rather bare stories: one is more general (689–95), concerning earlier hostility between the Pylians and the Epeians; the second is more specific (698–702), the story of the theft of Neleus' horses. The third episode (which develops in three stages) begins at 720–1: ἀλλὰ καὶ ὣς ἱππεῦσι μετέπρεπον ἡμετέροισι (even so I was pre-eminent among our own horsemen). This third episode includes within it a further tale, 738–46, which is introduced by the abstract: πρῶτος ἐγὼν ἕλον ἄνδρα, κόμισσα δὲ μώνυχας ἵππους, 738 (I was the first to kill a man, and I won his single-foot horses). In each of these larger episodes the story returns at its conclusion to the point promised in the abstract: the resolution of 675 echoes 672: ἔβλητ' ... ἐμῆς ἀπὸ χειρὸς ἄκοντι, κὰδ δ' ἔπεσεν (he was struck by a spear thrown from my hand and fell); the second phase of this first episode (initiated at 677) is completed with ἠλασάμεσθα (we drove) at 682.[19] The next resolution, which occurs at 703–5: ὁ γέρων ... ἐξέλετ' (the old man took for himself), echoes 696–7. The coda of 706 (ἡμεῖς ... διείπομεν (we administered (the spoil)) parallels the abstract of 687–8; the resolution of 743–4 echoes 738: ἤριπε δ' .... ἐγὼ δ' ἐς δίφρον ὀρούσας στῆν ῥα μετὰ προμάχοισιν (he dropped in the dust, whereupon I springing into his chariot took my place among the champions); and the coda, at 759–61, the focus of which is the celebration of Nestor's achievement echoes 720–1: πάντες δ' εὐχετόωντο θεῶν Διὶ Νέστορί τ' ἀνδρῶν (and all glorified Zeus among the gods, but among men Nestor). A fourth, transitional, episode (707–19) has no

---

[19] Notice the coda at 683–4, which draws together the two phases of this first episode and evaluates the young Nestor's performance: γεγήθει δὲ φρένα Νηλεύς (and Neleus was glad in his heart).

abstract. This element is implied (let me tell you what the Epeians did in their desire for revenge). The resolution of the tale (717–19), οὐδέ με Νηλεὺς εἴα θωρήσσεσθαι, ἀπέκρυψεν δέ μοι ἵππους (now Neleus would not let me be armed among them, and had hidden away my horses) makes no reference to this; rather, it serves as the prompt for the final episode (720–61), which has been discussed above.

We might observe eight rings in this long tale: a ring which is completed by entrance talk and exit talk, four consecutive rings, and three rings embedded within them.[20] Thus, when we examine Nestor's leisurely tale closely, we find that it is more firmly structured than we might at first have believed. His reminiscences resemble the tales which we tell in everyday contexts, in which, despite considerable expansion and a number of digressions, the point of the narrative is never forgotten. Nestor's ability, here as elsewhere, always to return in exit talk to the theme which introduced his tale reflects our own ability to retain in memory for sustained periods (including interruptions) the point of our stories in progress.

In the Niobe paradigm of *Il.* 24. 602–13 we find a story within a story within a larger segment. In the larger segment (599–620), Achilleus attempts to comfort Priam and to encourage him to resume the routines of life. On occasions like this, a relevant story will lend weight to a proposal. Hence the story of Niobe and her grief (602–13): Niobe was ready to eat, despite her grief. So, at 602, Achilleus begins the story of Niobe with an abstract which signals the point of the tale: καὶ γάρ τ' ἠΰκομος Νιόβη ἐμνήσατο σίτου (for even Niobe, she of the lovely tresses, remembered to eat). At 613 he repeats the phrase, now as a coda: ἡ δ' ἄρα σίτου μνήσατ' (but she remembered to eat . . .). That is, Achilleus' coda fulfils the promise of his abstract. But within this tale is a

---

[20] There is no single authoritative analysis of this long tale. See van Otterlo, *De Ringcompositie*, 18–22; Lohmann, *Die Komposition der Reden*, 73. My analysis accords in most respects with that of Gaisser, 'A Structural Analysis', 9–13. Although I find different points of correspondence for 738 and 761, I identify these as narrative boundaries, as does Gaisser. Thalmann, *Conventions*, 11, notes a comparable pattern in his discussion of the double frame of Eurykleia's story at *Od.* 19. 392–468. The functions of each of the rings, as Thalmann describes them, correspond (according to my analysis) to the functions of, first, entrance talk (392) and exit talk (467–8) and, second, abstract (393–4) and resolution (464–6).

self-contained story, the tale of how Niobe's children met their deaths, in which the abstract at 603 (τῇ περ δώδεκα παῖδες ἐνὶ μεγάροισιν ὄλοντο, [her] twelve children were destroyed in her palace) foreshadows the resolution, at 609 (τὼ δ' ἄρα καὶ δοιώ περ ἐόντ' ἀπὸ πάντας ὄλεσσαν, but the two, though they were only two, destroyed all the others). Achilleus' story yields two rings—abstract and coda and, within it, abstract and resolution.[21]

In the examples above, Labov and Waletzky's modified story framework accommodates itself readily to Homer's stories, some of which have been analysed elsewhere in terms of ring composition. What conclusions might we draw from the general correspondences which these two patterns of analysis reveal? Many of the structures in the Homeric texts which in recent years have been identified as examples of ring composition—that is, as repetitions consciously plotted by the poet—are, on the contrary, evidence that the poet is telling his story in accordance with the story format which underpins all oral anecdotes in the Western tradition. If we analyse Homer's story rings not as the products of a ring composition template but as the products of a strategy for oral storytelling, we again see that Homer understands storytelling in much the same way as we do.[22] With regard to any of the tales he tells, either in his own voice or in the voice of one of his actors, he prepares his listeners for the content and the direction of the narrative (through his abstract); and once the resolution has been reached, he will sometimes reiterate it or evaluate it (through his coda). And when any of his actors tell stories,

---

[21] Cf. van Otterlo, *De Ringcompositie*, 12; Lohmann, *Die Komposition der Reden*, 13–14 (and n. 3); Gaisser, 'A Structural Analysis', 9 (where the inner ring, of 603 and 609 (the embedded story), is overlooked). The correspondence (noted in Lohmann and Gaisser) between 601 (μνησώμεθα) and 618–19 (μεδώμεθα) has nothing to do with the framework of Achilleus' story. It is, I suggest, an integral part of the speech act *persuasion*. The limits of the speech act are marked off by the statement and restatement of the key element, as happens in many speech acts in Homer and in our own everyday speech, such as *exhortation* (cf. *Il.* 23. 403 and 414) and *defiance* (cf. *Il.* 24. 560 and 568). (For Thalmann's observations on this point, in connection with *Il.* 24. 524–50, see *Conventions*, 16; where also see his comments on a similar passage (at *Od.* 20. 61–82 a narrative is enclosed within a prayer).) For further discussion, see below.

[22] Cf. my discussion of his distinction between *complicating action* and *resolution* in Ch. 5, above.

he has them monitor their relationships with their listeners (through entrance talk and exit talk), just as we would.

THE ABSENCE OF A RING PATTERN

Sometimes Homer's presentation of his story will result in one or more rings; sometimes it will not. It is worth noting, however, that even those Homeric stories which do not exhibit ringlike patterns remain true to the story structure which Labov and Waletzky have identified. The absence of a ring pattern does not indicate that the story is in any way deficient. Nor need it indicate that the poet has developed, or selected, a different story format. Antenor's story, at *Il.* 3. 204–24, is a case in point. There is no *formal* repetition in the framework of Antenor's story. But note that Antenor's opening words express his agreement with the previous speaker. Helen has just described Odysseus (202) as εἰδὼς παντοίους τε δόλους καὶ μήδεα πυκνά ([familiar with] every manner of shiftiness and crafty counsels), despite his being the product of rugged Ithaka. Antenor's statement at 204, ἦ μάλα τοῦτο ἔπος νημερτὲς ἔειπες (surely this word you have spoken can be no falsehood) looks back to what has just been said; it allows *Helen's* words to serve as an evaluative abstract to *his* story, which will conclude (224) as it began with a confirmation in an evaluative coda of Helen's assessment: οὐ τότε γ' ὧδ' Ὀδυσῆος ἀγασσάμεθ' εἶδος ἰδόντες (then we wondered less beholding Odysseus' outward appearance). Gaisser, who regards Antenor's tale as exceptional in the *Iliad*, fails to recognize the displacement of the abstract; because she cannot find the repetition character-istic of ring composition, she classifies Antenor's tale as an example of a different—linear—technique, *Ritournellkom-position*.[23] This distinction, in my view, is meaningless. Rather, Antenor is simply doing what anyone does in conversation: he is picking up and developing a topic which has been already introduced into the conversation.

---

[23] On *Ritournellkomposition*, see Gaisser, 'A Structural Analysis', 5; on the Antenor tale, see ibid., 39–40. For other examples of stories without ring patterns, see *Il.* 10. 266–70 (the history of Meriones' helmet); *Od.* 3. 254–312; and see below.

It is this practice which accounts for the differences in structure between so many of the stories told in the *Odyssey* and those in the *Iliad*. Stories in the *Odyssey* are regularly, although not always, invited by another speaker.[24] Because the storyteller is responding to a request for information, which sets the agenda for his response, he will not provide the abstract to which the resolution or the coda of his tale might correspond. Such is the story which Demodokos tells the guests of Alkinoos, at Odysseus' request (*Od.* 8. 499–520). Odysseus has asked him to tell the story of the wooden horse. Demodokos does so. His tale, as Homer recounts it, omits entrance talk and abstract: entrance talk is unnecessary in the light of Odysseus' invitation to sing; and an abstract is unnecessary because the hero nominated the topic also (492–5), a request which serves as a résumé of what is to come:

> ἀλλ' ἄγε δὴ μετάβηθι καὶ ἵππου κόσμον ἄεισον
> δουρατέου, τὸν Ἐπειὸς ἐποίησεν σὺν Ἀθήνῃ,
> ὅν ποτ' ἐς ἀκρόπολιν δόλον ἤγαγε δῖος Ὀδυσσεύς,
> ἀνδρῶν ἐμπλήσας οἳ Ἴλιον ἐξαλάπαξαν.

> Come to another part of the story, sing us
> the wooden horse, which Epeios made with Athene helping,
> the stratagem great Odysseus filled once with men and brought it
> to the upper city, and it was these men who sacked Ilion.

The story which Odysseus tells Athene (*Od.* 13. 256–86) likewise commences without entrance talk or abstract. In this case Athene (in disguise) has called upon Odysseus (who is attempting to conceal his identity) to explain his presence on Ithaka (which has also been disguised). Entrance talk will be omitted, because the invitation to speak has been issued at 237–8: νήπιός εἰς, ὦ ξεῖν', ἢ τηλόθεν εἰλήλουθας, εἰ δὴ τήνδε τε γαῖαν ἀνείρεαι (you are some innocent, O stranger, or else you have come from far away, if you ask about this land). An abstract is omitted also, because the tale will explain Odysseus' presence on the

---

[24] Not all stories in the *Odyssey* are invited. Some follow the story format which I have set out above: e.g., note Odysseus' story of how he had constructed his bed (*Od.* 23. 187–202). This comprises abstract (188–9: this bed has a secret), the tale itself (190–201), and a coda (202: that is the secret of the bed) which corresponds to the abstract.

island and why he had had to ask its name: an abstract,
therefore, could be understood from both his earlier questions (233–5) and Athene's teasing response (237–49). That
such an abstract was implied is confirmed by the coda to the
tale at 286 (αὐτὰρ ἐγὼ λιπόμην ἀκαχήμενος ἦτορ, [b]ut I,
grieving at heart, was left behind here).[25]

Stories in the *Iliad* are for the most part not prompted in
this way. They are introduced into the discourse when one
of the participants wishes to influence the actions of another:
these are stories designed to persuade. And because the
storyteller introduces the story himself, there is every
chance that it will include an evaluative abstract and that
there will be some kind of correspondence between this and
the closing elements. That is, the variations in the structures
of the stories within the two epics represent natural
responses to differing circumstances in the story-world;
they are not evidence of different narrative styles, nor do
they represent, as Gaisser suggests, 'an evolutionary process
in the development of epic style'.[26]

RING PATTERNS AND THE PRAGMATICS OF STORYTELLING

Homer's ring patterns (those patterns, that is, which occur
in the context of storytelling) are, therefore, like our own.
We are considering a phenomenon which relates primarily
to the pragmatics of storytelling (getting the story told and
ensuring that it makes its point). Aesthetic and mnemonic
considerations (to the extent that they can be successfully
separated from the pragmatic) are secondary. Contrary to
what Edwards suggests, Homer's ring patterns do not mark

---

[25] For other examples of stories in which elements of the story format have been
transferred to other speakers, see *Od.* 4. 238–64 (Helen's evaluative abstract (239–
43) is taken up by Menelaos in an evaluative coda to her tale, 265–70); *Od.* 7. 241–
97 (Odysseus' summary abstract at 243 modifies but, nevertheless, addresses the
questions asked by Arete at 237–9); and, similarly, at *Od.* 14. 192, Odysseus'
introduction to his tale encompasses all the questions he has been asked by
Eumaios (186–90). Note in this last example that Odysseus has used entrance
talk (193–8) to arouse the swineherd's interest in and sympathy for his tale.

[26] Gaisser, 'A Structural Analysis', 43.

the poet as different from ourselves. Rather, in the light of Labov and Waletzky's study, which invites us to consider Homer's story patterns from, first, a pragmatic and, then, a cognitive point of view, we have evidence that Homer followed a story format closely akin to our own.

It is particularly satisfying to be able to relate our own everyday storytelling practice to the structures of traditional oral epic. This is not to say, however, that ring patterns in Homer are limited to the context of storytelling. A careful study of other speech acts, such as *persuasion, exhortation* and *defiance*, reveals examples of ring patterns of a similar kind. In each case the speech act is marked off by repeated elements, the first of which foreshadows the point of the speech act (as does a storyteller's abstract) and the second renders it in its logical position in the sequence of the argument (as does the resolution of a narrative).[27]

RING COMPOSITION IN TEXTS COMPOSED IN WRITING

So far I have discussed ring patterns which are context-based, being produced as a frame for this particular kind of speech act, the story. But there is another kind of ring—one which is not to be found in Homer. This kind of ring occurs as an ordering device; it governs the presentation of themes within a poem, for example, or even in expository prose.[28]

---

[27] There is, however, considerably more to be said about the apparent ring structure of speech acts. We have some evidence, partly from linguistic philosophy and principally from cognitive psychology, to support the notion of a series of procedural formats which structure the presentation of everyday speech acts in our world as well as that of speech acts expressed in Homer. What we lack, however, is any systematic study of the expression of a number of common speech acts, whether in English or another language. If this were available to us we could explain in more plausible terms the kind of repetition which has been identified by Lohmann, in particular, as ring composition (see *Die Komposition der Reden, passim*). For some introductory remarks from Homeric studies on this topic, however, see R. Martin, *The Language of Heroes: Speech and Performance in the Iliad* (Ithaca and London: Cornell University Press, 1989) 46–7.

[28] For commentary on the importance of ring composition as a structural principle of certain kinds of verse, see Cairns, *Tibullus*, ch. 8; and see above, n. 3. For the contrary view, see R. Peden, 'Endings in Catullus', in M. Whitby, P. Hardie, and

These rings occur in the very position where the occasional rings which we associate with the story format do not occur (that is, within the body of discourse, not at its periphery); their function, as far as we may judge it, is not to promote the telling of an acceptable story but is a stylistic, text-based choice. We must conclude that narrative rings of this second kind are a phenomenon different from, but not unconnected with, those ring patterns which we observe in the framework of the oral anecdote.

What might be the connection between the ring of written discourse and the ring pattern of oral storytelling? If a connection does exist, is it possible to explain it? I suggest, as a first hypothesis, that we might view the former (the rings of written discourse) as a development of the latter (the everyday rings). For support I turn again to Tannen's argument that literary language makes intensified and artful use of a number of features—such as repetition, alliteration—which in conversation are 'spontaneous, pervasive, and often relatively automatic'.[29] Tannen claims that many of the devices considered stylistic devices of literary texts (and which are thought of as being 'literary') are developments of patterns which we have always used in oral contexts—in storytelling in conversation, for example.

Let us consider the possibility that the elaborate, content-centred rings of Greek and, subsequently, Latin literature

M. Whitby (eds.), *Homo Viator: Classical Essays for John Bramble* (Bristol: Bristol Classical Press, 1987), 95–103, at 99 and n. 22. On the other hand, Cairns' reading, *Tibullus*, 197–201, of a passage from Homer (*Il.* 6. 343–68) as an example of complex ring composition does not persuade me that the success of the passage is in any way due to its 'conceptual symmetry'. (The somewhat simpler reading of Lohmann, *Die Komposition der Reden*, 101–2, still leaves the question unanswered: could these subtle correspondences have been intended by an *oral* poet, for a *listening* audience?) As for ring composition in written prose, it has been argued recently in considerable, but not entirely persuasive, detail that ring composition was indeed used in a highly sophisticated fashion as an ordering device within extended passages of written discourse: see J. Ellis, 'The Structure and Argument of Thucydides' Archaeology', *Classical Antiquity*, 10 (1991), 344–80.

[29] D. Tannen, 'Repetition in Conversation: Towards a Poetics of Talk', *Language*, 63 (1987), 574–605, esp. 581. Tannen has made this point elsewhere: see also 'Oral and Literate Strategies in Spoken and Written Narratives', *Language*, 58 (1982), 1–21; *Conversational Style: Analyzing Talk amongst Friends* (Norwood, NJ: Ablex, 1984), 168. And see Ch. 4, above.

(I refer now to written discourse) developed from the simple rings of oral discourse, of which story rings, perhaps, are the most notable. In the Homeric epics, as in everyday storytelling, correspondences of abstract and resolution or abstract and coda (and of entrance talk and exit talk) were often unpremeditated *as correspondences*. But once the Homeric epics were recorded and became the subjects for study, these pleasing patterns in the texts may have assumed a new significance for, at least, some of their readers. It is possible that writers in the ancient world noted these patterns within Homer's stories and, not comprehending the rationale which gave rise to them, sought to emulate them now for their own sake.[30] In the new, literate, context it came about that these repetitions lost their immediate, practical focus and took on a different aspect;[31] they came to be used self-consciously and artfully.[32] That is, the ringlike patterns which had framed and would continue to frame the oral anecdote became a literary device as well: an artificial, text-based, intellectual means for holding the attention of a reader.[33] They came to be

---

[30] It is quite likely that the rationale for the rings was not understood, given that implicit knowledge is 'unconscious' and 'nonreflective': see A. Reber, 'Implicit Learning and Tacit Knowledge', *Journal of Experimental Psychology: General*, 118 (1989), 219–35, at 222.

[31] The exception to this is the representation in written narrative of oral storytelling. In such circumstances the story framework has continued to be faithfully reproduced in the literary form: for examples from the classical world, observe the structure of storytellings in Apuleius, *Metamorphoses*. Here anecdotes are shared with the same zest and pleasure that we observe on Homer. The first story told in *Metamorphoses*, the story of Socrates (1. 5–19), for example, exhibits all the properties of the story format that we have studied in connection with Homer. For discussion of the survival of the formal properties of the story framework in English literary genres, see M. L. Pratt, *Towards a Speech-Act Theory of Literary Discourse* (Bloomington: Indiana University Press, 1977), ch. 2.

[32] Cairns, *Tibullus*, 213, asks whether poets used these structures consciously and whether readers perceived them. I would suggest that when the poet framed his narratives as he might do in everyday discourse, he was almost always unconscious of any pattern which he may have created. When the poet who composed in writing produced, in the body of his poem, what we could confidently identify as a series of rings, it is not possible that he acted unconsciously. Whether readers of the time perceived these artificial rings or not, we cannot say.

[33] Note that the scholars cited above, n. 3, all identify and discuss ring composition as a literate strategy—even when the patterns of repetition reflect the activity of oral storytelling, such as we have observed in the Homeric examples discussed above.

used in circumstances where they would not appear in oral discourse. Not only did they frame a unit of discourse but they shaped that unit, and not only did they prepare the listener for a message (and reiterate its point), but they presented the message and established its thematic unity.[34] The literate poets who observed this symmetry (whether they noted it in Homer or, perhaps, in casual discourse) may not have identified the pragmatic purpose which underpinned it. Nevertheless, they adopted what appeared to them to be a stylistic device and adapted it for their own ends.

The term 'ring composition', therefore, has been used by classicists to describe not one but two phenomena: first, the term identifies the occasional patterns which occur automatically in natural discourse—such as those which we find framing Homer's stories; and second, it identifies what appear to be premeditated patterns of reference and repetition across long stretches of discourse (such as we might find in Thucydides, or in Tibullus). Clearly we need to distinguish the two. We should separate the rings which may be produced when we refer to that story format which we hold in implicit memory (these rings, for this reason, we should *not* identify as ring composition) from the artificial rings of literary discourse.[35] Once we can make this distinction we shall be able to talk with greater understanding and greater sympathy about the poetics and pragmatics of oral story-telling, and about literary stylistics, in the ancient world.

---

[34] On thematic, but not necessarily logical, unity, see B. Gentili, *Poetry and its Public in Ancient Greece: From Homer to the Fifth Century*, trans. A. Cole (Baltimore and London: The Johns Hopkins University Press, 1988), 49. Some scholars, indeed, claim that ring composition may structure the presentation of narrative. It is not clear to me, however, why a system which doubles back on itself might promote the understanding or the enjoyment of material which is normally presented in linear form. For comment on this point, see Gaisser, 'A Structural Analysis', 42.

[35] We might refer to the occasional patterns produced when a storyteller follows the story format as 'ring patterns,' or as 'structural correspondence'. The term 'ring composition', which implies artifice, should be reserved for rings of literary discourse.

Epilogue
'Special' Storytelling:
Homer's 'Blameless Tales'

Egbert Bakker, in his examination of Homeric idiom, compares the ordinary speech which we use in everyday oral contexts and the 'special' speech which Homer uses in the telling of his tales.[1] On the basis of his observations he concludes that Homeric discourse is a stylization of ordinary discourse: it departs from it and yet retains, or even highlights, its most characteristic forms.[2] He makes the point that the language of Homer is special not because it is oral but because it is poetic.[3] Homer's language is 'poetry in speech': it is a special case of oral communication.

I make the same claim for the epics at the level of performance: the *Iliad* and the *Odyssey* are instances of 'special' storytelling. It is not because they are oral that they are special, because most oral storytelling falls into the category of 'ordinary' storytelling. There are other reasons for claiming that these epics are special; the evidence which supports such claims is to be found in the text of Homer. I shall base my discussion on two aspects of Homer's performances. The first is his recreation of storytellings in the course of the *Odyssey*—and the responses they elicit; the second is the evidence of certain features of his song.

There is merit in asking how Homer's poems might have been received in his own time: to what extent were they special in the eyes of his audiences? and in what respects? Homer, as the narrator of the *Odyssey*, reveals his views on

---

[1] E. Bakker, 'The Construction of Orality', *Poetry in Speech: Orality and Homeric Discourse* (Ithaca and London: Cornell University Press, 1997).

[2] Ibid., 17.

[3] Ibid., 17. Bakker claims, at 207, that all speech, including Homeric formulaic speech, should be considered as a medium in its own right, rather than as a style that is defined with respect to the written styles of later periods.

issues relating to communication and reception on those
occasions when he allows one of his actors to tell a story to
an audience within the story-world. I propose that we
consider some of these instanes, taking into account the
occasion, the teller and his intentions, and the reactions of
this internal audience.[4] These reactions will give us a
measure by which we can assess the anecdotes individually;
and they will lead us to some conclusions with respect to the
great tales themselves.[5] For the sake of contrast, however, let
us begin with the stories of the *Iliad*.

The stories told within the compass of the *Iliad* are with
few exceptions stories designed to persuade their listeners in
the story-world to a certain course of action—although, for
Homer's actual audience, they serve an evaluative purpose,
in bringing into perspective the action of the poem.[6] These
exemplary tales are regularly told by a figure of authority
within the story-world, with some urgency, at a time of need.
This we know from their context: Nestor tells stories from
his past to encourage others to act as he did on the battlefield,
as a responsible hero loyal to his comrades.[7] Phoinix works
with the same intention, when he tries to persuade Achilleus
to return to the fighting (9. 529–99). Achilleus tells Priam the
Niobe tale in order to encourage him to resume the activities
of day-to-day living (24. 602–17). When the listener in the
story-world hears and responds to a tale told in this context,

---

[4] I distinguish here between the internal audience of stories within the epic and
the actual audience of the poem—such as ourselves. For discussion of these
audiences, see L. Doherty, *Siren Songs: Gender, Audiences, and Narrators in the
Odyssey* (Ann Arbor: University of Michigan Press, 1995), chs. 1–3; B. Louden,
The Odyssey*: Structure, Narration, and Meaning* (Baltimore and London: The
Johns Hopkins University Press, 1999), ch. 3.

[5] See W. Wyatt, 'Homer in Performance: *Iliad* 1. 348–427', *CJ* 83 (1987–8),
289–97. Wyatt in his study of Achilleus' tale of woes to his mother in *Iliad* 1 works
on the same principle. The reactions of the audience within the poem are intended
to offer Homer's actual audience the evaluative cues which are necessary to them, if
they are to interpret events. For brief comment also, see C. Macleod, 'Homer on
Poetry and the Poetry of Homer', in C. Macleod, *Collected Essays* (Oxford:
Clarendon Press, 1983), 1–15, at 3.

[6] The tales told by Nestor show us how heroes are expected to behave; his stories
help us evaluate the behaviour of his comrades.

[7] Nestor tells tales from his past at *Il.* 1. 262–73; 7. 132–57; 11. 670–762, 765–90;
23. 629–43. Not all his tales are effective: his story at 1. 262–73 does not move
Agamemnon to give up his claim on Briseis. For commentary on the tales of
Nestor, see M. Schofield, 'Euboulia in the *Iliad*', *CQ* 36 (1986), 6–31.

it will not be with words of praise for the story and its telling. If the story is effective, his response will be action. Thus the Achaians will respond promptly to Nestor's exhortation to stand up against Hektor; Patroklos, in response to Nestor's exhortation, will return to Achilleus to beg him to be allowed to fight in his place; and Priam will consent to eat with Achilleus. Even the exchange of stories and story fragments which marks the *teichoskopia* of *Iliad* 3 does not amount to storytelling for its own sake. When Helen, on the walls of Troy with the Trojan elders, identifies the great heroes of the Achaians, the elders, at leisure, share stories about the men they see in the forces gathered below them (3. 146–244). The tale which one of the elders, Antenor, tells at 3. 205–24 is told to amplify and confirm a statement which Helen has made about Odysseus. He acknowledges this at 204. On its conclusion no member of his small audience makes any comment on it. The story, it appears, has served its purpose—as information. If it was intended as a tale designed to entertain, its audience has behaved in an extraordinary fashion, in not recognizing Antenor's contribution.[8]

Those who tell the stories within the *Odyssey*, on the other hand, openly admit that their tales are told to entertain their audience and, in many cases, to win sustenance or prestige for the teller.[9] These stories provide the parallel which we are seeking to the circumstances of oral song in public performance, whereas those of the *Iliad* do not. This is confirmed, indeed, by the performative context in which they occur: notably, the stories of Phemios and Demodokos in the palaces of Ithaka and Scheria; the stories told by Eumaios and Odysseus to pass long dark nights on Ithaka; and the long epic tale which Odysseus tells the Phaiakians

[8] For this reason it seems to me to be intended otherwise. In our own world we do not fail to show our appreciation of a story told simply to entertain. Our acknowledgement may be perfunctory, but it is a recognition of the storyteller's efforts.

[9] For commentary on this from within the *Odyssey*, see 8. 477–81, 14. 124–5, 23. 216–7. Most storytellers, however, seek no more than the praise due to a story well-told. Menelaos (266) recognizes the competence of his wife's telling (4. 239–64); and note the young Telemachos' enthusiastic response (4. 594–8) to Menelaos' tale (347–586).

on the second night after his arrival in their midst. The poet's purpose in depicting these storytellings is not limited to a concern with plot. Through these depictions, even as he is moving his story forwards, he is making a series of points about storytelling in general and, more precisely, about his own ambitions. The poet of the *Odyssey* wants us to recognize his mastery of his medium. He integrates his professional preoccupations—with poetry, with the social interaction of performance, and with narrative—into his song; his very self-consciousness, that is, his awareness of himself as a professional storyteller, becomes part of the performance itself.[10] A review of a number of the storytelling performances which the poet describes, all by accomplished singers, will illustrate my points.

WHAT MAKES A STORY INTERESTING? THE SONGS OF PHEMIOS AND DEMODOKOS

At *Od.* 1. 144–9 the suitors feast. After feasting they seek entertainment (151–2). The lyre is brought to the bard Phemios, the famous bard (ἀοιδὸς . . . περικλυτός, 325), who sings a fine song about the bitter homecomings of the Achaians returning from Troy (325–7). We do not hear the song, for it serves as a background to the interview of Athene and Telemachos. The suitors, however, do. And, reckless and thoughtless as they may be in so much of their behaviour to others, they now sit in silence, as respectful and attentive listeners (οἱ δὲ σιωπῇ ἧατ' ἀκούοντες, 325–6). The singer and his song exercise their power over the unruly crowd.

At *Od.* 8. 55 ff. the Phaiakian nobles are attending a feast, hosted by Alkinoos, in honour of Odysseus. When they have eaten, it is time for entertainment. Demodokos, the inspired

[10] For important commentary, see W. Suerbaum, 'Die Ich-Erzählungen des Odysseus', *Poetica*, 2 (1968), 150–77. Suerbaum identifies the stories told by Odysseus in the *Odyssey* as 'Rahmenerzählungen', 'stories within a story', which serve to mirror the circumstances of the poet within the work itself (166). For a recent study which takes the self-consciousness of the *Odyssey* as its theme, see Doherty, *Siren Songs, passim*.

singer (θεῖον ἀοιδόν, 43), has been summoned. Homer announces his arrival and commends him to us: Demodokos is a singer whom the Muse has loved greatly (τὸν πέρι Μοῦσ' ἐφίλησε, 63). The bard begins to sing. Whenever he pauses, his audience urges him to sing once more, since his stories give such pleasure. He will sing the quarrel of Achilleus and Odysseus (73–82), and, after a break for games, the story of Ares and Aphrodite (266–366). His audience is delighted (90–1, 367–9): Odysseus enjoys his song in his heart (τέρπετ' ἐνὶ φρεσὶν ᾗσιν, 368)—as do the Phaiakians. Finally, Demodokos sings the story of Odysseus and the sack of Troy (499–520).

Not all those who listen to the songs of these bards find pleasure in all their tales. When Phemios performs for the suitors in *Od.* 1, the suitors are spellbound, but Penelope is in tears (δακρύσασα, 336). She comes from her chamber to ask the singer to choose another song from amongst his repertoire, one which will not cause her such unforgettable sorrow (πένθος ἄλαστον, 342). She explains the cause: hearing of the returns of the Achaian heroes reminds her of her husband, for whom she longs (343–4). Odysseus, likewise, finds it difficult to listen unmoved to the tales which Demodokos tells about the quarrel of Achilleus and Odysseus and the sack of Troy. Indeed, at 8. 536–41, and 577–86, after Demodokos' second song about the action at Troy, Alkinoos, who has been observing Odysseus, infers that his grief is that of a man who has lost a kinsman or a companion before Troy.[11] In reporting the possibility that not all members of an audience will respond to the same song with the same enthusiasm, Homer reminds us of the complex dynamics of performance.

What is at issue here is the power of a story to engage its listeners. Three factors are critical, for all stories. First, there are certain topics which regularly catch our attention. Roger Schank calls these topics 'life themes' or 'absolute

---

[11] Alkinoos (94–5) had previously noted Odysseus' grief (83–9), when Demodokos had first sung. At that time he had discreetly suggested a diversion—the games. With Odysseus' second outpouring of grief, and in the light of his performance at the games, the king is clearly intrigued by his guest; he now presses him for further information.

interests'.[12] Stories which touch on death, danger, power, or
personal relationships, and which give rise to emotions such
as pity or fear are more likely to engage us than those which
do not.[13] All the stories told by Phemios and Demodokos in
the *Odyssey* touch on one or more of these categories. For
this reason they are intrinsically interesting to their listeners.
Second, no story, if it is to succeed, can comprise simply a
series of predictable, scripted, sequences. Rather, it should
contain elements of the unexpected, such as deviations from
scripts: quarrels, or troubled journeys, for example.[14] Third,
Schank draws attention also to the function of 'personal
relatedness', which operates as a factor in story enjoyment.[15]
Stories which include ourselves as actors, or which include
people close to us, are more likely to engage our listeners
than the same stories about strangers. 'Personal relatedness'
alone does not make for an interesting story; but it is a factor
in successful communication.

There is, however, a level of 'personal relatedness' which
makes the telling of a story so engaging that it is too painful
to hear. This is when the story concerns ourselves or people
close to us and the experience being narrated has not yet
been resolved in the real world; thus Odysseus grieves on
hearing of his own adventures at Troy, an expedition which
for him is not yet over (*Od.* 8. 83–92, 521–31), and Penelope
weeps on being reminded of her absent husband, whose
whereabouts are unknown to her (*Od.* 1. 328–44). Alkinoos
is close to the mark, therefore, when he suggests that
Odysseus is mourning the loss of a near kinsman
(*Od.* 8. 581–6); for Odysseus is, in a sense, mourning
himself. And Eumaios speaks wisely when later he tells his
master that, only after a man's trials have come to an end,
can he at last 'enjoy' them, that is, when he recreates them in

---

[12] See R. Schank, 'Interestingness: Controlling Inferences', *Artificial Intelligence*, 12 (1979), 273–97, at 278–91. Schank's concern, as a cognitive scientist, is the relationship between interest and inference in the understanding process.

[13] Such interests are culturally determined; they reflect our shared values, beliefs, and world view: see L. Polanyi, 'So What's the Point?', *Semiotica*, 25 (1979), 207–41, at 211–13.

[14] For comment on this point in the context of the narrative of the funeral games for Patroklos, see Ch. 1, above.

[15] Schank, 'Interestingness', 281.

story (μετὰ γάρ τε καὶ ἄλγεσι τέρπεται ἀνήρ, ὅς τις δὴ μάλα πολλὰ πάθῃ καὶ πόλλ' ἐπαληθῇ, *Od.* 15. 400–1).[16]

THE NEED FOR AUTHENTICITY: ODYSSEUS' STORIES FOR THE SWINEHERD

Through these stories by well-loved and highly-respected bards Homer shares with us his observations of the communicative aspects of storytelling. What he passes on is limited, however, by his decision to present Phemios' tale (*Od.* 1. 325–7) and two of the tales of Demodokos (*Od.* 8. 73–82, 499–520) in summary, as reported speech. There is yet more to be learned from the stories of a talented amateur, presented as *oratio recta*. I am referring here to the stories which Odysseus, in appearance a beggar, tells Eumaios against the simple background of the swineherd's hearth. In this episode, too, the poet gives due attention to the occasion, and to the participants and their intentions; but he also records the tale itself; and he reports the listener's evaluation of the story he has just heard. Eumaios has already shown himself in conversation to be discerning and sceptical;[17] Odysseus knows, therefore, that, whatever story he tells, his performance must be a performance of quality. In this intimate but challenging context Homer explores the art of making a story convincing.[18]

[16] For brief commentary on this point, from a slightly different perspective, see Macleod, 'Homer on Poetry', at 11 ('So the song which was to glorify the hero is felt by the hero himself as a moving record of the pain and sorrow he helped to cause.'). On personal involvement, see also A. Ford, 'Epic as Genre', in I. Morris and B. Powell, *A New Companion to Homer* (Leiden: E. J. Brill, 1997), 396–414, at 414.

[17] I read Eumaios as do F. Ahl and H. Roisman, *The* Odyssey *Re-Formed* (Ithaca: Cornell University Press, 1996), ch. 8; and Louden, *Structure, Narration, and Meaning*, at 62, who observes that Eumaios shows 'considerable, if unexpected sophistication'. Doherty, however, *Siren Songs*, 148–59, is less sympathetic to Eumaios: she sees the swineherd as 'dutiful and unimaginative'; he is a man of 'stolid dependability' (150). For a fine summary of Eumaios' role in the narrative and his reception of Odysseus' stories, see G. Dimock, *The Unity of the* Odyssey (Amherst, Mass.: University of Massachusetts Press, 1982), 189–98.

[18] The issue has been raised earlier in the epic: note Helen's comments at *Od.* 4. 238–9 (she asks her guests to enjoy her storytelling, because she will offer them a plausible tale (ἐοικότα γὰρ καταλέξω, 239)).

At *Od.* 14. 183–90 Eumaios seeks distraction from his concern for his master and for his estate. He asks that his guest tell him something of his own history. The form of his request at 185 outlines the compass of the tale and his expectations of its content:

ἀλλ' ἄγε μοι σύ, γεραιέ, τὰ σ' αὐτοῦ κήδε' ἐνίσπες
Come now, aged sir, recite me the tale of your sorrows

Odysseus obliges; he begins his story (192–359) with a preamble, a reflection on those conditions which best promote a successful storytelling. According to Odysseus, the prerequisites for success are ample time, an audience at leisure, to whom he can respond (193–7), and narratable material. To meet this last demand Odysseus, speaking as a beggar, will tell of his many sorrows (197–8). His preamble serves as an evaluative abstract, in which he supplies Eumaios with certain cues to the reading of the story which is to come. Odysseus suggests that his life-story is far too eventful to be reduced to a compact after-dinner tale. The story he will tell, he implies, will represent a selection from the material available (196–8). Note Odysseus' measured approach to his task; he appears to be deferring the telling until he has his thoughts in order. By contrast with the story which Odysseus tells the Phaiakians (9. 2–12. 453), and like the tale he will later tell Penelope (19. 165–202), this 'history' will be an invention: it is a mock-autobiographical tale, designed to complement his disguise. Odysseus is aware, nevertheless, that if it is to be acceptable to his audience it must ring true; it must be plausible.

The beggar begins his tale. He passes over some elements, which are not relevant or appropriate to the present circumstances; he dwells on others, which are. For he needs to win Eumaios' sympathy. For this reason he echoes in his tale the experiences and sufferings of his host.[19] Thus he can be

---

[19] For commentary on Odysseus' false tales, see Doherty, *Siren Songs*; esp. 148–58; Ahl and Roisman, *The* Odyssey *Re-Formed*; ch. 8; Dimock, *Unity*, bk. 14; S. D. Olson, *Blood and Iron: Stories and Storytelling in Homer's* Odyssey (Leiden: E. J. Brill, 1995), ch. 6; C. Trahman, 'Odysseus' Lies (*Odyssey*, Books 13–19)', *Phoenix*, 6 (1952), 31–43; A. Haft, 'Odysseus, Idomeneus and Meriones: The Cretan Lies of *Odyssey* 13–19', *CJ* 79 (1983–4), 289–306. Trahman (39), Haft (300), Olson (129), and Ahl and Roisman (187) all identify the key to Odysseus' effectiveness as a

certain of Eumaios' cognitive and emotional involvement in the tale; and the swineherd will be more likely to believe what he hears. The shape of Odysseus' tale, however, is supplied by his own wanderings—although his adventures, in the cause of plausibility, now remain within the bounds of human experience. Indeed, he mentions Odysseus and his homeward journey in his narrative (14. 321–33), for a false story is more plausible if it has a foothold in reality. Taken as a whole, the false autobiography which the beggar offers his host is a formidable creation: a cunning blend of fact, truth, half-truth, and fiction.

The beggar's coda—ἔτι γάρ νύ μοι αἶσα βιῶναι (life is still my portion, 359)—closes off the action in the story-world and returns him and his listener to the conversational present. Now is the moment for Eumaios to express his views on the tale. The swineherd evaluates Odysseus' telling. He reports on his own reaction: ἦ μοι μάλα θυμὸν ὄρινας (truly you troubled the spirit in me, 361). He summarizes what he has heard (362). And, through reference to the Odysseus anecdote, he connects the beggar's story to the conversation from which it arose. Thus he confirms his understanding of the narrative and his appreciation of the beggar's contribution to the conversation. In terms of the etiquette of storytelling, this is the co-operative response of an exemplary listener. But, despite the beggar's efforts in the interests of authenticity (his reference to Odysseus; his precise references to place and time) Eumaios is not wholly satisfied with the tale. He was convinced by that part of the story which described the beggar's sufferings (that part which had been assimilated to his own experience); but he was suspicious of that portion which reported an encounter with Odysseus.[20] Because

storyteller: he has in this false history aimed to manipulate Eumaios' sympathy by fashioning a tale which parallels the actual sufferings of the swineherd himself (sufferings of which we, the audience, are still unaware).

[20] We, the audience, know that that portion which suggests that Odyseus is alive is perhaps the only true element in the tale: for discussion of this point, see Doherty, *Siren Songs*, at 149–50. The irony generated in this scene by Odysseus' disguise, Eumaios' ignorance, and our knowledge, is to be repeated again and again through the rest of the epic. For discussion of irony and deception in this episode, and its consequences for our reading of the rest of the *Odyssey*, see E. Minchin, 'Homer Springs a Surprise: Eumaios' Tale at *Od.* o 403–484', *Hermes*, 120 (1992), 259–66, at 263–6; A. Rengakos, 'Spannungsstrategien in den homerischen Epen',

Eumaios cannot believe that his master is still living, he refuses to accept what the beggar says on that point. And he accuses his guest of lying (364–5):

> τί σε χρὴ τοῖον ἐόντα
> μαψιδίως ψεύδεσθαι;

Why should a man such as you are lie recklessly to me?

This part of the tale, he decrees, is not as it should be, οὐ κατὰ κόσμον (363).

Although his first effort at storytelling was rejected as implausible, Odysseus tries again. He volunteers a second story, a boastful story, which, he tells Eumaios, he would not share if he were sober (463–7). But his story (468–503) reveals no want of control. Odysseus, clad in his beggar's garb, feels the chill of the night air; he decides to probe the swineherd, to see how well-disposed he is to him. His test is simple: will Eumaios take off his cloak and give it to him? or will he tell one of his men to give up his cloak for him (459–61)? He does not ask for a cloak directly; he tells a tale which begins with the problem of being too cold and which recounts the solution which Odysseus devised to address it. Because the tale is set in the time of the Trojan War, the beggar's reference to Odysseus will not be unacceptable to Eumaios; this encounter is plausible. The beggar recounts how once, on setting out on a night mission, he was the only one of his companions to leave his quarters without a cloak. He was caught outdoors, unprepared, and bitterly cold. How was he to survive until dawn? We know from the outset that the tale in the strictest sense cannot be true: the beggar who tells the tale is a fiction. The problem at the heart of the story, however, is resolved in the story-world in a completely plausible fashion: only Odysseus could devise and put into effect the solution described, which turned upon the hero's powers of prompt invention, his cunning, his discretion, and his authority within the Achaian army. Because the tale captures what is essentially Odyssean about Odysseus, it

in J. Kazazis and A. Rengakos (eds.), *Euphrosyne: Studies in Ancient Epic and its Legacy in Honour of Dimitris N. Maronitis* (Stuttgart: Franz Steiner, 1999), 308–38, at 323–4, 327–35.

represents that broader truth of plausibility which we seek in storytelling. For this reason it satisfies Eumaios. In response he commends the tale warmly: this tale is blameless, he says (αἶνος . . . ἀμύμων, 508); it is absolutely right (οὐδέ τί πω παρὰ μοῖραν, 509). Odysseus, the creative poet, has made the false seem true.[21]

INVOLVING ONE'S LISTENERS: THE IMPORTANCE OF STORY STRUCTURE

The beggar's tale is blameless, first, in terms of its format. The teller has used his implicit knowledge about the presentation of stories to shape a tale that his audience can process without confusion. We note in the tale all the elements of the story format discussed in my Introduction and in Chapter 6: *entrance talk* at 462–3; an evaluative *abstract* at 463; further *entrance talk* at 463–8; *orientation* at 469–72; *complicating action* at 473–9; further *orientation* at 480–2; *complicating action* at 483–501; *resolution* at 501–2; and *exit talk* at 503. Evaluative information is included in the abstract (this, the beggar tells us, is a boastful tale, 463) and within the narrative (Odysseus' name is sufficient to forewarn an audience of guileful action, 470; but the beggar also characterizes the hero, at 491: he is the foremost in battle and in counsel).[22]

If a storyteller were to organize his tale so as to promote his listeners' ready comprehension, he would simply report events as they had happened, in chronological sequence; and his narrative would transmit the narrative sequence as information.[23] This strategy, however, will not result in a

---

[21] Eumaios immediately sees the point of the tale: as Ahl and Roisman, *The Odyssey Re-Formed*, 179, phrase it (in the terminology of our literate culture), he is able to read between the lines of the narrative. After the tale is done, without further prompting by Odysseus, Eumaios discusses the limited availability of cloaks. His perceptiveness here confirms our assessment of him as an intelligent listener.

[22] Odysseus' cunning—and discretion—is revealed also in the whisper in which he addresses the beggar (492). He urges his companion, the beggar, not to betray himself at a potentially embarrassing moment.

[23] In such a case we are considering not a story but a chronicle: a report of one

particularly effective story. Stories are designed to engage
and entertain; and those which are most effective are rarely
either shaped or ordered in this straightforward fashion.
First, as Lang suggests, a process of selection or subordina-
tion is necessary, if the storyteller is to produce a story-
path which is satisfying.[24] Second, the event sequence of a
good story is most often organized in a non-sequential
order. The consequence of this is that listeners are obliged
to pay close attention to the narrative in order to learn the
true sequence of events: that is, to be able to form a causal
chain.

Brewer and Lichtenstein identify three discourse-
structures which are responsible for the enjoyment of a
large proportion of stories.[25] These are related to reactions
in the audience of surprise, suspense, or curiosity. When the
storyteller defers an eagerly-awaited climax, he is structuring his story to arouse suspense; when he witholds information which the audience could not otherwise know or infer,
he is aiming to arouse surprise; when he suppresses a crucial
event but gives his audience enough information to know
that something has been suppressed, he arouses curiosity.[26]
Listeners are absorbed by tales structured on these lines
because they cannot complete the causal chain of a narrative
without what has been withheld, whether it is an event or an
explanation. Their interest and involvement are, in the first
instance, of a cognitive kind: they remain attentive, because
they are awaiting the missing clue. It is essential, however,
that storytellers resolve the suspense or the curiosity which
they have produced, or offer a rationale for the surprising
event which has been introduced. Resolution is essential to
the structure of the tale. An audience cannot relax until the
storyteller has completed the causal chain and everything, as
we say, 'falls into place'.

The beggar's cloak tale, which was discussed above,

---

event after another. This is, in some respects, as Lang observes, 'too much like life':
see M. Lang, 'Homer and Oral Techniques', *Hesperia*, 38 (1969), 159–68, at 168.

[24] Lang, 'Homer and Oral Techniques', 168.

[25] See W. Brewer and E. Lichtenstein, 'Stories are to Entertain: A Structural-
Affect Theory of Stories', *Journal of Pragmatics*, 6 (1982), 473–86.

[26] On this ibid., 480–2.

offers a neat instance of an event-structure which is designed to arouse both curiosity and surprise. The beggar omits from his narrative chain an explanation of what Odysseus, as an actor in the cloak tale, has in mind when he forms his plan (490) to find a cloak for his companion, and when he speaks to his companions, telling them of his dream. It is only with the conclusion of the tale (501), when Thoas leaves behind his cloak to run back to the ships, that the listener realizes what was in Odysseus' mind all along. The audience, therefore, has felt from the outset a general curiosity about how the beggar's problem, of being without a cloak, might be addressed; once Odysseus enters the action, listeners feel a more specific curiosity, because they are sure that he has been able to devise a solution which they cannot predict; and they feel a certain surprise—and amusement—at discovering what information the beggar had withheld and in seeing how cunningly Odysseus has addressed the problem. Indeed, by these structural adjustments the beggar's tale captures the experience of 'being there'.[27] In telling the story in such a way as to reflect his own puzzlement, because, in the story-world, the beggar would not have been aware of the plan which Odysseus had formed until it had been executed, the beggar arouses in his audience (Eumaios) those same emotions which he, the beggar, would have felt at the time. Thus he recreates through artificial means the experience of being part of those events as they occurred. This contributes to the authenticity of the tale.

As we have noted in earlier discussions, a story is deemed by its listeners to be more enjoyable if they have been encouraged to play an active role in the storytelling: when, as in the cloak tale, they are obliged to reconstruct the causal chain of the tale in the light of new information; or when the storyteller assigns to his or her listeners the task of discovering for themselves the opinion which he or she wishes them to hold about the action described.[28]

---

[27] For Macleod's comments on this theme, and the epic poet's valuing of the eyewitness account, the gift of the Muse, see 'Homer on Poetry', at 6.

[28] See above. See also Ch. 1, on reconstructing the causal chain of a story; and Ch. 3, on internal and external evaluation.

Storytellers encourage this kind of self-sufficiency in their listeners when they avoid offering explicit commentary on the action. Instead, preserving dramatic continuity, they convey so-called internal cues. In the absence of explicit direction from the storyteller, the audience is obliged to observe closely, or identify with, the characters in the story-world in order to interpret the action. The point of the cloak tale, for example, is not expressed. But we conclude from the fact that Odysseus is the hero of the tale, that its immediate aim is to share a moment of recognition and delight in Odysseus and his quick think-ing, and to build on it.[29] The beggar's subsequent wish that someone might give him a cloak is built on that positive response. To return to a point made in Chapter 3, it is because evaluative cues, conveyed indirectly, engage the audience in locating the meaning or the point of the narrative, that a presentation which relies largely on internal evaluation makes for a more absorbing story. And, because the narrator does not impose his views on the audience, the story itself may appear more persuasive. For this reason, too, it will be a better story.

AN EPIC TALE: SCALE AND PACE

The stories discussed above are on a relatively small scale. Some have been told as after-dinner entertainment, by bards, others have been told in conversation. Provided that we set aside the question of the special formulaic language of epic, these tales are tales which any competent storyteller might tell. The beggar's cloak tale is on the same scale as stories which we would tell to friends in casual encounters. Eumaios' life story is long, but not of such extraordinary length that we could not imagine a similar telling today. The story of Ares and Aphrodite, as told by Demodokos, is, in Kirk's terms, a 'normal' story, which would have been known to many singers; and some of its

---

[29] Ahl and Roisman, *The* Odyssey *Re-Formed*, read more than this into the tale: for their commentary on what they see as Eumaios' failure, see 179–81.

listeners, at least, could have retold the tale with much the same detail and with similar success.[30] There is, however, one performance within the *Odyssey* which is not unlike the *Odyssey* itself. This is the long tale which Odysseus tells to the Phaiakians (9. 2–12. 453).

At *Od.* 8. 548–86 Alkinoos requests that Odysseus tell his own story. As a guest in the palace, Odysseus has little choice but to oblige. After some graceful entrance talk (9. 5–11), through which he reminds us of the context in which he is about to perform (the backdrop being the eager guests seated in order down the palace hall, abundant food, and wine, and an assiduous steward), the hero begins a tale that will rival those told by the bard Demodokos. Odysseus looks back over the ten years which have passed since the fall of Troy and prepares to give his own account of the challenges which he has encountered in that time. He begins his tale with an evaluative abstract (9. 12–13):

σοὶ δ' ἐμὰ κήδεα θυμὸς ἐπετράπετο στονόεντα
εἴρεσθ', ὄφρ' ἔτι μᾶλλον ὀδυρόμενος στεναχίζω·

But now your wish was inclined to ask me about my mournful sufferings, so that I must mourn and grieve even more.

At 9. 14–15 he puts into words the concern natural to any storyteller about to embark on an ambitious project: he ponders his choice of material and the most efficacious arrangement of the narrative itself (he deliberates, 14–15; he makes a decision, 37–8). These are the preoccupations of an experienced teller of tales. Even at this early point in Odysseus' story, we sense that this tale is going to be superior in a number of ways to the tales we have already studied. His leisured preamble to his telling and the self-consciousness that we identify with ambitious storytelling are both present.

At 9. 16 Odysseus begins the narrative proper. The tale which he tells is, like his preamble, a leisurely telling; it contrasts strongly with the version which he is reported to have given his wife, when they have been reunited (23. 310–41). At 11. 330–2 he pauses. He gives the Phaiakians the

---

[30] For his discussion of 'normal' as opposed to 'special' storytelling, see G. S. Kirk, *The Iliad: A Commentary*, i (Cambridge: Cambridge University Press, 1985), at 12.

opportunity to call a halt or to ask him to continue.[31] The audience, however, is spellbound (333–4):

> Ὣς ἔφαθ', οἱ δ' ἄρα πάντες ἀκὴν ἐγένοντο σιωπῇ,
> κηληθμῷ δ' ἔσχοντο κατὰ μέγαρα σκιόεντα.

So he spoke, and all of them stayed stricken to silence,
held in thrall by the story all through the shadowy chambers.

Alkinoos praises not only the content of the song but Odysseus' telling (367–9):

> σοὶ δ' ἔπι μὲν μορφὴ ἐπέων, ἔνι δὲ φρένες ἐσθλαί,
> μῦθον δ' ὡς ὅτ' ἀοιδὸς ἐπισταμένως κατέλεξας,
> πάντων Ἀργείων σέο τ' αὐτοῦ κήδεα λυγρά.

You have
a grace upon your words, and there is sound sense within them,
and expertly, as a singer would do, you have told the story
of the dismal sorrows befallen yourself and all of the Argives.

The terms of his praise nicely complement the earlier reflections of Odysseus on the content and shape of the story he proposed to tell. And, equally, they complement Odysseus' praise of Demodokos' song. The two tributes taken together reveal what it is that makes a song successful. There is truth in Odysseus' stories, Alkinoos says; they are well-structured, so that the audience can follow the story and see its point; and they reveal that logic which is at the base of our own broad experience of life. They have the ring of authenticity, in contrast with the inadequacies of the tales of a poor storyteller: these are lies, from which no one could learn anything (ψεύδεά τ' ἀρτύνοντας, ὅθεν κέ τις οὐδὲ ἴδοιτο, 366). Odysseus has told his tale as would a professional singer, who understands the principles of choosing, structuring, and presenting a song for best effect. As a result, Alkinoos is convinced and engaged by the tale: in its unfinished state it has aroused his curiosity (Did you meet any of your companions in Hades?, 370–2); he feels its suspense (I could hold out till dawn, if you would keep telling, 375–6); and his emotions are engaged (. . . if you could

---

[31] Demodokos, at *Od.* 8. 87, is said to have broken his performance for the same purpose: to test the mood of the audience. Compare A. B. Lord's comments on the singer and his audience in *The Singer of Tales* (Cambridge, Mass.: Harvard University Press, 1960; New York: Atheneum edn., 1965), 16–17.

bear to tell us more of your sorrows, 376). He asks that the tale continue, without a pause. And he indicates the pace at which the teller should proceed (11. 373–6)—the slowest possible pace:

νὺξ δ᾽ ἥδε μάλα μακρὴ ἀθέσφατος· οὐδέ πω ὥρη
εὕδειν ἐν μεγάρῳ· σὺ δέ μοι λέγε θέσκελα ἔργα.
καὶ κεν ἐς ἠῶ δῖαν ἀνασχοίμην, ὅτε μοι σὺ
τλαίης ἐν μεγάρῳ τὰ σὰ κήδεα μυθήσασθαι.

Here is a night that is very long, it is endless. It is not time yet to sleep in the palace. But go on telling your wonderful story. I myself could hold out until the bright dawn, if only you could bear to tell me, here in the palace, of your sufferings.[32]

He offers Odysseus the rest of the night for his telling. It will be one of those extraordinary, once-in-a-lifetime performances; its listeners will forgo all sleep to hear it through.

Odysseus resumes his telling. And, in time, the tale is at an end (12. 453). The performance, however, is not yet complete. The poet has yet to describe the response of the audience. The silent wonder of the proud Phaiakians, a discriminating audience, expresses their evaluation of the tale (13. 1–2 = 11. 333–4). Such a response, along with Alkinoos' comments when Odysseus had earlier broken off, is the tribute which any storyteller seeks: to know that his story has succeeded, that its point has been taken, and, above all, that his listeners recognize his own active role in the telling. This profound silence—the silence of the spellbound—is a proper tribute, because Odysseus' performance has been a sustained and deliberately measured composition, in which astonishing events and astonishing figures have been assembled and woven into a persuasive whole.[33] There are qualities which are important to the success of any story, independent of the context of the telling: its 'interestingness'; its plausibility; and its structure. But the qualities of scale and pace, which Alkinoos had identified, are

---

[32] Telemachos' comments on Menelaos' story are similar: see 4. 594–8.
[33] Much later in the *Odyssey*, Eumaios will speak with the same warmth about Odysseus' storytellings: at 17. 514–21 he describes how he was as charmed by Odysseus' song as he might have been by a singer whose gifts were god-given.

distinguishing features of great epic song: the kind of song to which we might apply Kirk's descriptive term, 'monumental'.[34] These are the qualities which endow epic song with its special grandeur. Through Odysseus' careful regulation of the pace of the song he performs for the Phaiakians, he creates a tale which is akin to the *Odyssey* itself.

From an audience's point of view, oral song on a grand scale differs from storytelling in conversation in the heightened expectations which we hold of it, and in the storyteller's strategies of response. Several factors—the reputation of the performer, the large audience, perhaps the physical setting, and certainly the sense of occasion—arouse in listeners far greater expectations of epic performance, and of the performer, than they hold of a casual anecdote.[35] They expect a performance of high quality; they seek to forget the distractions of the real world for more than a moment and they long, in Homer's terms, to be caught up in the action of the tale and to be 'enchanted'.[36] Since the monumental tale is on a larger scale and of greater breadth than 'normal' storytelling, it allows the poet to explore his subject at greater leisure than do most other forms of storytelling.[37] And, in trying to meet the higher expectations of his audience, the poet looks to some narrative strategies of a different order.

---

[34] See Kirk, *The* Iliad: *A Commentary*, i, at 12.

[35] Richard Bauman makes this point in the course of his important discussion on the need to integrate the social and the poetic in a discussion of oral literature: see R. Bauman, *Story, Performance, and Event: Contextual Studies of Oral Narrative* (Cambridge: Cambridge University Press, 1986), 1–10, at 3.

[36] Cf. Homer's descriptions of the effect of song on its listeners at *Od.* 1. 337; 11. 333–4; 13. 1–2; 17. 514–21. Listeners, that is, find temporary relief or distraction from affairs of the real world. But, if the story is well-told, they are not passive. They will be called upon to follow the tale and to make judgements about it. Alkinoos, Eumaios, and Odysseus, are, on occasion, just such listeners: they appreciate the story itself, and they are alive to the skill of the telling. See also G. B. Walsh, *The Varieties of Enchantment: Early Greek Views of the Nature and Function of Poetry* (Chapel Hill and London: University of Carolina Press, 1984), 14; Ahl and Roisman, *The* Odyssey *Re-Formed*, at 176–7.

[37] For Aristotle's observations on the scale of epic, see *Poetics*, 1459b. For other comments on the amplitude of epic, see, for example, E. Tillyard, 'The Nature of the Epic', in A. C. Yu (ed.), *Parnassus Revisited* (Chicago: American Library Association, 1973), 42–52; R. Martin, *The Language of Heroes: Speech and Performance in the* Iliad (Ithaca and London: Cornell University Press, 1989), 224–5.

In terms of story structure, Fenik observes that the epic poet at many points of his narrative rejects the 'efficient, perfectly linear development of his action'; he strives instead to slow the action, or hold it back.[38] It is, indeed, by the related strategies of retardation, deferment, and elaboration that epic song differs from other storytelling genres. Homer fills out his narrative line with associated, but not essential, anecdote; or he suspends the action of his principal story-line for an interval during which he will follow a secondary narrative thread, such as the Telemachos thread in the *Odyssey*; or he expands the scene he is describing through elaboration on its sequences. It is his repertoire of strategies for elaboration that interests me, in the context of my discussion of memory and its resources.

The scale of telling in both epics demands 'special' techniques. One of these is the breaking down of the major events of the story into their lesser components and the expression of scripted details; another is detailed description of objects; a third is the expansion of similes; and a fourth is the use of lists or catalogues. These techniques, which slow the pace of any performance, are not only the characteristic features of the Homeric epics, but they are also components of Odysseus' night-long perform-ance for the Phaiakians, in which I have identified a similar concern, on the poet's part, for scale and pace. We may identify in that performance typical scenes such as the killing of an enemy (10. 161–6);[39] the preparation of a meal (12. 353–65); bathing a guest (10. 358–67); dining (10. 368–74); beaching a ship (9. 543–7); and boarding a ship and putting out to sea (9. 560–4). We find a number of passages of description: Maron's wine (9. 196–211); the door to the Kyklop's cave (9. 240–3); Kirke's house (10. 210–19); and the island of Ithaka (9. 21–7). The poet/Odysseus uses similes. Some of these are brief (9. 289, 314); but a number (9. 384–6, 391–3; 10. 410–15; 12. 251–4) are of the extended kind which we find in the narrative which Homer claims to be his own. And there is a list: the famous Catalogue of Women of *Od.* 11, elaborated as catalogues always are by

[38] See B. Fenik, *Studies in the* Odyssey (Wiesbaden: Franz Steiner, 1974), at 104.
[39] The enemy here being a beast, not a human foe.

small stories within its structure (11. 235–330). All these devices slow the pace of the poem and allow the poet the scope in which to develop other aspects of his telling. Their presence in his song proclaims his intention: that he is undertaking a grand project which requires the special skills of the professional.

By contrast, none of these strategies is present in the small tales told in the course of the *Odyssey*.[40] The only places we find such modes are either in Odysseus' long epic of his wanderings or in Homer's own narration. If we examine, first, the long tale which Menelaos tells (*Od.* 4. 351–586), we do not find these devices of extension. He refers to the preparation of an evening meal as we might, through brief reference to the script (4. 429, 574); the simile Menelaos uses is brief (535); and description is limited to a single description of place (354–9). If we turn now to the story which Odysseus tells Eumaios (*Od.* 14. 192–359), we find only one expansion of a script into a typical scene: Odysseus' 'undressing' at 276–7. This, brief as it may be, is for dramatic effect. There is also a certain slowing of the action at another dramatic point of the story, Odysseus' tale of his escape from Thesprotian pirates (334–59): the forward movement of his escape narrative is carefully regulated (344–55). But Odysseus, as storyteller, does not otherwise call on special techniques of expansion in rendering this tale.

In earlier chapters I examined aspects of Homer's practice as storyteller and compared these with our practices in everyday conversation today. We have been able to observe that Homer's strategies are in most cases elaborations of our own. As stylized versions of ordinary stories, his epic tales enhance and intensify a number of standard features of everyday storytelling practice. Like us, Homer refers to scripts; but, unlike us, he expresses lower-level details of scripts. He readily refers to his memory for stories (that is, his repertoire of causal chains) to give us more information about people, places, and significant items. These are incorporated into his descriptive segments, his lists, and

---

[40] The only regular exception are the scripted speech acts, which rely on implicit memory. These are expressed in both the shorter and longer tales of the *Odyssey*.

his similes. We have studied how he works with visual, spatial, semantic, and aural memory in the production of his remarkable lists and catalogues; and we have observed his reference to visual and semantic memory in his so-called extended similes, another characteristic feature of Homeric song. What we have learnt is that in composing a song on this scale, of this scope, the poet makes extraordinary use of the only resources he has, those of his mind. He has accommodated his presentation to its strengths. And yet, even as the storyteller calls upon these devices to support him as he sings, they contribute equally to the audience's pleasure in the performance. They work for the audience through their insistent appeal to the very same resources of memory—auditory memory, visual memory, spatial memory, and episodic memory—which assist the poet as he performs.

The poet of the *Odyssey* shares with his audience what he has learnt, by observation and practice, about storytelling. In reproducing a series of storytellings within his song, Homer, through repetition, draws our attention to the etiquette of storytelling and to storytelling as a communicative event. He encourages us to identify those principles which we for the most part unconsciously observe when processing or telling stories; he demonstrates those principles which hold good whenever a storyteller encounters an audience which is alert, experienced, and responsive. His representations of storytelling, therefore, are evaluative cues in themselves, designed to function as a commentary on the tale in which they are embedded, the *Odyssey* itself. He uses these means to promote his actual audience's understanding of the event in which they are taking part: for he wishes us to evaluate his performance of the *Odyssey* against these small-scale performances. He invites us, that is, to pause and to recognize in his performance a story planned, arranged, and elaborated so as to hold our attention and to fill us with wonderment. The poet of the *Odyssey* wishes us to vouch for its authenticity, and to describe it, as Eumaios described Odysseus' song, as ἀμύμων, οὐδέ . . . παρὰ μοῖραν (14. 508–9): as a blameless tale, which could not be faulted. He wishes us to appreciate the scope and quality of his song and to recognize his skill in rendering it—his ability to perform sustained lists and catalogues, his delightful descriptive segments, his expanded similes, and his familiar, but never unwelcome, typical scenes. He wants his audience to believe, as he does, that he is inspired, as Demodokos must have been, by the Muse or Apollo (8. 488). For, according to Odysseus, the man who sings as well as Demodokos did is prized beyond all others (8. 487). Homer's performance, as the singer of the *Iliad* and the *Odyssey*, is more ambitious and more remarkable than the songs of Demodokos; it is more ambitious than Odysseus' night-long performance for the Phaiakian nobles, which left its audience speechless with wonder. This is 'special' storytelling. And, although we now are able to identify some of the creative ways in which the poet worked with memory as he composed, his songs cannot lose their power to enchant.

Bibliography

Abelson, R., 'Psychological Status of the Script Concept', *American Psychologist*, 36 (1981), 715–29.

Ahl, F., and H. Roisman, *The* Odyssey *Re-Formed* (Ithaca: Cornell University Press, 1996).

Andersson, T. M., *Early Epic Scenery: Homer, Virgil, and the Medieval Legacy* (Ithaca and London: Cornell University Press, 1976).

Arend, W., *Die typischen Scenen bei Homer* (Berlin: Weidmannische Buchhandlung, 1933).

Armstrong, J., 'The Arming Motif in the *Iliad*', *AJP* 79 (1958), 337–54.

Auerbach, E., *Mimesis: The Representation of Reality in Western Literature*, trans. W. Trask (Princeton, NJ: Princeton University Press, paperback edn., 1968).

Austin, J. L., *How to Do Things with Words* (Oxford: Clarendon Press, 1962).

Austin, N., 'The Function of Digressions in the *Iliad*, *GRBS* 7 (1966), 295–312.

Baddeley, A., *Human Memory: Theory and Practice* (Hove and London: Lawrence Erlbaum, 1990).

Bakker, E., 'Homeric Discourse and Enjambement; A Cognitive Approach', *TAPA* 120 (1990), 1–21.

—— 'Discourse and Performance: Involvement, Visualization and "Presence" in Homeric Poetry', *Classical Antiquity*, 12 (1993), 1–29.

—— 'Noun–Epithet Formulas, Milman Parry, and the Grammar of Poetry', in J. P. Crielaard (ed.), *Homeric Questions* (Amsterdam: J. C. Gieben, 1995), 96–125.

—— *Poetry in Speech: Orality and Homeric Discourse* (Ithaca and London: Cornell University Press, 1997).

—— 'Storytelling in the Future: Truth, Time, and Tense in Homeric Epic', in E. Bakker and A. Kahane (eds.), *Written Voices, Spoken Signs: Performance, Tradition, and the Epic Text* (Cambridge, Mass.: Harvard University Press, 1997), 11–36.

Bakker, E., The Study of Homeric Discourse', in I. Morris and B. Powell (eds.), *A New Companion to Homer* (Leiden: E. J. Brill, 1997), 284–304.

—— 'Homeric *OYTOΣ* and the Poetics of Deixis', *Classical Philology*, 94 (1999), 1–19.

Bartlett, F., *Remembering: A Study in Experimental and Social Psychology* (Cambridge: Cambridge University Press, 1932; reprint edn., 1950).

Bassett, S. E., *The Poetry of Homer* (Berkeley and Los Angeles: University of California Press, 1938).

Bateson, G., 'Totemic Knowledge in New Guinea', in U. Neisser (ed.), *Memory Observed: Remembering in Natural Contexts* (San Francisco: W. H. Freeman, 1982), 269–73.

Bauman, R., *Story, Performance, and Event: Contextual Studies of Oral Narrative* (Cambridge: Cambridge University Press, 1986).

Beaugrande, R. de, 'The Story of Grammars and the Grammar of Stories', *Journal of Pragmatics*, 6 (1982), 383–422.

Becker, A. L. 'Text-building, Epistemology, and Aesthetics in Javanese Shadow Theatre', in A. L. Becker and A. Yengoyan (eds.), *The Imagination of Reality: Essays in Southeast Asian Coherence Systems* (Norwood, NJ: Ablex, 1979), 211–43.

Becker, A. S. 'The Shield of Achilles and the Poetics of Homeric Description', *AJP* 111 (1990), 139–53.

—— *The Shield of Achilles and the Poetics of Ekphrasis* (Lanham, Md.: Rowman and Littlefield, 1995).

Beye, C. R., 'Homeric Battle Narratives and Catalogues', *HSCP* 68 (1964), 345–73.

Black, J., and G. Bower, 'Story-Understanding as Problem-Solving', *Poetics*, 9 (1980), 223–50.

Block, E., 'The Narrator Speaks: Apostrophe in Homer and Vergil', *TAPA* 112 (1982), 7–22.

Bower, G., J. Black, and T. Turner, 'Scripts in Memory for Text', *Cognitive Psychology*, 11 (1979), 177–220.

Bowra, C. M., *Tradition and Design in the* Iliad (Oxford: Clarendon Press, 1930).

—— *Heroic Poetry* (London: Macmillan, 1952).

—— *Homer* (London: Duckworth, 1972).

Bransford, J. D., *Human Cognition: Learning, Understanding and Remembering* (Belmont, Calif.: Wadsworth, 1979).

Brewer, W., 'To Assert that Essentially All Human Knowledge and Memory is Represented in Terms of Stories is Certainly Wrong', in R. Wyer, *Knowledge and Memory: The Real Story* (Hillsdale, NJ: Lawrence Erlbaum, 1995), 109–19.

——and E. Lichtenstein, 'Stories are to Entertain: A Structural-Affect Theory of Stories', *Journal of Pragmatics* 6 (1982), 473–86.

Broadbent, D., P. FitzGerald, and M. Broadbent, 'Implicit Knowledge and Explicit Knowledge in the Control of Complex Systems', *British Journal of Psychology*, 77 (1986), 33–50.

Butterworth, J., 'Homer and Hesiod', in J. H. Betts, J. T. Hooker, J. R. Green (eds.), *Studies in Honour of T. B. L. Webster*, i (Bristol: Bristol Classical Press, 1986), 33–45.

Byatt, A. S., *Possession: A Romance* (London: Vintage, 1991).

——*Still Life* (Harmondsworth: Penguin, 1986).

——'The Glass Coffin', in *The Djinn in the Nightingale's Eye* (London: Vintage, 1995), 3–24.

Cairns, F., *Generic Composition in Greek and Roman Poetry* (Edinburgh: Edinburgh University Press, 1972).

——*Tibullus: A Hellenistic Poet at Rome* (Cambridge: Cambridge University Press, 1979).

Calame, C., *The Craft of Poetic Speech in Ancient Greece*, trans. J. Orion (Ithaca and London: Cornell University Press, 1995).

Chadwick, H. M. and N. K., *The Growth of Literature*, 3 vols. (Cambridge: Cambridge University Press, 1932–40).

Chafe, W., 'Some Things that Narratives Tell Us about the Mind', in B. Britton and A. Pellegrini (eds.), *Narrative Thought and Narrative Language* (Hillsdale, NJ: Lawrence Erlbaum, 1990), 79–98.

Chatman, S., *Story and Discourse* (Ithaca: Cornell University Press, 1978).

Clay, J. Strauss, *The Wrath of Athena: Gods and Men in the Odyssey* (Princeton: Princeton University Press, 1983).

Coffey, M., 'The Function of the Homeric Simile', *AJP* 78 (1957), 113–32.

Damon, P., *Modes of Analogy in Ancient and Medieval Verse* (Berkeley and Los Angeles: University of California Press, 1961).

de Jong, I., *Narrators and Focalizers: The Presentation of the Story in the* Iliad (Amsterdam: B. R. Grüner, 1987).

——'Homer as Literature: Some Current Areas of Research', in J. P. Crielaard, *Homeric Questions* (Amsterdam: J. C. Gieben, 1995), 127–46.

Dickinson, O., 'Homer, the Poet of the Dark Age', in I. McAuslan and P. Walcot (eds.), *Homer* (Oxford: Oxford University Press, 1998), 19–37.

Dijk, T. van, *Text and Context: Explorations in the Semantics and Pragmatics of Discourse* (London and New York: Longman, 1977).

Dimock, G., *The Unity of the* Odyssey (Amherst, Mass.: University of Massachusetts Press, 1989).

Doherty, L., *Siren Songs: Gender, Audiences, and Narrators in the* Odyssey (Ann Arbor: University of Michigan Press, 1995).

Dube, E., 'Literacy, Cultural Familiarity, and "Intelligence" as Determinants of Story Recall', in U. Neisser (ed.), *Memory Observed: Memory in Natural Contexts* (San Francisco: W. H. Freeman, 1982), 274–92.

Duckworth, G., *Foreshadowing and Suspense in the Epics of Homer, Apollonius and Vergil* (Princeton, 1933; reprint edn., New York: Haskell House, 1966).

Dunkle, J. R., 'Some Notes on the Funeral Games: *Iliad* 23', *Prometheus*, 7 (1981), 11–18.

—— 'Nestor, Odysseus, and the Mêtis–Biê Antithesis: The Funeral Games, *Iliad* 23', *CW* 81 (1987), 1–17.

Dyer, M., *In-Depth Understanding: A Computer Model of Integrated Processing for Narrative Comprehension* (Cambridge, Mass.: MIT Press, 1983).

Edwards, M., 'Type-Scenes and Homeric Hospitality', *TAPA* 105 (1975), 51–72.

—— 'The Structure of Homeric Catalogues', *TAPA* 110 (1980), 81–105.

—— 'Homer and Oral Tradition: The Formula, Part I', *Oral Tradition*, 1 (1986), 171–230.

—— *Homer: Poet of the* Iliad (Baltimore and London: The Johns Hopkins University Press, 1987).

—— 'Homer and Oral Tradition: The Formula, Part II', *Oral Tradition*, 3 (1988), 11–60.

—— *The* Iliad: *A Commentary*, v (Cambridge: Cambridge University Press, 1991).

—— 'Homer and Oral Tradition: The Type-Scene', *Oral Tradition*, 7 (1992), 284–330.

Eide, T., 'A Note on the Homeric ΧΕΙΡΙ ΠΑΧΕΙΗΓ', *Symbolae Osloenses*, 55 (1980), 23–6.

Ellis, J., 'The Structure and Argument of Thucydides' Archaeology', *Classical Antiquity*, 10 (1991), 344–80.

Emmott, C., *Narrative Comprehension: A Discourse Perspective* (Oxford: Clarendon Press, 1997).

Ervin-Tripp, S., and A. Küntay, 'The Occasioning and Structure of Conversational Stories', in T. Givón (ed.), *Conversation: Cognitive, Communicative and Social Perspectives* (Amsterdam and Philadelphia: J. Benjamins, 1997), 133–66.

Farah, M. J., 'Is Visual Imagery Really Visual? Overlooked

Evidence from Neurophysiology', *Psychological Review*, 95 (1988), 307–17.

Fenik, B., *Typical Battle Scenes in the* Iliad: *Studies in the Narrative Techniques of Homeric Battle Description* (Wiesbaden: Franz Steiner, 1968).

—— *Studies in the* Odyssey (Wiesbaden: Franz Steiner, 1974).

—— *Homer and the Niebelungenlied: Comparative Studies in Epic Style* (Cambridge, Mass.: Harvard University Press, 1986).

Finkelberg, M., 'A Creative Oral Poet and the Muse', *AJP* 111 (1990), 293–303.

—— *The Birth of Literary Fiction in Ancient Greece* (Oxford: Clarendon Press, 1998).

Finnegan, R., *Oral Poetry: Its Nature, Significance and Social Context* (Cambridge: Cambridge University Press, 1977).

Fitzgerald, R., *Homer: The* Odyssey (Garden City, NY: Anchor Books, 1963).

Fleischman, S., *Tense and Narrativity: From Medieval Performance to Modern Fiction* (Austin: University of Texas Press, 1990).

Foley, H., '"Reverse Similes" and Sex-Roles in the *Odyssey*', *Arethusa*, 11 (1978), 7–26.

Foley, J. Miles, *The Theory of Oral Composition* (Bloomington and Indianapolis: Indiana University Press, 1988).

—— *Immanent Art: From Structure to Meaning in Traditional Oral Epic* (Bloomington: Indiana University Press, 1991).

Ford, A., *Homer: The Poetry of the Past* (Ithaca and London: Cornell University Press, 1992).

—— 'Epic as Genre', in I. Morris and B. Powell (eds.), *A New Companion to Homer* (Leiden: E. J. Brill, 1997), 396–414.

Fowler, R., *The Nature of Early Greek Lyric: Three Preliminary Studies* (Toronto: University of Toronto Press, 1987).

Fränkel, H., *Die homerischen Gleichnisse* (Göttingen: Vandenhoeck and Ruprecht, 1921; repr. 1977).

Gaisser, J., 'A Structural Analysis of Digressions in the *Iliad* and the *Odyssey*', *HSCP* 73 (1969), 1–43.

Gentili, B., *Poetry and its Public in Ancient Greece: From Homer to the Fifth Century*, trans. A. Cole (Baltimore and London: The Johns Hopkins University Press, 1988).

Gentner, D., 'The Mechanisms of Analogical Learning', in S. Vosniadou and A. Ortony (eds.), *Similarity and Analogical Reasoning* (Cambridge: Cambridge University Press, 1989), 199–241.

Gernet, L., 'Jeux et droit (remarques sur le XXIIIe chant de l'*Iliade*)', *Revue historique de droit français et étranger*, 26 (1948), 177–88.

Glenberg, A., and W. Langston, 'Comprehension of Illustrated Text: Pictures Help to Build Mental Models', *Journal of Memory and Language*, 31 (1992), 129–51.

Goatly, A., *The Language of Metaphors* (London and New York: Routledge, 1997).

Goffman, E., *The Presentation of Self in Everyday Life* (Edinburgh: Edinburgh University Press, 1958).

——*Interaction Ritual: Essays on Face-to-Face Behaviour* (Harmondsworth: Penguin, 1972).

——'On Face-Work: An Analysis of Ritual Elements in Social Interaction', in J. Laver and S. Hutcheson (eds.), *Communication in Face-to-Face Interaction* (Harmondsworth: Penguin, 1972).

——*Frame Analysis: An Essay on the Organization of Experience* (Harmondsworth: Penguin, 1975).

——'Replies and Responses', *Language in Society*, 5 (1976), 257–323.

Goodwin, C., 'Designing Talk for Different Types of Recipients', in *Conversational Organization: Interaction between Speakers and Hearers* (New York: Academic Press, 1981), 149–66.

Griffin, J., *Homer on Life and Death* (Oxford: Clarendon Press, 1980).

——'Freshly Perceived Epics', *TLS* 4, 433 (March 18–24, 1988), 312.

Groningen, B. A. van, *La Composition littéraire archaïque grecque: Procédés et réalisations* (Amsterdam: Noord-Hollandsche Uitg. Mij., 1958).

Gülich, E., and M. Quasthoff, 'Storytelling in Conversation: Cognitive and Interactive Aspects', *Poetics*, 15 (1986), 217–41.

Gunn, D. M., 'Narrative Inconsistency and the Oral Dictated Text in the Homeric Epic', *AJP* 91 (1970), 192–203.

Haft, A., 'Odysseus, Idomeneus and Meriones: The Cretan Lies of *Odyssey* 13–19', *CJ* 79 (1983–4), 289–306.

Hainsworth, B., *The Iliad: A Commentary*, iii (Cambridge: Cambridge University Press, 1993).

Havelock, E., *The Muse Learns to Write: Reflections on Orality and Literacy from Antiquity to the Present* (New Haven and London: Yale University Press, 1986).

Heubeck, A., 'Homeric Studies Today', in B. Fenik (ed.), *Homer: Tradition and Invention* (Leiden: E. J. Brill, 1978), 1–17.

——S. West, and J. B. Hainsworth, *A Commentary on Homer's Odyssey*, i (Oxford: Clarendon Press, 1988).

—— and A. Hoekstra, *A Commentary on the* Odyssey, ii (Oxford: Clarendon Press, 1989).

Hidi, S., and W. Baird, 'Interestingness—A Neglected Variable in Discourse Processing', *Cognitive Science*, 10 (1986), 179–94.

Hohendahl-Zoetelief, I., *Manners in the Homeric Epic* (Leiden: E. J. Brill, 1980).

Hope Simpson, R., and J. F. Lazenby, *The Catalogue of Ships in Homer's* Iliad (Oxford: Clarendon Press, 1970).

Jachmann, G., *Der homerische Schiffskatalog und die* Ilias (Köln: Westdeutscher Verlag, 1958).

Janko, R., *The* Iliad*: A Commentary*, iv (Cambridge: Cambridge University Press, 1992).

Jefferson, G., 'Sequential Aspects of Storytelling in Conversation', in J. Schenkein (ed.), *Studies in the Organization of Conversational Interaction* (New York: Academic Press, 1978), 219–48.

Jousse, M., *Le Style oral rythmique et mnémotechnique chez les Verbo-moteurs* (1st pub. Paris, 1925), trans. E. Sienaert and R. Whitaker (New York: Garland, 1990).

Katz, A., 'On Choosing the Vehicles of Metaphors: Referential Concreteness, Semantic Distances, and Individual Differences', *Journal of Memory and Language*, 28 (1989), 486–99.

Kirk, G. S., *The* Iliad*: A Commentary*, i (Cambridge: Cambridge University Press, 1985).

—— *The* Iliad*: A Commentary*, ii (Cambridge: Cambridge University Press, 1990).

Labov, W., *Language in the Inner City: Studies in the Black English Vernacular* (Philadelphia: University of Pennsylvania Press, 1972).

—— and J. Waletzky, 'Narrative Analysis: Oral Versions of Personal Experience', in J. Helm (ed.), *Essays on the Verbal and Visual Arts* (Seattle: University of Washington Press, 1967), 12–44.

Lakoff, G., and M. Turner, *More than Cool Reason: A Field Guide to Poetic Metaphor* (Chicago: Chicago University Press, 1989).

Lamberton, R., *Hesiod* (New Haven and London: Yale University Press, 1988).

Lang, M., 'Homer and Oral Techniques', *Hesperia*, 38 (1969), 159–68.

Lattimore, R., *The* Iliad *of Homer* (Chicago: University of Chicago Press, 1951).

—— *The* Odyssey *of Homer* (New York: Harper & Row, 1965).

Leaf, W., and M. Bayfield, *The* Iliad *of Homer* (London: Macmillan, 1895).

Lee, D. J. N., *The Similes of the* Iliad *and the* Odyssey *Compared* (Melbourne: Melbourne University Press, 1964).

Lessing, G. E., *Laocoön* (1st pub. 1766), trans. E. A. McCormick (Baltimore: The Johns Hopkins University Press, paperback edn., 1984).

Levy, D., 'Communicative Goals and Strategies: Between Discourse and Syntax', in T. Givón (ed.), *Discourse and Syntax* (New York: Academic Press, 1979), 183–210.

Lewandowsky, S., J. Dunn, and K. Kirsner (eds.), *Implicit Memory: Theoretical Issues* (Hillsdale, NJ: Lawrence Erlbaum, 1989).

Liddicoat, A., 'Discourse Routines in Answering Machine Communication in Australia', *Discourse Processes*, 17 (1994), 283–309.

Linde, C., 'The Organization of Discourse', in T. Shopen and J. M. Williams (eds.), *Style and Variables in English* (Cambridge, Mass.: Winthrop, 1981), 84–114.

Lodge, D., *Small World* (London: Secker & Warburg, 1984).

—— *The Art of Fiction* (London: Secker & Warburg, 1992).

Lohmann, D., *Die Komposition der Reden in der* Ilias (Berlin: de Gruyter, 1970).

Lord, A. B., 'Composition by Theme in Homer and Southslavic Epos', *TAPA* 82 (1951), 71–80.

—— *The Singer of Tales* (Cambridge, Mass.: Harvard University Press, 1960; New York: Atheneum edn., 1965).

—— *Epic Singers and Oral Tradition* (Ithaca and London: Cornell University Press, 1991).

Louden, B., *The* Odyssey*: Structure, Narration, and Meaning* (Baltimore and London: The Johns Hopkins University Press, 1999).

Lukács, G., 'To Narrate or Describe?', trans. Hanna Loewy, from *Probleme des Realismus* (Berlin: Aufbau-Verlag, 1955), repr. in G. Steiner and R. Fagles (eds.), *Homer: A Collection of Critical Essays* (Englewood-Cliffs, NJ: Prentice-Hall, 1962), 86–9.

Lynn-George, M., *Epos: Word, Narrative, and the* Iliad (Basingstoke and London: Macmillan, 1988).

McDaniel, M., and G. Einstein, 'Bizarre Imagery as an Effective Memory Aid: The Importance of Distinctiveness', *Journal of Experimental Psychology: Learning, Memory, and Cognition*, 12 (1986), 54–65.

McDonald, W. A., 'Early Greek Attitudes toward Environment', *Names*, 6 (1958), 208–16.

Macleod, C., *Collected Essays* (Oxford: Clarendon Press, 1983).

Mandler, G., 'Organization and Memory', in K. W. and J. T. Spence (eds.), *The Psychology of Learning and Motivation*, i (New York: Academic Press, 1967), 327–72.

——and P. Dean, 'Seriation: Development of Serial Order in Free Recall', *Journal of Experimental Psychology*, 81 (1969), 207–15.

——and N. Johnson, 'Remembrance of Things Parsed: Story Structure and Recall', *Cognitive Psychology*, 9 (1977), 111–51.

Marschak, M., 'Imagery and Organization in the Recall of Prose', *Journal of Memory and Language*, 24 (1985), 734–45.

——and R. Reed Hunt, 'A Reexamination of the Role of Imagery in Learning and Memory', *Journal of Experimental Psychology: Learning, Memory, and Cognition*, 15 (1989), 710–20.

Martin, R., *The Language of Heroes: Speech and Performance in the* Iliad (Ithaca and London: Cornell University Press, 1989).

——'Similes and Performance', in E. Bakker and A. Kahane (eds.), *Written Voices, Spoken Signs: Performance, Tradition, and the Epic Text* (Cambridge, Mass.: Harvard University Press, 1997), 138–66.

Mayer, R. E., 'Can You Repeat That? Qualitative Effects of Repetition and Advance Organizers on Learning from Science Prose', *Journal of Educational Psychology*, 75 (1983), 40–9.

Miller, D. Gary, 'A New Model of Formulaic Composition', in J. Miles Foley (ed.), *Comparative Research on Oral Traditions: A Memorial for Milman Parry* (Columbus, Ohio: Slavica, 1987), 351–93.

Miller, G., 'The Magical Number Seven, Plus or Minus Two: Some Limits on our Capacity for Processing Information', *Psychological Review*, 63 (1956), 81–97.

——'Images and Models, Similes and Metaphors', in A. Ortony (ed.), *Metaphor and Thought*, 2nd edn. (Cambridge: Cambridge University Press, 1993), 357–400.

Minchin, E., 'The Interpretation of a Theme in Oral Epic: *Iliad* 24. 559–70', *G&R* 33 (1986), 11–19.

——'Homer Springs a Surprise: Eumaios' Tale at *Od.* o 403–484', *Hermes*, 120 (1992), 259–66.

——'Scripts and Themes: Cognitive Research and the Homeric Epic', *Classical Antiquity*, 11 (1992), 229–41.

Minchin, E., 'The Poet Appeals to His Muse: Homeric Invocations in the Context of Epic Performance', *CJ* 91 (1995–6), 25–33.

234   *Bibliography*

Minchin, E., 'Ring-Patterns and Ring-Composition: Some Observations on the Framing of Stories in Homer', *Helios*, 22 (1995), 23–35.

—— 'Lists and Catalogues in the Homeric Epics', in I. Worthington (ed.), *Voice into Text: Orality and Literacy in Ancient Greece* (Leiden: E. J. Brill, 1996), 1–20.

—— 'Describing and Narrating in Homer's *Iliad*', in E. Anne Mackay (ed.), *Signs of Orality: The Oral Tradition and its Influence in the Greek and Roman World* (Leiden: E. J. Brill, 1999), 49–64.

—— 'Similes in Homer: Image, Mind's Eye, and Memory', in J. Watson (ed.), *Speaking Volumes* (forthcoming).

Minsky, M., 'A Framework for Representing Knowledge', in P. H. Winston (ed.), *The Psychology of Computer Vision* (New York: McGraw-Hill, 1975), 211–17.

Minton, W., 'Homer's Invocations of the Muses: Traditional Patterns', *TAPA* 91 (1960), 292–309.

—— 'Invocation and Catalogue in Hesiod and Homer', *TAPA* 93 (1962), 188–212.

Moulton, C., *Similes in the Homeric Poems* (Göttingen: Vandenhoeck and Ruprecht, 1977).

Muellner, L., 'The Simile of the Cranes and Pygmies: A Study of Homeric Metaphor', *HSCP* 93 (1990), 59–101.

Munro, D. B., and T. W. Allen (eds.), *Homeri Opera*, i–iv (Oxford: Clarendon Press, 1902).

Murray, P., 'Poetic Inspiration in Early Greece', *JHS* 101 (1981), 87–100.

Nagler, M., *Spontaneity and Tradition: A Study in the Oral Art of Homer* (Berkeley: University of California Press, 1974).

Neisser, U. (ed.), *Memory Observed: Remembering in Natural Contexts* (San Francisco: W. H. Freeman, 1982).

—— 'Domains of Memory', in P. Solomon, G. Goethals, C. Kelley, and B. Stephens (eds.), *Memory: Interdisciplinary Approaches* (New York and Berlin: Springer-Verlag, 1988), 67–83.

—— 'What is Ordinary Memory the Memory Of?', in U. Neisser and E. Winograd (eds.), *Remembering Reconsidered* (Cambridge: Cambridge University Press, 1988), 356–73.

Nilsson, M., *Homer and Mycenae* (London: Methuen, 1933).

Nimis, S., *Narrative Semiotics in the Epic Tradition: The Simile* (Bloomington, Indiana: Indiana University Press, 1987).

Notopoulos, J., 'Continuity and Interconnexion in Homeric Oral Composition', *TAPA* 82 (1951), 81–101.

Bibliography 235

Olson, S. D., *Blood and Iron: Stories and Storytelling in Homer's Odyssey* (Leiden: E. J. Brill, 1995).

Ong, W., *Orality and Literacy: The Technologizing of the Word* (London and New York: Methuen, 1982).

Ortony, A., 'Beyond Literal Similarity', *Psychological Review*, 86 (1979), 161–80.

Otterlo, W. van, *De Ringcompositie als Opbouwprincipe in de Epische Gedichten van Homerus* (Amsterdam: Noord-Hollandsche Uitg. Mij., 1948).

Page, D. L., *History and the Homeric* Iliad (Berkeley: University of California Press, 1959).

Paivio, A., *Imagery and Verbal Processes* (New York: Holt, Rinehart & Winston, 1971).

—— 'The Mind's Eye in Arts and Science', *Poetics*, 12 (1983), 1–18.

—— *Mental Representations: A Dual Coding Approach* (New York: Oxford University Press, 1986).

—— and M. Walsh, 'Psychological Processes in Metaphor Comprehension and Memory', in A. Ortony (ed.), *Metaphor and Thought*, 2nd edn. (Cambridge: Cambridge University Press, 1993), 307–28.

Parry, A. (ed.), *The Making of Homeric Verse: The Collected Papers of Milman Parry* (Oxford: Clarendon Press, 1971).

Pawley, A., and F. D. Syder, 'Two Puzzles for Linguistic Theory: Nativelike Selection and Nativelike Fluency', in J. Richards and R. Schmidt (eds.), *Language and Communication* (London and New York: Longman, 1983), 191–226.

Peden, R., 'Endings in Catullus', in M. Whitby, P. Hardie, and M. Whitby (eds.), *Homo Viator: Classical Essays for John Bramble* (Bristol: Bristol Classical Press, 1987), 95–103.

Pedrick, V., 'The Muse Corrects: The Opening of the *Odyssey*', *YCS* 29 (1992), 39–62.

Polanyi, L., 'So What's the Point?', *Semiotica*, 25 (1979), 207–41.

—— 'On Telling the Same Story Twice', *Text*, 1 (1981), 315–36.

—— 'Linguistic and Social Constraints on Storytelling', *Journal of Pragmatics*, 6 (1982), 509–24.

—— 'Literary Complexity in Everyday Storytelling', in D. Tannen (ed.), *Spoken and Written Language* (Norwood, NJ: Ablex, 1982), 155–70.

Powell, B., 'Word Patterns in the Catalogue of Ships (B494–709): A Structural Analysis of Homeric Language', *Hermes*, 106 (1978), 255–64.

Pratt, M. L., *Towards a Speech-Act Theory of Literary Discourse* (Bloomington: Indiana University Press, 1977).

Querbach, C., 'Conflicts between Young and Old in Homer's *Iliad*', in S. Bertman (ed.), *The Conflict of Generations in Ancient Greece and Rome* (Amsterdam: B. Grüner, 1976), 55–65.

Reber, A., 'Implicit Learning and Tacit Knowledge', *Journal of Experimental Psychology: General*, 118 (1989), 219–35.

Redfield, J., *Nature and Culture in the* Iliad: *The Tragedy of Hector* (Chicago and London: Chicago University Press, 1975; Phoenix edn., 1978).

Reece, S., *The Stranger's Welcome: Oral Theory and the Aesthetics of the Homeric Hospitality Scene* (Ann Arbor: University of Michigan Press, 1993).

Rengakos, A., 'Spannungsstrategien in den homerischen Epen', in J. Kazazis and A. Rengakos (eds.), *Euphrosyne: Studies in Ancient Epic and its Legacy in Honor of Dimitris N. Maronitis* (Stuttgart: Franz Steiner, 1999), 308–38.

Richardson, N., *The* Iliad: *A Commentary*, vi (Cambridge: Cambridge University Press, 1993).

Richardson, S., *The Homeric Narrator* (Nashville, Tenn.: Vanderbilt University Press, 1990).

Rubin, D., 'Learning Poetic Language', in F. S. Kessel (ed.), *The Development of Language and Language Researchers: Essays in Honor of Roger Brown* (Hillsdale, NJ: Lawrence Erlbaum, 1988), 339–51.

—— 'Stories about Stories', in R. Wyer (ed.), *Knowledge and Memory: The Real Story* (Hillsdale, NJ: Lawrence Erlbaum, 1995), 153–64.

—— *Memory in Oral Traditions: The Cognitive Psychology of Epic, Ballads, and Counting-out Rhymes* (New York and Oxford: Oxford University Press, 1995).

—— W. Wallace, and B. Houston, 'The Beginnings of Expertise for Ballads', *Cognitive Science*, 17 (1993), 435–62.

Rumelhart, D., 'Notes on a Schema for Stories', in D. Bobrow and A. Collins (eds.), *Representation and Understanding* (New York: Academic Press, 1975), 211–36.

Russo, J., 'Homer against His Tradition', *Arion*, 7 (1968), 275–95.

—— M. Fernandez-Galiano, and A. Heubeck, *A Commentary on Homer's* Odyssey, iii (Oxford: Clarendon Press, 1992).

Rüter, K., *Odysseeinterpretationen: Untersuchungen zum ersten Buch und zur Phaiakis* (Göttingen: Vandenhoeck and Ruprecht, 1969).

Sale, M., 'In Defence of Milman Parry: Renewing the Oral Theory', *Oral Tradition*, 11 (1996), 374–417.

Schank, R., 'Interestingness: Controlling Inferences', *Artificial Intelligence*, 12 (1979), 273–97.

—— *Dynamic Memory: A Theory of Reminding and Learning in Computers and People* (Cambridge: Cambridge University Press, 1982).

—— and R. Abelson, *Scripts, Plans, Goals and Understanding: An Inquiry into Human Knowledge Structures* (Hillsdale, NJ: Lawrence Erlbaum, 1977).

—— —— 'Knowledge and Memory: The Real Story', in R. Wyer (ed.), *Knowledge and Memory: The Real Story* (Hillsdale, NJ: Lawrence Erlbaum, 1995), 1–85.

Schofield, M., 'Euboulia in the *Iliad*', *CQ* 36 (1986), 6–31.

Scott, W., *The Oral Nature of the Homeric Simile* (Leiden: E. J. Brill, 1974).

Scribner, S., and M. Cole, *The Psychology of Literacy* (Cambridge, Mass.: Harvard University Press, 1981).

Segal, C., 'Transition and Ritual in Odysseus' Return', *La Parola del Passato*, 22 (1967), 321–42.

—— *Singers, Heroes, and Gods in the* Odyssey (Ithaca and London: Cornell University Press, 1994).

Shipp, G. P., *Studies in the Language of Homer* (Cambridge: Cambridge University Press, 1972).

Shive, D., *Naming Achilles* (New York and Oxford: Oxford University Press, 1987).

Slings, S. R., 'Written and Spoken Language: An Exercise in the Pragmatics of the Greek Sentence', *Classical Philology*, 87 (1992), 95–109.

Small, J. P., *Wax Tablets of the Mind: Cognitive Studies in Memory and Literacy in Classical Antiquity* (London and New York: Routledge, 1997).

Sperber, D., and D. Wilson, 'Pragmatics', *Cognition*, 10 (1981), 281–6.

Stanley, K., *The Shield of Homer: Narrative Structure in the* Iliad (Princeton: Princeton University Press, 1993).

Suerbaum, W., 'Die Ich-Erzählungen des Odysseus', *Poetica*, 2 (1968), 150–77.

Tannen, D., 'What's in a Frame? Surface Evidence for Underlying Expectations', in R. O. Freedle (ed.), *New Directions in Discourse Processing* (Norwood, NJ: Ablex, 1979), 137–81.

—— 'Oral and Literate Strategies in Spoken and Written Narratives', *Language*, 58 (1982), 1–21.

Tannen, D., 'The Oral/Literate Continuum in Discourse', in D. Tannen (ed.), *Spoken and Written Language: Exploring*

Orality and Literary, Advances in Discourse Processes, 9 (Norwood, NJ: Ablex, 1982), 1–16.

—— *Conversational Style: Analyzing Talk amongst Friends* (Norwood, NJ: Ablex, 1984).

—— 'Relative Focus on Involvement in Oral and Written Discourse', in D. Olson, N. Torrance, and A. Hildyard (eds.), *Literacy, Language, and Learning: The Nature and Consequences of Reading and Writing* (Cambridge: Cambridge University Press, 1985), 124–47.

—— 'Repetition in Conversation: Towards a Poetics of Talk', *Language*, 63 (1987), 574–605.

—— *Talking Voices: Repetition, Dialogue, and Imagery in Conversational Discourse* (Cambridge and New York: Cambridge University Press, 1989).

Taplin, O., 'The Shield of Achilles within the *Iliad*', *G&R* 27 (1980), 1–21.

—— *Homeric Soundings: The Shaping of the* Iliad (Oxford: Clarendon Press, 1992).

Thalmann, W., *Conventions of Form and Thought in Early Greek Epic Poetry* (Baltimore and London: The Johns Hopkins University Press, 1984).

Thomas, R., *Oral Tradition and Written Record in Classical Athens* (Cambridge: Cambridge University Press, 1992).

Thorndyke, P., and F. Yekovich, 'A Critique of Schema-Based Theories of Human Story Memory', *Poetics*, 9 (1980), 23–49.

Thornton, A., *Homer's* Iliad: *Its Composition and the Motif of Supplication* (Göttingen: Vandenhoeck and Ruprecht, 1984).

Tillyard, E., 'The Nature of the Epic', in A. C. Yu (ed.), *Parnassus Revisited* (Chicago: American Library Association, 1973), 42–52.

Tourangeau, R., and L. Rips, 'Interpreting and Evaluating Metaphors', *Journal of Memory and Language*, 30 (1991), 452–72.

Trabasso, T., and L. Sperry, 'Causal Relatedness and Importance of Story Events', *Journal of Memory and Language*, 24 (1985), 595–611.

—— and P. van den Broek, 'Causal Thinking and the Representation of Narrative Events', *Journal of Memory and Language*, 24 (1985), 612–30.

Trahman, C., 'Odysseus' Lies (*Odyssey*, bks. 13–19)', *Phoenix*, 6 (1952), 31–43.

Wallace, W., and D. Rubin, ' "The Wreck of the Old 97": A Real Event Remembered in Song', in U. Neisser and E. Winograd (eds.), *Remembering Reconsidered* (Cambridge: Cambridge University Press, 1988), 283–310.

Walsh, G. B., *The Varieties of Enchantment: Early Greek Views of the Nature and Function of Poetry* (Chapel Hill and London: University of Carolina Press, 1984).

Wardhaugh, R., *How Conversation Works* (Oxford: Basil Blackwell, 1985).

Wild, S., 'Australian Aboriginal Theatrical Movement', in B. Fleshman (ed.), *Theatrical Movement: A Bibliographical Anthology* (Metuchen, NJ: Scarecrow Press, 1986), 601–17.

Willcock, M., 'The Funeral Games of Patroclus', *BICS* 20 (1973), 1–11.

—— 'Antilochos in the *Iliad*', in E. Delebecque, *Mélanges Edouard Delebecque* (Aix-en-Provence: University of Provence, 1983), 477–85.

—— 'The Search for the Poet Homer', *G&R* 37 (1990), 1–13.

Willis, W., 'Athletic Contests in the Epic', *TAPA* 72 (1941), 392–417.

Wood, M., *In Search of the Trojan War* (London: BBC Books, 1985).

Wyatt, W., 'Homer in Performance: *Iliad* 1. 348–427', *CJ* 83 (1987–8), 289–97.

Yates, F., *The Art of Memory* (London: Routledge & Kegan Paul, 1966).

Young, K. G., *Taleworlds and Storyrealms: The Phenomenology of Narrative* (Dordrecht: Martinus Nijhoff, 1987).

Zeitlin, F., 'Figuring Fidelity in Homer's *Odyssey*', in B. Cohen (ed.), *The Distaff Side: Representing the Female in Homer's* Odyssey (New York and Oxford: Oxford University Press, 1995), 117–52.

General Index

Index Locorum

DATE DUE

MAY 3 0 2006	
MAY 2 5 2008	